'The essays are accessible without being simple. ... ...ading the entire book will encounter a range of theoretical approaches being skillfully and productively applied to *The Chronicles of Narnia*.' - **Richard C. Burke**, *Lynchburg College, USA*

Beginning with the publication of *The Lion, the Witch and the Wardrobe* in 1950 and concluding with the appearance of *The Last Battle* in 1956, C. S. Lewis's seven-book series chronicling the adventures of a group of young people in the fictional land of Narnia has become a worldwide classic of children's literature.

This stimulating collection of original essays by critics in a wide range of disciplines explores the past place, present status, and future importance of *The Chronicles of Narnia*. With essays ranging in focus from textual analysis to film and new media adaptations, to implications of war/trauma and race and gender, this cutting-edge New Casebook encourages readers to think about this much-loved series in fresh and exciting ways.

Introduction by Lance Weldy. Essays by: Gili Bar-Hillel, Rhonda Brock-Servais & Matthew B. Prickett, Aaron Clayton, Keith Dorwick, Melody Green, Nanette Norris, Susana Rodriguez, Joseph Michael Sommers, Jennifer Taylor, Rachel Towns.

Michelle Ann Abate is Associate Professor of English at Hollins University, USA.

Lance Weldy is Associate Professor of English at Francis Marion University, USA.

This latest series of *New Casebooks* consists of brand new critical essays specially commissioned to provide students with fresh thinking about key texts and writers. Like the original series, the volumes embrace a range of approaches designed to illuminate the rich interchange between critical theory and critical practice.

D1141608

New Casebooks

Collections of all new critical essays

CHILDREN'S LITERATURE

ROBERT CORMIER
Edited by Adrienne E. Gavin

ROALD DAHL
Edited by Ann Alston & Catherine Butler

C. S. LEWIS: *THE CHRONICLES OF NARNIA*
Edited by Michelle Ann Abate & Lance Weldy

J. K. ROWLING: *HARRY POTTER*
Edited by Cynthia J. Hallett & Peggy J. Huey

FURTHER TITLES ARE CURRENTLY IN PREPARATION

For a full list of published titles in the past format of the New Casebooks series, visit the series page at www.palgrave.com

New Casebooks Series

Series Standing Order
ISBN 978–0–333–71702–8   hardcover
ISBN 978–0–333–69345–2   paperback
(Outside North America only)

You can receive future titles in this series as they are published by placing a standing order. Please contact your bookseller or, in case of difficulty, write to us at the address below with your name and address, the title of the series and the ISBN quoted above.

Customer Services Department, Macmillan Distribution Ltd, Houndmills, Basingstoke, Hampshire RG21 6XS, England

New Casebooks

C. S. LEWIS
THE CHRONICLES OF NARNIA

Edited by

MICHELLE ANN ABATE & LANCE WELDY

First published 2012 by
PALGRAVE MACMILLAN

Palgrave Macmillan in the UK is an imprint of Macmillan Publishers Limited, registered in England, company number 785998, of Houndmills, Basingstoke, Hampshire RG21 6XS.

Palgrave Macmillan in the US is a division of St Martin's Press LLC, 175 Fifth Avenue, New York, NY 10010.

Palgrave Macmillan is the global academic imprint of the above companies and has companies and representatives throughout the world.

Palgrave® and Macmillan® are registered trademarks in the United States, the United Kingdom, Europe and other countries.

ISBN 978–0–230–30124–5   hardback
ISBN 978–0–230–30125–2   paperback

This book is printed on paper suitable for recycling and made from fully managed and sustained forest sources. Logging, pulping and manufacturing processes are expected to conform to the environmental regulations of the country of origin.

A catalogue record for this book is available from the British Library.

A catalog record for this book is available from the Library of Congress.

10   9   8   7   6   5   4   3   2   1
21 20 19 18 17 16 15 14 13 12

Printed in China

Contents

Series Editor's Preface	vii
Preface	viii
Notes on Contributors	x
Introduction *Lance Weldy*	1

PART I: TEXT AND CONTEXTS

1 "Turkish Delights and Sardines with Tea": Food as a
  Framework for Exploring Nationalism, Gender, and
  Religion in *The Lion, the Witch and the Wardrobe*   15
  Rachel Towns

2 Scapegoating and Collective Violence in *The Lion,
  the Witch and the Wardrobe*   38
  Melody Green

PART II: APPLICATIONS AND IMPLICATIONS

3 Moving Beyond "All That Rot": Redeeming Education
  in *The Chronicles of Narnia*   53
  Keith Dorwick

4 War and the Liminal Space: Situating *The Lion, the
  Witch and the Wardrobe* in the Twentieth-Century
  Narrative of Trauma and Survival   71
  Nanette Norris

5 C. S. Lewis's Manifold Mythopoeics: Toward a
  Reconsideration of Eschatological Time in the
  Construction of *The Chronicles of Narnia*   90
  Joseph Michael Sommers

PART III: ADAPTATIONS AND MEDIATIONS

6 The Author, the Movie, and the Marketing: *The Lion,
   the Witch and the Wardrobe* and Early Reader Adaptations   113
   Rhonda Brock-Servais and Matthew B. Prickett

7 The Lion, the Witch, and the Wii: Lewis's Theology
   in the Narnia Video Game   126
   Aaron Clayton

PART IV: CONFLICTS AND CONTROVERSY

8 Lewis and Anti-Lewis: On the Influence of
   The Chronicles of Narnia on *His Dark Materials*
   by Philip Pullman   145
   Gili Bar-Hillel

9 "Beautiful Barbarians": Anti-Racism in *The Horse and
   His Boy* and Other *Chronicles of Narnia*   161
   Jennifer Taylor

10 Boy-Girls and Girl-Beasts: The Gender Paradox
    in C. S. Lewis's *The Chronicles of Narnia*   186
    Susana Rodriguez

Further Reading   199

Index   208

Series Editor's Preface

Welcome to the latest series of New Casebooks.

Each volume now presents brand new essays specially written for university and other students. Like the original series, the new-look New Casebooks embrace a range of recent critical approaches to the debates and issues that characterize the current discussion of literature.

Each editor has been asked to commission a sequence of original essays which will introduce the reader to the innovative critical approaches to the text or texts being discussed in the collection. The intention is to illuminate the rich interchange between critical theory and critical practice that today underpins so much writing about literature.

Editors have also been asked to supply an introduction to each volume that sets the scene for the essays that follow, together with a list of further reading which will enable readers to follow up issues raised by the essays in the collection.

The purpose of this new-look series, then, is to provide students with fresh thinking about key texts and writers while encouraging them to extend their own ideas and responses to the texts they are studying.

Martin Coyle

Preface

As Roderick McGillis notes in the Preface of his edited book, *Voices of the Other: Children's Literature and the Postcolonial Context*, "The best laid schemes, we know, often go awry,"[1] and while he refers to schemes in terms of the ideological structuring and organization of his book, I am referring to it in terms of how this finished book project came to be. I would not necessarily refer to the turn of events of this book project as something that has gone "awry," as I am sure that most any book project undergoes a considerable amount of unforeseen turns. Rather, I would say that the extent of my work on this New Casebook was an unexpected surprise. I had already been attached to this book as a contributor but, through a series of events, I was asked to assume leadership of the project when the original editor, Michelle Ann Abate, could no longer do so. As such, this project represents our combined efforts: Michelle's at the beginning, and mine at the end. During the first few weeks of the transition, I can still remember the trepidation I felt at the thought of maintaining the quality of the project that Michelle had established. That pressure has always remained in the back of mind, and I trust that I will not disappoint Michelle or the others who contributed to make this project possible.

I would like to offer my thanks and gratitude to the help of many people. Gwen Tarbox served as an indefatigable sounding board on many occasions, selflessly giving of her time and offering me advice when I desperately needed it, even when she herself was juggling five times the amount of work. I would also like to formally thank Michelle Ann Abate for trusting in my capabilities in finishing the book project for her. I say with all sincerity that Michelle truly did the "lion's share" of the work (yes, with all puns intended) in everything from doing the background research on Lewis and Narnia to getting the book proposal and project successfully launched and beyond. And I certainly owe all the contributors a round of thanks for their patience and willingness to put up with my editorial idiosyncrasies. Also, Sonya Barker, Felicity Noble, and the rest of the team at Palgrave Macmillan were incredibly patient with me at every stage.

Finally, I would like to acknowledge the influence of my mother, Glenda Seaborg Weldy. It is hard to believe that, more than 20 years ago, my mother served as what composition theorist Deborah Brandt calls a "sponsor of literacy"[2] when she gave me *The Lion, the Witch and the Wardrobe* to read. As a lifelong educator, my mother was known for reading through the entire Narnia series out loud to her students, and, knowing that I was a reader, she wanted me to enter this world too. I approached her as soon as I had finished the book and can still visualize the enthusiasm on her face as she began to ask me questions about the allegorical implications of the text. (As this New Casebook will show, the question regarding the existence, traces, or elements of allegory in Narnia is one that is still much discussed, questioned, and analyzed.) Of course, I didn't realize it at the time, but this was probably one of my first—though brief—discussions involving liter-ary analysis. There was no way either my mother or I could have envisioned that my introduction to Narnia and fantasy literature analysis would have prepared me further down the road to discuss my own critical responses to Narnia in international conferences and, ultimately, this New Casebook. I trust that my critical enthusiasm for Narnia studies is adequately represented throughout this project.

Lance Weldy

Notes

1. Roderick McGillis, "Preface," in *Voices of the Other: Children's Literature and the Postcolonial Context* (New York: Garland Publishing, 1999): xi–xiii, at xi.
2. Deborah Brandt, "Sponsors of Literacy," *College Composition and Communication* 49(2) (1998): 165–85.

Notes on Contributors

Michelle Ann Abate is an Associate Professor of English at Hollins University, Virginia. She is the author of *Raising Your Kids Right: Children's Literature and American Political Conservatism* (Rutgers University Press, 2010) and *Tomboys: A Literary and Cultural History* (Temple University Press, 2008). With Kenneth B. Kidd, she co-edited *Over the Rainbow: Queer Children's and Adolescent Literature* (University of Michigan Press, 2011), and, with Annette Wannamaker, she is the co-editor of *Global Perspectives on Tarzan: From King of the Jungle to International Icon* (Routledge, 2012).

Gili Bar-Hillel is a publisher and translator of children's books. She runs the "Young Graff" imprint for Graff Publishing in Tel Aviv, which publishes books by Rick Riordan, Cassandra Clare, Diana Wynne Jones, and many others. As a translator she made her name by translating the Harry Potter books into Hebrew; she has also translated classics such as *The Wizard of Oz*, and translated and annotated an authoritative edition of J. M. Barrie's *Peter and Wendy*. As well as running her publishing company and raising three children with her husband Haim, she is also enrolled in the graduate Program on Children's and Youth Culture Studies at Tel Aviv University.

Rhonda Brock-Servais is a department Chair and full Professor at Longwood University, Virginia, where she teaches Children's and Young Adult Literature classes, as well as the History of Literature for Young Readers for the Children's Literature minor. In addition, she is a member of Hollins University's summer program for Children's Literature. There she teaches History and Criticism as well as special topics courses on fairy tales. With coauthor Matt Prickett, this is their second piece on classic children's books and adaptation; the first, focused on *Anne of Green Gables*, was published in *The Lion and the Unicorn*. They have other endeavors in the planning stages.

Aaron Clayton is an Assistant Professor of English at Frederick Community College, Maryland. He is writing a dissertation titled "Legion of Consumers: Corporeal Capital, Nature, and (In)Human Beasts in a Zombie Nation" as a doctoral candidate at Binghamton University. He has recently published essays in *Conradiana* and the

International Journal of Comic Art, and is a contributor to the forthcoming collection *Global Perspectives on Tarzan* (Routledge, 2012).

Keith Dorwick, an Associate Professor of English at the University of Louisiana at Lafayette and editor of the online journal *Technoculture*, has several interests. He is a visual artist who works primarily with video and audio; artistic director and producer of The Plastic Theater of Lafayette; and author of both critical articles in journals such as *Computers and Composition* and *The Journal of Bisexuality*, and book chapters in such edited collections as *Mediated Boyhoods* (Peter Lang, 2011).

Melody Green earned her PhD in English Studies with a specialization in Children's Literature from Illinois State University in 2008, and is currently teaching composition at Lewis University. She has published essays on various topics, including the British television series Doctor Who, as well as the authors Neil Gaiman and George MacDonald. Recently her article "Death and Nonsense in the Poems of George MacDonald's *At the Back of the North Wind* and Lewis Carroll's *Alice* Books" was published in the 2011 issue of *North Wind: A Journal of George MacDonald Studies*. Melody is a member of ChLA and the Mythopoeic Society.

Nanette Norris is Assistant Professor of English at Royal Military College Saint-Jean, where she teaches undergraduate courses in twentieth-century literature. Her work has appeared in *Images of the Child* (Bowling Green, 1994), *Engaging the Enemy: Canada in the 1940s* (Dinefwr Press, 2006), and *The D. H. Lawrence Review*, among others. She co-edited (with Colette Balmain) *Uneasy Humanity: Perpetual Wrestling with Evils* (ID Press, 2009). Most recently, she has broadened her studies from D. H. Lawrence and modernism to war and trauma. An article on Paris in Tim O'Brien's *Going After Cacciatio* is forthcoming in *Paris in American Literature*, from Fairleigh Dickinson University Press. She is currently editing a volume of ecocritical essays, entitled *Words for a Small Planet*, for Lexington Books.

Matthew B. Prickett is a PhD student in the Childhood Studies Department at Rutgers University-Camden, New Jersey. He has published on such topics as Pete Hautman, L. M. Montgomery's *Anne of Green Gables* (along with Rhonda Brock-Servais), representations of female predators in the media, and the supernatural in children's literature. He has also been featured on NPR's *With Good Reason*.

Susana Rodriguez is a PhD candidate in Illinois State University's English Studies program specializing in children's literature. Her publications include "Researching, or How I Fell in Love with Post-Its" (Fall 2011) and "Reading Visual Texts: A Bullet For Your Arsenal" (Fall 2010, reprinted Spring 2012) in the *Grassroots Writing Research Journal*, the primary text for ISU's Writing Program general education courses; and "Deadly Fun: *Jouissance* and Carnival in *Alice in Wonderland* and *Peter Pan*" (Spring 2010) in *Polyglossia*, Sigma Tau Delta's English Studies journal at ISU. "Boy-Girls and Girl-Beasts: The Gender Paradox in C. S. Lewis's *The Chronicles of Narnia*" is her first book chapter.

Joseph Michael Sommers is an Assistant Professor of English at Central Michigan University where he teaches courses in Children's and Young Adult Literature as well as courses in modern and contemporary literature, visual narratives, and popular culture. He has published work on figures such as Gary Paulsen, Hunter Thompson, Denise Levertov, and Judy Blume. Most recently, he has brought out chapters and articles on the culture of childhood in nineteenth-century women's journalism, the maturation of Marvel Comics' characters in the Post-9/11 Moment, Hellboy amongst the Melungeon People, Christopher Nolan's *The Dark Knight*, *Twilight*, and his first book-length anthology (co-edited with Todd A. Comer), entitled *Sexual Ideology in the Works of Alan Moore* (McFarland, 2011). Currently, he is completing his next book-length project on the narrative intersection between video games and movies.

Jennifer Taylor earned an MA in Children's Literature at Hollins University, Virginia. Her areas of interest include Western religious art, Christian symbolism in literature, classic fairy tales, and women's studies; she has presented on various topics at conferences, such as religion and death in Katherine Paterson's work, art symbols in classic fairy tales, racism in C. S. Lewis's fiction, and the female Satan in *The Chronicles of Narnia*. Currently she is researching ways that authors of fairy tales and fantasy help children to identify and handle abuse. In 2011, she received the Honor Essay Award from the Children's Literature Association of America.

Rachel Towns is a teacher of English, History, and Religion at St. John's Regional College in Dandenong, Victoria, Australia. She has completed a Bachelor of Arts, Bachelor of Letters (Honors), Graduate Diploma in Education (Secondary), Masters in Arts (Theology), and a Graduate Diploma of Arts (Writing). This is her first academic paper to be published; however, she has also had two fiction stories published: "Grace's Fire" in *Stories from the Hearth: Heartwarming Tales of Appalachia* (Woodland Press, 2011), and "The Memory-Thief" in Swinburne University's journal of writing and practice-led research, *Bukker Tillibul*. She is currently working on constructions of violence in Victorian Literature.

Lance Weldy, Associate Professor of English at Francis Marion University, teaches Children's and Young Adult Literature. His most recent publication is the edited anthology, *Crossing Textual Boundaries in International Children's Literature* (Cambridge Scholars Publishing, 2011). He is currently co-editing a special issue of the *Children's Literature Quarterly* on Sexualities and Children's Culture with Thomas Crisp.

Introduction

Lance Weldy

Overview of Narnia

It all started with an image of a faun; at least, this is the famous statement from C. S. Lewis that has been reprinted in countless essays and
scholarship about *The Chronicles of Narnia*. Specifically, Lewis said:
"All of my seven Narnia books, and my three science fiction books,
began with seeing pictures in my head. At first they were not a story,
just pictures. The *Lion* all began with a picture of a Faun carrying
an umbrella and parcels in a snowy wood."[1] This image of the faun
remains one of the most iconic images of the Narnia series and serves
as a good starting point for this introduction to *The Chronicles of Narnia*
New Casebook. On one level, I hope that with the mention of the
faun, I have already conjured for the reader a positive, almost oneiric
mental picture, perhaps one of fanciful nostalgia for feelings of that
first encounter with Narnia, be it through the story of Tumnus or
Lucy or otherwise.

However—and as a somewhat simple illustration regarding the
general purpose of this Casebook—I want to consider this image
of the faun on another level so that it becomes deconstructed, scrutinized, problematized. As mentioned by several scholars, including
Owen Dudley Edwards, this scene of a young girl walking home with
a complete stranger whose own mythological roots trace back to a
healthy reputation around sexualization certainly gives one pause. And
even though Edwards notes that "*The Lion, the Witch and the Wardrobe*
can only work with an absolute suspension of concerns about sex and
paedophilia, since it turns on a faun inviting a little girl to tea while
secretly intending to betray her," he does concede that "fauns in the
sense Lewis was employing are companions to Silenus and similar
voluptuaries in Rubens paintings or to Comus and damnable entou-
rage in Milton masque."[2] In other words, the kinds of characteriza-
tions affiliated with fauns in the traditional literary sense were bawdy
at best and hedonistic at worst. Additionally, J. R. R. Tolkien famously
provided his feedback to Lewis's Narnia story, specifically concerning the faun, as told to Roger Lancelyn Green: "'I hear you've been

reading Jack's children's story. It really won't do, you know! I mean to say: "*Nymphs and their Ways, the Love-Life of a Faun.*" Doesn't he know what he's talking about?"[3] Of course, Tolkien's cheeky reference to the kinds of books that could possibly be in Tumnus's personal library can be interpreted several ways, but Colin Duriez believes the remark means that "Tolkien is more bothered with what he sees as a serious error of taste than he lets on."[4] This "error of taste" could very well refer to Lewis's incorporating into his children's book the figure of a faun, whose sensual reputation in artistic and literary history seems at odds with the implied reader of his narrative. And remember, the faun is one of the most iconic images of the whole series.

This one small example of the faun symbolizes the complexities of *The Chronicles of Narnia* and also represents just one of the critical approaches that the scholars in this anthology undertake. True, it might be taking the "fun" out of Narnia, as many of our children's literature students would say, but, as Peter Hunt notes, "we have to accept that children's books are *complex*."[5] What Hunt means by this is that we have to accept that texts written for children require the same amount of scrutiny as would a text for adults—even more so because of the implicit and explicit ideological influences inherent. Because of this, the essays in this New Casebook seek to extend upon previous scholarship and explore new ways of critically assessing the Narnia texts.

The Chronicles of Narnia series consists of seven fantasy books that were published between 1950 and 1956. The narrative chiefly is set in a secondary world called Narnia, where different children from the primary world of England cross a threshold in various ways (a wardrobe, a painting, etc.) into Narnia to help the good talking animals of Narnia battle evil and restore order. Each time the children enter Narnia, it is because the lion Aslan has called them. Though the publication history of the series conflicts with the internal chronology and composition history of the series, it is safe to say that, overall, the series recounts the story of Narnia from its creation in *The Magician's Nephew* through to its devastation in *The Last Battle*. Out of the seven books, the Pevensie children are arguably the best known protagonists, most likely because of their presence in the first published, and most well-known, book of the series, *The Lion, the Witch and the Wardrobe*, even though they are not present in all seven books. Furthermore, Lucy and Edmund Pevensie are present in the series most often, serving both as protagonists in three novels and in more minor roles in two others, one of which is *The Horse and His Boy*, which is the only novel in the series where the visiting children are not the protagonists of the story.

As I mentioned above, the Narnia series becomes complicated when discussing the chronology of the narrative versus its composition and publication, and the ordering of the books for reprints of the series has been quite controversial. For example, Lewis conceived the Narnia story in 1939 with the advent of World War II, did not finish writing *The Lion, the Witch and the Wardrobe* until 1949, and then published it in 1950. However, *The Magician's Nephew* (which recounts the creation of Narnia) was the sixth book published in the series in 1955, but was actually the last book to be written, because *The Last Battle* (which tells of the destruction of Narnia) was published in 1956, but actually finished in 1953. To illustrate the confusion about the reading order of the series, here is an excerpt from a letter written by Lewis in 1957 to Laurence Krieg, an American boy who suggested reading the series according to the chronology of Narnia time—*The Magician's Nephew* (1955); *The Lion, the Witch and the Wardrobe* (1950); *The Horse and His Boy* (1954); *Prince Caspian* (1951); *The Voyage of the Dawn Treader* (1952); *The Silver Chair* (1953); and *The Last Battle* (1956):

> I think I agree with your order for reading the books more than with your mother's. The series was not planned beforehand as she thinks. When I wrote *The Lion* I did not know I was going to write any more. Then I wrote *P. Caspian* as a sequel and still didn't think there would be any more, and when I had done *The Voyage* I felt quite sure it would be the last. But I found I was wrong. So perhaps it does not matter very much in which order anyone reads them. I'm not even sure that all the others were written in the same order in which they were published. I never keep notes of that sort of thing and never remember dates.[6]

As Lewis says, his books were published in a different order than that in which they were written. The series itself was not given its proper title of *The Chronicles of Narnia* until 1951. Paul Ford also notes that Lewis apparently went through four different "spurts of creative energy" when it came to writing the Narnia stories: the first concerned *The Lion, the Witch and the Wardrobe* "and a rough draft of *The Magician's Nephew*;" the second produced *Prince Caspian* and *Voyage of the Dawn Treader*; third came *The Horse and His Boy*; and finally, *The Silver Chair*, *The Last Battle*, and *The Magician's Nephew*.[7] The publishing of this series has involved considerable controversy since the late twentieth century, when HarperCollins acquired the rights and decided to publish the books according to the chronology of Narnia (as Laurence Krieg suggested approximately 40 years earlier), using Lewis's letter to Krieg as support for such a decision.

However, many believe this new ordering detracts from the aesthetic and stylistic value of Lewis's narrative, such as is voiced in the second chapter of Peter Schakel's *The Way into Narnia: A Reader's Guide*.[8]

The critical reception of the series has been predominantly positive. Not only has the series remained commercially successful by staying in print since the mid-1950s, but it also received critical success by being awarded the Carnegie Medal—which honors outstanding literature for children—for *The Last Battle* in 1956. However, not all of the reception has been so glowing, especially among several contemporary popular writers: J.K. Rowling, Neil Gaiman, and Philip Pullman. Both Rowling and Gaiman are concerned with the manner in which Susan Pevensie's character becomes represented, or, better put, becomes absented in *The Last Battle*, referred to by her brother as "no longer a friend in Narnia." Several others who know Susan in this scene chip in to say her absence is because Susan is more concerned with "nylons and lipstick and invitations" than with Aslan and Narnia.[9] Rowling interprets Susan's condition of being "irreligious basically because she found sex" as highly problematic.[10] Gaiman, of the same mindset, wrote a short story whose title has become eponymous with the issue: "The Problem of Susan." In this story, Gaiman provides an intriguing conversation between a young reporter and a retired professor named Susan who has, oddly (or conveniently), experienced the same loss of family that Susan Pevensie experienced in the Narnia series. Greta, the young reporter, serves as the voice of Lewis enthusiasts when she says, "even though Susan had refused Paradise then, she still had time while she lived to repent." Through a series of statements, Susan the Professor refutes the idyllic notions from Narnia apologists such as Greta and positions the death of the Pevensie family in a realistic setting for the reader, specifically in having to identify the bodies: "'A god who would punish me for liking nylons and parties by making me walk through that school dining room, with the flies, to identify Ed, well … he's enjoying himself a bit too much, isn't he?'"[11]

Pullman's statements could be considered the most vitriolic of the three. In his famous article in the *Guardian* in 1998, "The Dark Side of Narnia," Pullman marvels at how Lewis has become a literary celebrity who is "beyond the reach of ordinary criticism."[12] While recognizing Lewis's scholarly contributions, Pullman is not shy about saying the Narnia series "is one of the most ugly and poisonous things I've ever read." He gives several reasons, including the much-talked-about scene in *The Last Battle*, where the children learn they are already dead: "To slaughter the lot of them, and then claim they're better off, is not honest storytelling: it's propaganda in the service of life-hating ideology. But that's par for the course. Death is better than life; boys are better than girls; light-coloured people are better than dark-coloured people."[13] In this oft-quoted passage from Pullman and elsewhere in his article, he has hit upon several points of controversy that will be addressed by several chapters in this New Casebook, especially dealing with the topics of racism and sexism and "The Problem of Susan."

But Alan Jacobs, a Narnia apologist, both addresses Gaiman's "The Problem of Susan" and refutes Pullman's claims that Susan cannot enter heaven because of her budding sexuality. Instead, Jacobs suggests two reasons this is not so: that her exile resulted from her desiring "social acceptance," and also because she was not dead and so could not be officially denied entrance into heaven.[14] He also mentions a portion of Lewis's oft-quoted 1957 letter to Martin Kilmer, a young boy who had questions about Susan's fate. Lewis writes, "The books don't tell us what happened to Susan. She is left alive in the world at the end, having by then turned into a rather silly, conceited young woman. But there is plenty of time for her to mend, and perhaps she will get to Aslan's country in the end—in her own way."[15] While the debate over Narnia's more controversial elements proves too complex to detail in its entirety here, this brief summary of some of the kinds of critical inquiry and scrutiny into the Narnia series should serve as justification for a New Casebook about this complex fantasy cycle.

Most who are familiar with C. S. Lewis's reputation as a Christian apologist, known for his numerous works such as *The Screwtape Letters*, realize that religious imagery plays a significant role in the Narnia series, so it is no surprise that *The Chronicles of Narnia* still resonate largely with a Christian audience. Even Pullman recognizes the celebrity status of Lewis when he acknowledges that Lewis's own conversion story (and its connection with Tolkien) has been mythologized. However, James Russell claims that Lewis's "books remain extremely popular with readers across the world, many of whom are unaware of, or uninterested in, their Christian subtext."[16] It is safe to say that Lewis's popularity is not limited to Christian circles; he is also well known for his contributions to the fields of medieval literature, science fiction, fantasy, and children's literature. His Narnia series, which certainly falls under the category of the last two fields mentioned, rests securely in the twenty-first-century canon of literature, and would be taught today in classes of all ages. Furthermore, like Tolkien's fiction, Lewis's Narnia series is considered one of the landmark fantasy texts from the second half of the twentieth century and has influenced a wide range of authors, even Pullman, whose *His Dark Materials* series can be viewed as a response to Narnia, and Rowling, who attributes Lewis's influence, especially crossing the threshold into Narnia via the wardrobe, on Harry Potter's crossing the threshold at Kings Cross Station into Hogwarts. Also, the enormous breadth of scholarship still written today about Narnia reinforces its canonicity and relevance. A simple MLA Bibliography search of the word "Narnia" found 81 hits for the past ten years alone. It seems that Narnia rests comfortably in both critical and popular circles, as evidenced by the numerous radio, stage, and television adaptations of Narnia. Of course, the most recent film adaptations by Walden Media are certainly at the forefront of contemporary awareness of Narnia. Russell observes that Walden Media's first Narnia film in 2005 was produced because of the fantasy bandwagon effect: their desiring to be included in the same successful box office cinematic history as the *Harry Potter* and *The Lord of the Rings* films.[17]

Aside from the more global and obvious religious themes, *The Chronicles of Narnia* certainly cover others, such as the importance of family. One of the catalysts for *The Lion, the Witch and the Wardrobe* was Lewis's own personal experience with British evacuee children, like the Pevensies, seeking refuge from the city during the beginning part of World War II. Three girls, Margaret, Mary, and Katherine, stayed with Mrs. Moore, where Lewis was living at the time. Scholars have also noted how this theme of "parentlessness" in Narnia finds parallels in Lewis's own life. Ford notices how "the death of his mother when he was nine" deeply affected him, and the image of an ailing parent or dead parents can be seen with Digory in *The Magician's Nephew* and with Caspian in *Prince Caspian*.[18] Arguably, one of the most important overarching themes of the series is that of redemption, oftentimes because of an act of betrayal, greed, pride, or some other personal sin; and the redemption of Edmund by Aslan on the Stone Table serves as one of the most iconic acts of redemption in the series. Redemption by means of deliverance can be found when Prince Caspian, with the help of the Pevensies, reclaims Narnia and the missing lords, respectively, in *Prince Caspian* and *The Voyage of the Dawn Treader*; when Jill and Eustace rescue Prince Rilian in *The Silver Chair*; when Bree and Shasta seek redemption from slavery in *The Horse and His Boy*; and when Aslan redeems the wrongs by Digory in *The Magician's Nephew* and Shift in *The Last Battle*.

Much has been written about the existence—or the lack thereof—of Christian allegory in the *Chronicles*. Walter Hooper, one of the foremost Lewis scholars and biographers of the last half-century (partly because of his close relationship with Lewis), insists that Lewis and Tolkien believed their books were not allegories because they used a different definition of the word. According to Hooper's 1974 essay,

"Narnia: The Author, the Critics, and the Tale," they believed an allegory operates from concrete to the abstract—"the use of something real and tangible to stand for that which is real but intangible," and if they operated on a system that went from concrete to concrete, it would not fit the definition of allegory.[19] James Como is less than enthusiastic in his account of the recent (as of 1982) body of work written by "allegorizers":

> The Chronicles of Narnia have been particularly harassed, for the "allegorizers"—equivocating, narrow and not disinterested—have had the field largely to themselves. When not simply psychologizing (ordinarily as a means of attack on Lewis' Christian premises), these interpreters have produced little more than enthusiastic cartographies ... In short, much current work on Lewis, posturing as scholarship, consists of diatribe, pedantic analyses, or cheerleading formulas.[20]

What is significant about Como's perspective is that allegory is an instrument used not by Lewis enthusiasts alone, but also by Lewis detractors.

However, more recently, Jean E. Graham uses allegory to refute Peter Schakel's notion in *Reading with the Heart* that the White Witch cannot be an allegory for the Devil. She argues that the White Witch, if indeed she is a form of the Lilith literary figure, can have demonic relations of one kind or another, and can also be considered an immortal figure if we take the possibility of her resurrection in *Prince Caspian* into account.[21] In the same year, Amanda Rogers Jones extensively scrutinized the use of allegory in Narnia: "Although Lewis disclaimed much use of allegory, I find the term has since been explained by Piehler to correspond closely to Lewis' actual use of symbolic imagery in Narnia."[22] It seems that Jones's combination of Christianity and psychology provides a new strategy for appropriating the term "allegory." Edwards seems to believe Lewis was writing an allegory, saying, "Tolkien denied its [*The Lord of the Rings*] being an allegory, which his friend Lewis would create on Christ's Crucifixion in *The Lion, the Witch and the Wardrobe*. *The Lord of the Rings* seems something allied but opposite: a parable."[23] Also, Rebecca Davies notes that Elizabeth Baird Hardy's book concerning the literary sources of Lewis emphasizes the fact that "all of the texts discussed were intended to be allegorical, including the *Chronicles* ... [and thereby] provides an explanation for the virgin/whore dichotomy that appears to afflict the representation of many female characters in all the texts,"[24] including John Milton and Edmund Spenser. Clearly, the debate about the degree or existence of allegory in the *Chronicles* continues to provide new opinions and suggestions from different viewpoints, and selected essays in this New Casebook continue this discussion, such as Joseph Michael Sommers's essay (Chapter 5), which argues that the Narnia series is not allegorical. Nevertheless, it is important to note that, with regard to Como's statement about the nature of "allegorizers," the majority of the publications I have mentioned in the past two paragraphs did not come from vanity or religious presses.

Methodology and organization of the collection

To begin this section, I want to continue with Peter Hunt's own introduction to his edited collection to serve as a rationale for the methodology and ideological emphasis that this New Casebook seeks to employ when analyzing the Narnia series as a complex text. Hunt provides in his introductory chapter an explanation and a defense of studying children's literature in academia, arguing that

> we can reflect on the direct or indirect influence that children's books have, and have had, socially, culturally, and historically. They are overtly important educationally and commercially—with consequences across the culture, from language to politics: most adults, and almost certainly the vast majority in positions of power and influence, read children's books as children, and it is inconceivable that the ideologies permeating those books had no influence on their development.[25]

What makes Hunt's remarks here so important to my undertaking of this New Casebook is how we can interchange the phrase "the Narnia series" for "children's books." Through this chapter and the subsequent chapters, we will be discussing the importance of looking at the Narnia series through a critical lens of literary, popular, and cultural analysis, highlighting topics that have formerly been over-looked or discussed in new ways, such as the presence of violence, racial and gender politics, and cinematic and commercial adaptations. As several essays will argue, the commercial success not only of the book series but also of the recent Hollywood movie and game series is significant for showing how Narnia has had a lasting influence on popular culture. The following sections illustrate the rationale behind the organization of the essays.

Part I: Text and Contexts

The chapters in this section provide new contexts for reading the rest of the Narnia series. Rachel Towns (Chapter 1) observes that food in Narnia affects characterization, both in terms of gender and nationality, and serves as an indicator of morality; and Melody Green (Chapter 2) takes a closer look at how *The Lion, the Witch and the Wardrobe* in its various textual adaptations employs the theoretical model of scapegoating as a means of appeasing violence.

Part II: Applications and Implications

The second section explores various uses and misuses of Lewis's Narnia series in realms ranging from the public school classroom, treatment of war trauma, and secular interpretations of the apocalypse. Keith Dorwick (Chapter 3) analyzes the representation of formal education as it plays out in the Narnia series and argues that Lewis prized "experiential education" over rote memorization. Nanette Norris (Chapter 4) situates *The Chronicles of Narnia* as part of the post-traumatic cultural recovery of the twentieth century; and Joseph Michael Sommers (Chapter 5) incorporates Bahktin's chronotope as a means to explore Lewis's construction of various kinds of time and space.

Part III: Adaptations and Mediations

The essays in this next section examine the textual evolutions of the Narnia series itself with the presence of these narratives in realms other than merely print culture, such as television shows, feature-length films, and even in new media technologies like video games. Rhonda Brock-Servais and Matthew B. Prickett (Chapter 6) examine how the 2005 Walden Media film adaptation of *The Lion, the Witch and the Wardrobe* becomes itself adapted into early reader texts and what this means for adaptation studies. Aaron Clayton (Chapter 7) continues this examination into the digital world by discussing how Lewis's theology becomes problematically translated from *The Lion, the Witch and the Wardrobe* book to the video game based on the 2005 Walden Media movie adaptation of the same name.

Part IV: Conflicts and Controversy

The final part focuses on some of the most recent and heated critical debates regarding the series, which includes the series' influence on Philip Pullman and the complicated portrayal of race and gender. Gili Bar-Hillel (Chapter 8) recognizes the differences in beliefs between Pullman and Lewis before making a thought-provoking case for how these two authors have much more in common than initially believed, arguing that Lewis is a "literary father" to Pullman. Jennifer Taylor (Chapter 9) approaches the controversial racial elements in the Narnia series, specifically in *The Last Battle* and *The Horse and His Boy*, from a different angle than previous scholars, noting that neither side of the racism debate has considered the thematic purpose of racial representation, and arguing that these elements work together to expose and condemn offensive racial viewpoints. Finally, Susana Rodriguez (Chapter 10) addresses the Narnia series from a gender perspective, arguing that the Narnia stories convey a gender paradox and also imply the problematic position of a sexualized girl,[26] especially in Susan's case.

I finish this Introduction with a return to the image of the faun. I mentioned that this image lends itself to at least two levels of responses: the nostalgic, oneiric one, and also a problematic, sexualized one. But there could also be a third level—a heterogeneous communal response. Lewis said his image contained a faun carrying parcels. Who were these parcels for? The narrator of the novel is led to believe they are Christmas presents. Even though we learn it is not Christmas in Narnia at the beginning of the story, the diverse, unlikely pair of Tumnus and Lucy certainly builds a long-lasting community, and so it is with those who enter the world of Narnia through multiple forms of readerly participation. I believe it is safe to say that this community of Narnia participants actually consists of a combination of both the first and second. As the essays in this New Casebook suggest, there are as many doors to enter the study of Narnia as there are critical perspectives and textualities, and who is to say that a scholar cannot also be a fan?

Notes

1. C. S. Lewis, "It All Began with a Picture," in Walter Hooper (ed.), *Of Other Worlds: Essays and Stories* (London: Geoffrey Bles, 1966): 42–3, at 42.
2. Owen Dudley Edwards, *British Children's Fiction in the Second World War* (Edinburgh: Edinburgh University Press, 2009): 155.
3. Roger Lancelyn Green and Walter Hooper, *C. S. Lewis: A Biography* (New York: HarperCollins, 2002): 307.
4. Colin Duriez, *Tolkien and C. S. Lewis: The Gift of Friendship* (Mahwah, NJ: Paulist Press, 2003): 131.
5. Peter Hunt, "Introduction: The World of Children's Literature Studies," in Peter Hunt (ed.), *Understanding Children's Literature: Key Essays from the International Companion Encyclopedia of Children's Literature* (London: Routledge, 1999): 1–14, at 2.
6. Paul F. Ford, *Companion to Narnia: A Complete Guide to the Magical World of C. S. Lewis's The Chronicles of Narnia* (New York: HarperCollins, 2005): 23–4.
7. *Ibid.*: 16.
8. Peter Schakel, *The Way into Narnia: A Reader's Guide* (Grand Rapids, MI: Eerdmans, 2005).

9. C. S. Lewis, *The Last Battle. The Chronicles of Narnia* (New York: HarperCollins, 2001): 665–767, at 741.

10. Lev Grossman, "J.K. Rowling Hogwarts and All," *Time*, July 17, 2005: www.time.com/time/printout/0,8816,1083935,00.html (accessed May 15, 2011).

11. Neil Gaiman, "The Problem of Susan," in *Fragile Things: Short Fictions and Wonders* (New York: William Morrow, 2006): 181–90, at 186–7.

12. Philip Pullman, "The Dark Side of Narnia," *Cumberland River Lamp Post*, September 2, 2001: www.crlamppost.org/darkside.htm (accessed May 15, 2011).

13. Pullman's article, originally published at http://reports.guardian.co.uk/articles/1998/10/1/p-24747.html, is no longer available. I found a reprint at the *Cumberland River Lamp Post* website, given in note 12 above.

14. Alan Jacobs, *The Narnian: The Life and Imagination of C. S. Lewis* (San Francisco, CA: HarperSanFrancisco, 2005): 260.

15. C. S. Lewis, *C. S. Lewis's Letters to Children*, ed. Lyle W. Dorsett and Marjorie Lamp Mead (New York: Touchstone, 1985): 67.

16. James Russell, "Narnia as a Site of National Struggle: Marketing, Christianity, and National Purpose in *The Chronicles of Narnia: The Lion, the Witch and the Wardrobe*," *Cinema Journal* 48(4) (2009): 59–76, at 64.

17. *Ibid*.: 65.

18. Ford: 105.

19. Walter Hooper, "Narnia: The Author, the Critics, and the Tale," *Children's Literature* 3 (1974): 12–22, at 15.

20. James Como, "Mediating Illusions: Three Studies of Narnia," *Children's Literature* 10 (1982): 163–8, at 164.

21. Jean E Graham, "Women, Sex, and Power: Circe and Lilith in Narnia," *Children's Literature Association Quarterly* 29(1–2) (2004): 32–44, at 39–40; Peter J. Schakel, *Reading with the Heart: The Way into Narnia* (Grand Rapids, MI: Eerdmans, 1979): 9.

22. Amanda Rogers Jones, "The Narnian Schism: Reading the Christian Subtext as Other in the Children's Stories of C. S. Lewis," *Children's Literature Association Quarterly* 29(1–2) (2004): 45–61, at 47.

23. Edwards: 308.

24. Rebecca Davies, Review of *Milton, Spenser and The Chronicles of Narnia: Literary Sources for the C.S Lewis Novels* by Elizabeth Baird Hardy, *Children's Literature Association Quarterly* 32(4) (2007): 400–2, at 401.

25. Hunt: 1.

26. This past summer, as I was watching Walden Media's *The Voyage of the Dawn Treader* (2010) as it was being broadcast on the Tilt Train from Bundaberg to Brisbane, Australia, it became even more clear to me just how much the concept of sexual maturity does not belong in Narnia, especially near the end of the film when Aslan tells Lucy and Edmund that they have grown up and are not allowed back in Narnia.

Part I
Text and Contexts

1

"Turkish Delights and Sardines with Tea": Food as a Framework for Exploring Nationalism, Gender, and Religion in *The Lion, the Witch and the Wardrobe*

Rachel Towns

Food grabs our attention, right from the beginning of *The Lion, the Witch and the Wardrobe*. The very first meals in the new land of Narnia provide a contrast through which characters' identities are constructed. Their meal choices both reveal their personalities and position them as positive or negative. Food transforms from a mere necessity of life to an integral part of the narrative, as characters' choices about food and involvement with meals shape how they are perceived. Food is presented in such a way as to be connotative of meanings and understandings beyond its own literal reality.

Specific fare is clearly associated with particular nationalities, signposting the identity of the characters who eat that food as connected to that country. Furthermore, the preparation or offering of food brings gender into the construction of identity, as it communicates perceptions of what is acceptable or unacceptable. As characters conform to or subvert gender roles, they are correspondingly identified as good or evil. Food is also used to connect the narrative with Christianity, as the transformation of Narnian characters from human to "meal" echoes the transformation of Jesus revealing important concepts within Christianity.

British is best: British food as a signifier of good character

Jean Anthelme Brillat-Savarin once said, "Tell me what you eat and I will tell you who you are."[1] Although written in 1826, that comment rings true for *The Lion, the Witch and the Wardrobe*, published in 1950. Food is used as a signifier of identity, demarcating good and evil characters based on the nationality of their food. Countries share meals, ensuring that "the commonality of food is a linchpin of group identification."[2] Normally, this is a kind of "gastro-nationalism,"[3] where the national identity of a country is bound up in the food choices that members of this nationality make, thus endowing the food with characteristics of that nationality. However, in Narnia, nationality becomes a food-created concept, as the attributed food nationality is used to create the "national" identity of those who eat it. This "national identity" applied through food is one which is constructed outside of Narnia and then placed upon its landscape. Thus protagonists—the good, main characters—in Narnia are always associated with eating "good" traditional British fare, while antagonists make "foreign" or "other" food choices, correspondingly constructing their characters as "other."

The four children—Peter, Susan, Edmund, and Lucy—are all British, and therefore their connection to British food makes sense, for "loyalty to familiar food is emphasised in children's literature,"[4] thus consolidating their national identity. Any meals these children eat which have the "hallmark of English cooking,"[5] such as "roast meat and vegetables, stews, pies and pasties, … steam puddings"[6] or "afternoon tea,"[7] only helps to construct their British identity. All the children only eat British food, with the exception of Edmund, and are identified as good characters, beginning the connection between British food and good actions.

Choice of food by the Narnian characters strengthens the connections of food, nationality, and identity, as good Narnian characters are equally constrained to meals of British construction. This appears more unusual, for one would expect a fantasy world with fantastical environments and creatures to have interesting food; however, the food is not "a feast befitting a wondrous kingdom,"[8] but rather a reversion to familiar, comforting, and, above all, British food. These good characters are so anglicized by their food choices that they are more British than Narnian. Indeed Mr. and Mrs. Beaver are almost more British than the children, living in a "literally Northernised" environment of "a log cabin with snow shoes, rocking chair, stove, sewing machine and fishing tackle."[9] Even their environment does not escape the connection to food, for on their ceiling is British fare of "hams and strings of onions."[10]

British food can even assuage concerns about characters, for when the children first meet Mr. Beaver, they are concerned by questions of "are we to go to it?" based on their fears of following "a guide we know nothing about."[11] It is only when he suggests going to his house for "a real talk and also dinner" that none of them "felt any difficulty about trusting the Beaver now …"[12] This potentially dangerous situation of going to a strange location with a stranger is defused by the powerful goodness associated with British food.

In this new world the four children are unable to recognize signs to indicate the internal nature of characters. They even originally fear that some of their strongest allies might really be enemies.[13] In their own world they are able to identify dangerous people, based on their experience. In this world, it is characters like Mr. Beaver who are able to identify characters as "good" or "evil" based on their appearance. It is he who identifies Edmund's connection to the White Witch because "[h]e had the look of one who has been with the Witch."[14] The children, unused to this world, are unable to see the evil in their brother. However, even Mr. Beaver uses food as a guide, for his recognition of Edmund's nature stems from him having "eaten his food."[15] This food not only changes Edmund's internal nature, but also begins to alter his external appearance, so that his body shows his internal corruption. Without experience in Narnia, the children are forced to rely on the ingestion of good stolid healthy food as a signifier of goodness in others. It is a powerful signpost to characters' natures as it helps them to identify allies in the Beavers and even has transformative powers.

Evil impulses can even be overcome by the power of British food. The first meal eaten in Narnia was an afternoon tea for Lucy Pevensie, hosted by Mr. Tumnus the faun. From Lucy's first meeting with him, there is a contradiction between his external appearance as a foreign and otherworldly faun and his very British umbrella. He is identified as "a very strange person," whose appearance ranges from the normal, wearing a "red woolen muffler," to the abnormal: "his legs were shaped like a goat."[16] These features posit him as foreign and threatening. As he invites her into his house, he epitomizes the fears of "don't trust a stranger." However, this is contrasted with the food used to entice her; it is not stereotypical lollies, but rather food of more British construction. When he first invites her for "tea," she protests that she needs to return home, until he mentions the specific food of "toast—and sardines—and a cake," which allays Lucy's fears as she appears to regard those food choices as safe.[17] The meal itself is an afternoon tea, the quintessential English meal.[18] It was a "wonderful tea" full of good hearty food, from a "nice brown egg … [to] sardines on toast … [and even] a sugar topped cake."[19] It is all rich food, but it is also correspondingly British food, an idealization of the traditional

English afternoon tea—almost utopian when compared to the restrictions of wartime Britain. The nationality of the food changes the potential paradigm of the meal as enticement of the child, Lucy, to one which transforms the adult, Mr. Tumnus.

As a faun, a strange otherworldly male creature, he engenders ideas of enticement and kidnapping. This is in fact his intended role, since he was recruited by the Witch to bring her any humans he met.[20] However, the food itself is what saves Lucy, for it anglicizes Mr. Tumnus. Instead of being some kind of foreign, strange creature, he now "lives in a cave and serves tea," embodying an Oxbridge don, dispensing knowledge and afternoon tea from his academic "cave," rather like C. S. Lewis himself: "If a faun could be found living in an English wood his home would certainly be like this," and also his meals.[21] By taking Lucy in and feeding her, he assists in his own redemption through food. Originally, he "pretended to be your [Lucy's] friend and asked you [Lucy] to tea,"[22] but once they ate together "the items ingested sa[id] something meaningful about … themselves"[23] so that their relationship changed from pretension to friendship to real friendship. After they eat together he realizes: "I can't give you up to the Witch, not now I know you."[24] How did he know her so quickly? Above all, he learned her identity—and created his own—when they ate together. Their identities are now clearly connected to both good and Britain. This afternoon tea is so powerful a force for good that it overcomes even the fear of injury, for he risks being maimed or turned into stone if he helps Lucy. [25] The food Mr. Tumnus ingests transforms him into the stereotype of a British gentleman, who would save Lucy from her fate to the detriment of his own.

Characters that provide the good, sustaining British food are therefore connected to stereotypical British qualities and are confirmed as protagonists. The food that they consume is like them: it is plain, but honest and good. The "plain economical food"[26] is glorified through the descriptive language used, connecting it to the power of good. Instead of milk, fish, and cake, it is "a jug of creamy milk … a big lump of deep yellow butter, … [and] there's nothing to beat good freshwater fish."[27] Healthy, life-giving food with beautiful colors and smells sustains the characters and confirms the positive qualities of all who are satisfied with these meals. Edmund, although he apparently eats the British meal with the others, is not satisfied with it, because he focused on his former meal of Turkish Delight, which "spoils the taste of good ordinary food."[28] His lack of satisfaction with English-style meals is a reflection of his morally ambivalent nature at this point.

Foreign foods are not to be trusted: British nationalism and war shape foreigners as "other"

The representation of food in the novel is strongly influenced by the contemporary situation of World War II as present in the "real" world and also as it contributes to the xenophobic views that connect good and bad characters to specific food choices. As Susan Rowland suggests, one cannot divorce the war from Narnia because in many respects this story is an attempt "to contain and rewrite the terrible story of a war."[29] The Pevensie children "'escape' to the Professor's House in the country"[30] for safety from the Nazis in a war they have no control over. When "they 'escape' again to Narnia ... [they] encounter another criminal regime."[31] However, this regime is one that the children can combat and ultimately are able to destroy. Significantly, one of the important elements used in the Narnian war is food, which is used to identify whether characters are good or bad as well as being one of the weapons used to transform the nature of the consumer.

In the Narnian war, the association of British food and good becomes more than simple patriotic rhetoric, as it comes to identify which side they are allied with. As a "signifier of national identity,"[32] it turns the battleground of Narnia into a nationalistic debate of the British good and the evil "other." Evil characters, in particular the White Witch and Edmund, are damned by their food choices to be seen as "other." They are not necessarily Germanicized; *The Lion, the Witch and the Wardrobe* was not intended as a literal comparison to World War II, but rather constructs identities in opposition: there is the good British, and the foreign "other." There is clearly an ideal-ization of English products beyond the reality of England and the English experience of food during the war, so Narnia is not the reality of England, but rather "*England* as it should be,"[33] a reimagining of England in a simpler time, with correspondingly idealized qualities of warrior mentality and appropriate performance of gender roles.

The "other" does not represent specific countries from the Axis, but a generalized nationally based xenophobia of foreigners. As the concept of England is idealized, so those identified as "others" or foreigners are correspondingly demonized. Consequently, when the two characters, later identified as evil, first meet, their food choices very quickly enter into the debate of foreign as "other" and evil. As British food protected the good nature of Mr. Tumnus, "foreign" food corrupts and destroys the moral worth of those who eat it. Edmund, although English, is open to the moral corruption of Turkish Delight through his "preoccupation with food and his greed"[34] as well as his already morally ambivalent nature, making him "spiteful"[35] when he can find an appropriate target. Edmund's meal serves as a contrast to Lucy's first meal as he experiences a foreign food. In children's literature, foreign food "is often viewed as threatening"[36] and is therefore associated with more evil or ambiguous characters.

Labeling of characters as good or bad through their food choices is never shown more clearly than in the case of Edmund. Although Edmund had appeared "unpleasant"[37] in the events previous to entering Narnia, it is only there that he actively turns to the evil side. Previously, his bad actions were explained away, as he "was tired … which always made him bad-tempered."[38] So, although showing a proclivity toward nastiness, there is an understanding of the character's motivations, allowing him to be partially redeemed. Once he enters Narnia, instead of Lucy's positive experience with good, British-style food which protects her, he meets the White Witch. Her food is as exotic as her appearance, "white like snow or paper or icing sugar."[39] Although she is not stereotypically "foreign" in her appearance, there is an unreality to her face that highlights her lack of true humanity.

The appearance of the Witch as being like icing sugar presages her first meal with Edmund of excessively sweet food and drink. It is also reminiscent of the deception of gingerbread houses that promise much, but offer little. She appears good on the outside like sweet sugar, Turkish Delight, and the unknown drink that is so readily offered; in reality, all this sugar is not positive and has its own consequences, hidden behind its sweet appearance. This food also hides its secret poisonous nature, for it is "enchanted" so "anyone … would want more and more of it" to the detriment of their own health.[40] Therefore, this exotic food is unhealthy not only because of its own nature, but also because of its addictive qualities. It is bad for Edmund's health, but also bad for his nature because it transforms him into one of the evil characters: "The temptational aspect of evil is represented symbolically in the texts, by Turkish Delight"[41]; its sweet seduction begins by leading Edmund to perceive the White Witch positively, but ultimately leads to the betrayal of his family.

As with Lucy, when Edmund first meets a Narnian he is offered food. His greed leads him to ignore his instinctive fear of the White Witch, so that by the end of his meal, he "felt much better"[42] about her. However, this feeling of security, developed through consuming her meal, is a deceptive one, for both the food and the drink are foreign to him. The drink was "something he had never tasted before" and so foreign to his British palate, while the food, although

Edmund's choice, is equally exotic—Turkish Delight.[43] The very name of this food indicates its foreign qualities, and there is an insidious "racism [that] is implicit in the [association of] evils ... [with] 'Turkish Delight.'"[44] This sweet slowly starts to change Edmund: he moves from "remember[ing] that it is rude to speak with one's mouth full"[45] to ignoring polite convention in the satiation of his greed. This is a minor change that reflects the stronger seduction that transforms him from being annoying to someone who betrays his own family "in order to gain self-satisfaction and power."[46] This connection of betrayal to foreign sweets thereby suggests that the quality of betrayal is one foreign to a true English identity.

Food is used as a weapon by the White Witch to bring Edmund to her side, but it also leads to her loss in the Narnian war. It is successful as a weapon in turning him to her side; however, when Edmund returns to her without his siblings, she punishes him and uses food to do it. Instead of a sweet seduction into evil with Turkish Delight, Edmund's "policy and guile are appropriately rewarded"[47] with the prosaic reality of bread and water. Tauntingly described as "Turkish Delight for the little Prince,"[48] it awakens Edmund to the nature of his betrayal, the extent of the Witch's deception, as well as to his own self-deception. Once her true colors are shown, there is a clear contrast between the Witch's false meal and "the Beaver's true meal."[49] This starts to turn Edmund, the Witch's first real weapon in the war against Aslan, from an ally to a potential enemy. The Witch knows that she will be defeated if two Sons of Adam and two Daughters of Eve are able to ascend the thrones at Cair Paravel.[50] However, instead of appeasing Edmund's desire for Turkish Delight in order to alienate him from his family and prevent the prophecy's fulfillment, she gives in to anger and uses food as her weapon. Lack of hospitality from the Witch makes Edmund more aware of food: first for himself, as usual, thinking "about breakfast,"[51] before moving to concern for others. The Animal's Christmas party that the White Witch meets on her way to Aslan is a direct affront to the Witch, for it threatens her rule of "always winter and never Christmas."[52] This food is not the "phantasmic food [of the Witch that] will not nourish,"[53] for there is eating and merriment rather than obsession. Destruction of this meal helps Edmund because when the Witch turns all the creatures eating their traditional (British) Christmas dinner into statues, his moral nature is reawakened. Despite not partaking of the Christmas meal, the incident allows Edmund to develop a sense of what is really important: "for the first time in this story, [he] felt sorry for someone besides himself."[54] For Edmund, food is a powerful signifier of, and transformer of, identity. When he eats the Turkish Delight he is prepared to betray his family; when he is given crusts of bread, he reevaluates the Witch and becomes aware of her deception of him; but it is only when he sees the British meal being eaten and then silenced into stone by the Witch that he returns to his positive and patriotic British roots of right and wrong. When Edmund is rescued by Aslan's army, it triggers two events which lead the defeat of the Witch: it is he who in the battle "had the sense to bring his sword smashing down on her wand,"[55] destroying the White Witch's power, and it is his betrayal and redemption that triggers Aslan's sacrifice, leading to the defeat and destruction of the Witch. However, if the Witch had continued to placate Edmund with food, there would have been no sacrifice by Aslan, no deeper magic, and no fourth occupant for the thrones at Cair Paravel. Her use of food as a weapon to punish Edmund for his failure ultimately becomes the source of her defeat.

Women in the kitchen, men outside: appropriate gender roles in meal preparation

Meal preparations are used to highlight whether characters conform or subvert gender stereotypes. As traditional British food is highlighted as the food of good people in Narnia, so conforming to "traditional" gender roles is indicated as the only appropriate behavior: "Sexual difference is arbitrary and must be constantly reconstructed"[56] in society. Therefore, referring to the gender roles as being "traditional" reflects the context that *The Lion, the Witch and the Wardrobe* was constructed in—a context in which the author "saw feminism as a modern evil"[57] and perceived the subversion of gender roles as a degenerative activity. The confirmation or subversion of gender roles is often demonstrated through the preparation or offering of food.

"[D]ominant ideas about masculinity and femininity"[58] are explored through the interactions that the characters have with food. Thus the good male characters have very little to do with the cooking of food, and even when food is brought forth by male characters, there is never any real reference to them making the meal. The meal provided by Father Christmas is offered without reference to him "creating" the meal. In some senses his offering is not a meal at all, for all he provides is sugar, cream and a pot of tea. It only becomes a meal when it is joined with the ham and bread, packed by Mrs. Beaver, reestablishing meal preparation as part of the feminine domestic domain. Presentation of these provisions by Father Christmas develops a mysterious quality because "nobody quite saw him do it,"[59] which distances him from the action of preparing a meal.

This distancing of food preparation from men, even when they provide food, is one which is frequently encountered in the text. When Lucy first meets Mr. Tumnus, he invites her to come and have tea, but when they are in his house, there is no mention of him cooking or toasting the bread, only the innocuous mention of "setting out the tea things."[60] The closest he comes to food creation is not connected to food, but rather to tea as he "put a kettle on."[61] Both of the meals offered by Mr. Tumnus and Father Christmas limit the extent to which men are involved in the production of food, removing them from almost every action connected to food, except making tea. However, this can be connected to their identification as British, since tea is a "fragile yet enduring *symbol* of Englishness. The cup of *tea* goes hand in hand, moreover, with a particular disposition towards the natural world"[62] of colonial and imperialistic British oppression, thereby reflecting traditionally masculine ideals of "[w]ar and warrior worship,"[63] and thus making a feminine domestic beverage a symbol of colonial masculinity and strength.

Positive associations of men and appropriate involvement with food are highlighted by Mr. Beaver and Peter who exhibit a "manly self-image [as they embody the] ... traditional good of hunter-warriors"[64] when catching "a beautiful trout"[65] for dinner. By involving Peter, but not Edmund, this "hunt [is re-interpreted] as initiation"[66] into acceptable masculinity. These characters conform to traditional masculine roles in relation to food by embodying hunter roles or through bringing forth food without actually cooking it. It is only the good male characters who embody these traditional gender roles in relation to food; other male characters demonstrate more ambiguous interactions.

Female characters, on the other hand, are expected to be involved in the production of food since "[f]ood then becomes a way of measuring the worth of the mother [women] of the house, for a home with good domestic values is expected to provide a 'proper' meal."[67] As Mr. Beaver was the embodiment of the masculine "Man of the house," his wife "Mrs. Beaver ... [portrays the embodiment of an] Earth Mother ... [who, despite being] surprised to have visitors," manages to produce from the oven "a great and gloriously sticky marmalade roll."[68] Her involvement with food includes all the nitty-gritty elements of food production. Even the miraculous marmalade roll, although emerging unexpectedly, comes from the prosaic location of the oven, dispelling enchantment and magic in favor of demonstrating domestic ideals of good organization and cooking ability. As a good female character, Mrs. Beaver is shown to be involved in the production of good and healthy food. Food is not just magically offered; it is made from beginning with every step documented as a symbol of femininity. It is simple and plain food, but one in which she and the two girls, Lucy and Susan, are involved in completely. There is the drawn-out process of mutually working together to "fill the kettle and lay the table and cut the bread and put the plates in the oven to heat."[69] On the face of it, this appears to be an unnecessary passage. Why explain that it was Susan who drained the potatoes or that it was Lucy who helped Mrs. Beaver? The reason is that it more definitively confirms their performance of appropriate gender roles.[70] The worth of the girls is being shown through the good food that they create, while the worth of the boys is shown when they catch food or when they provide food without appearing to create that food.

Subversive eating, subversive behaviors: food preparation that subverts gender roles subverts the personality as well

In opposition to these appropriate behaviors with food, the designated evil characters show more ambivalent interactions with food. Edmund, who becomes the center of the war between good and evil, is often shown to have an uncertain relationship with food. While in the Beavers' house the two girls assist Mrs. Beaver to cook and Peter helps Mr. Beaver to catch the fish for dinner, Edmund is conspicuously absent. Edmund remains unmentioned in the text until after the meal is consumed, despite being present until the end of the meal.[71] Edmund does not fulfill his masculine role since he does not assist in the hunting, but he does not subvert it by adopting feminine roles either. Instead he is silenced until after they have eaten, which implicitly removes him from the action of eating the British food.

Edmund's absence from the performance of gender roles could be connected to the idea that although he has turned to the evil side by joining with the Witch, ultimately he is still redeemable. Unlike the Witch who easily transgresses gender roles, Edmund is largely removed from the gender debate. However, in some senses, his desire for Turkish Delight could be perceived as emasculating because of its "oriental and romantic overtones,"[72] which makes it both "other" and feminine. Symbolism connected to this food is amplified since it is identified as what Edmund would "like best to eat,"[73] and instead of choosing food like "[m]eat [which is perceived to bring] qualities of strength, aggression, passion, [and] sexuality,"[74] he opts for the feminized, orientalized qualities of sugar. Edmund's relationship with food is one in which he fails to conform to male gender stereotypes, leaving him absent rather than subversive.

Subversion of the Witch's femininity develops in two ways. As a woman she is confined to the "virgin-mother-crone (or whore) dialectic."[75] Her appearance places her as a virgin or mother, and she plays and subverts both roles in relation to food.

As a food provider she plays a kind of destructive mother role to Edmund. Right from the start, Edmund is the "most resistant to the new house ... [and to the] separation from his parents, or more precisely his mother."[76] He avoids Susan's attempts to be a mother— "Don't go on talking ... like mother"[77]—but is clearly still searching for a mother figure, which he finds in the Witch. Her maternal qualities are communicated through the provision of food, the exotic Turkish Delight and the unfamiliar drink, "something he had never tasted before, very sweet."[78] Alston suggests that providing food is the action of a good mother in children's literature, for the "putting of food in the children's stomachs was the ultimate test of mother-hood ...."[79] The Witch appears to follow traditional female roles by proffering food.

However, by presenting sweet, exotic, foreign food and, more importantly, by offering the child a choice, she "subvert[s] this [maternal] role in providing him with the food he desires, rather than the foods he needs."[80] Instead of giving food that is healthy and wholesome, she provides the sweet Turkish Delight, so that Edmund becomes "[p]oisoned by the toxic mother's sugar."[81] He is poisoned not only by the sweet nature of the food itself, but also by its super-natural quality of creating an insatiable greed in the consumer.

Sweets are used by the Witch to disarm Edmund's suspicion of her and lead her to offer a false mothering of him: "I want a nice boy whom I could bring up as a Prince."[82] Identified as the Queen of Narnia, she is implicitly offering herself as a maternal substitute. However, this role is a destructive one, for when Edmund fails her she shows her true side and the promised Turkish Delight becomes stale bread and water. Her true destructive maternity is finally embodied through the averted sacrifice of Edmund. As the Witch realizes that she has been unable to prevent the other children meeting Aslan, her plans change from the destruction of them all, to the meal of Edmund. The preparations for his death echo those for a meal, for he is bound, like a trussed bird for roasting, and the Witch wished to kill him on a "table."[83] However, it is her weapon that most strongly indicates that the death of Edmund will also be a meal, for she is using a "knife"[84] to kill him. Where in the Beavers' House there was celebration of the femininity of Lucy, Susan, and Mrs. Beaver in their food preparation, in this scene the femininity of the Witch is most perverted in her preparations for this unnatural meal. She orders him to be prepared by her male dwarf, continuing the subversion of gender roles through the emasculation of her servant, both in his size and in his subservient preparatory role. The Witch's use of a knife is rendered horrific as she engages in the domestic action of sharpening a knife in order to kill him. This contrasts the offer of mothering with the reality of her destruction of him. She is not only a destructive mother at this point, but a devouring mother: a "vampire, a drawer of life from things to herself,"[85] consuming the life of her nation, including her own "child."

Labeling the Witch as a devouring mother contrasts with her other subversion of femininity, "virgin." The label of virgin is intended as a temporary phase and not as an eternal role. Although the Witch appears as a virgin in her youthful appearance and lack of a husband, her enchantment of Narnia for a hundred years and her connection to food renders her as an eternal virgin which subverts the traditional understanding of the role. The traditional role of virgin is a temporary role of innocence and purity as a child, which is transformed by motherhood. Because the witch is eternally virgin, she makes no transition to "real" motherhood, although she pretends to offer it, and her focus on death and power is a contrast to the values of innocence and purity that is implicitly indicated by her virginal status.

Her failure to consume is central to this subversion of femininity. Food is central to this novel, yet it is an experience she never engages in. Although she provides food to Edmund, the nature of the food as being either too much or too little suggests a dislocation of herself from food: anorexia in a world of consumption. Through her lack of physical food she is able to develop a body that never changes, just like the white, unchanging landscape of Narnia. She creates her own rules for the world that rely on an unchanging environment for her own security. The Witch through her lack of food becomes a static, unchanging environment, "unappealing not only sexually but gustatorily."[86] Nobody would want to eat her, for her body "is a symbol for disease (or dis-ease) by means of her whiteness,"[87] and nobody would want to have sex with her, which then avoids initiation into an adult female body and behavior. She externalizes her own battle with food and sexuality onto the landscape so that both her body and Narnia demonstrate the same pale, white sterility. By making Narnia white and limiting its fertility, she recreates the country as virginal and removes the possibility of Narnia bringing forth life. Avoiding food also subverts her mother role, for by refusing "food and body fat and femaleness [she] obviates the need to refuse motherhood. The anorexic *can't* be mother,"[88] just as the Witch "ha[s] no children of [her] own."[89] If she ate, she would lose control, just as she would lose control of the land if she let Narnia change through the seasons.

The Witch does not desire change, for under her rule Narnia becomes "always Winter and never Christmas."[90] To her, the joys of food and happiness that Father Christmas brings interrupt her idea of order and conformity. Christmas would feed Narnia, taking it outside of her consumptionless power. She actively destroys the Christmas food of others as a revenge for its having the potential to take away her power. Any change is perceived by her to be a threat to her sense of control and must be destroyed. Edmund's intrusion into Narnia is met first by one weapon, her wand, before being replaced by a much more insidious weapon, food, her own feared object, creating a kind of prolonged death. Her displaced fears of food are then transplanted onto others and used to destroy them. The enchanted Turkish Delight provided by the Witch is a clear weapon of death—her own fear of food leads to the creation of a meal which allows people to kill themselves by giving in to greed. Her own ability to avoid eating the addictive food shows her control over herself in relation to food.

Provision of this Turkish Delight also subverts traditional feminine roles because she does not cook and prepare this food; instead it magically arrives. It is an unreal food without the physical reality that cooking and preparing would give it. She assumes a masculine role in relation to food since it is provided without real creation. The Witch does not desire the feminine roles which are celebrated in the good female characters of domesticity—the bearing of children and the creation of food—because her world is made up solely of her fears: seeing Edmund makes her fear that her reign will end. She tries to hide from these fears, avoiding living her life in her attempts to prolong it. As the eternal virgin/anorexic, the Witch "has only one notion of reality."[91] She is unable to change her ideas and is therefore doomed when the world around her changes.

Betrayal and false gods: Edmund as a Judas figure

There is a strong connection between Narnia and Christianity. This connection is frequently highlighted through the medium of food, as meals are used connotatively to illustrate important messages in Christianity. Food is used to reinterpret messages from Christianity through the lens of Narnia, connecting Edmund and Aslan to biblical figures. Aligning the fantasy story with biblical events and characters connects meals with the opposing concepts of betrayal and redemption.

This concept of betrayal through food is explored through two characters: Edmund from *The Lion, the Witch and the Wardrobe* and Judas from the New Testament. Their characters are connected on many levels, so that Edmund "is made to play the part of Judas."[92] Originally both characters were incorporated within their groups: Edmund within the Pevensie family and Judas as part of the new family of apostles that Jesus created.[93] However, both characters demonstrate how their inclusion is not as deserved as the other members. Edmund is a continually "grumbling" character overly concerned with food: "we haven't even got anything to eat."[94] His moral weakness is demonstrated when he allows his appetite to shape his interactions in the new world. Judas is represented negatively when he objects to the use of expensive nard to anoint Jesus.[95] Ostensibly, this was because it could be used for "the poor," but really because "he was a thief," highlighting his objectionable nature.[96] As this anointing is a prelude to Jesus' death and the Last Supper, ultimately he is objecting to the transformation of Jesus from human to divine meal/sacrifice. This is mirrored in Narnia, when Edmund is dismissive of the divine nature of Aslan, believing the Witch superior. Edmund and Judas are represented as undesirable, with their obsessions becoming their downfall. They both become betrayers to their "families": Edmund by offering up his family for more Turkish Delight, and Judas by offering up his leader for "thirty pieces of silver."[97] For Edmund, the use of food as a tool of betrayal turns this action into both "the act of a thoroughly naughty boy and as a piece of primal treachery requiring the ultimate sacrifice on Aslan's part."[98] Judas's betrayal is also communicated through food, for during the Last Supper Jesus identifies that "[h]e who has shared my bread has turned against me."[99] Not only are past meals and previous table fellowship broken down by this accusation, but in that particular meal "it is the one to whom I give this piece of bread"[100] who is the betrayer.

Food is the communicant of betrayal and sin: the Turkish Delight is enchanted to make Edmund crave it above anything else, and it is when "Judas took the bread" given to him as the betrayer that "Satan entered into him."[101] Judas therefore does not betray simply for thirty pieces of silver but also through the semiotic power of food. Meals become connected to betrayal because these two characters are so caught up in their obsession that food or money/food becomes more important than other features of their lives. They have turned their obsession into a false idol, so it is both the object and themselves that they worship in their consumption. Both Judas and Edmund are more concerned with taking than giving, until the end, ensuring that their needs are satiated first. They also put their trust in characters "who would be gods unto themselves"[102] rather than ones who would be gods for others. Edmund places his trust in the Witch, a dangerous and powerful woman, because she gives him food. Her positive representation of herself as a woman is compromised when she had Mr. Tumnus taken away. However, Edmund continues to question the idea of perceiving her as evil.[103] He instinctively turns to the Witch because "[h]er flattery [had] appeal[ed] to his pride and her magical Turkish delight to his gluttony."[104] Judas also turns to people who are not worthy of the faith he puts in them. As a counterpart to the White Witch who styles herself Queen, his false gods are the "chief priests"[105] who in their hereditary religious positions believed that they were the only source of religious knowledge and understanding. They "feared the popularity of Jesus" because he threatened their authority by "refus[ing] to respond clearly to"[106] them and because he engaged in table fellowship with those deemed by the chief priests "as hopelessly excluded from the kingdom of God."[107]

Both of these false gods fear losing their positions to the real religious figure of Aslan/Jesus. The chief priests look for any reason, even "false evidence against Jesus, so they could put him to death."[108] Similarly, the Witch does everything in her power to destroy Aslan and his followers, even by cheating, promising Aslan she will kill only him as a sacrifice to protect his people, while planning to kill his followers. Therefore these "false gods" use "false" food/money as a counter to the "true meal" of Jesus and Aslan. These meals encourage the betrayal of figures whose very role as apostles or as one of the kings would most wound the real messianic figure. Both Edmund and Judas realize, too late, that their betrayal was not worth the cost. For Edmund this was when the Witch's promises of rooms of Turkish Delight turn into stale bread and water, and for Judas it is when his "remorse" means that he "returned the thirty pieces of silver" but still fails to save Jesus, the bread of life.[109] The meals of Judas and Edmund after they have betrayed highlight the true nature of their false gods, whose promises are as false as their divine/religious nature. As a false god the Witch has no real power, and her meals are tasteless once the illusion of seductive betrayal is removed. Stale food that is provided by the Witch echoes her stale promises and serves to awaken Edmund to the nature of his betrayal. Equally, the chief priests who represented themselves as being on the side of truth and God follow neither since their need to remove Jesus overrides their concern for their own religion. The money they gave becomes blood money once Jesus is sentenced, and Judas is left with no real lasting meal as he abandons their impure meal of money. This contrasts with Jesus and Aslan, who transform themselves into never-ending meals. Both provide living water and living meal, and those who eat and drink their meal "will never thirst."[110]

Edmund and Judas both face death for their betrayal: Judas "went away and hanged himself"[111] because he had caused Jesus' death; Edmund is nearly killed by the Witch and only saved by Aslan's own sacrifice. False food destroys their moral quality and their family, leading to the death of Jesus/Aslan. Food makes them both betrayers as well as the betrayed, adhering to the promises of false gods or false religious leaders over the words of the true God and then being betrayed in turn.

Messiahs and meals: Eucharist and sacrifice in Christianity and Narnia

This theme of betrayal through food is balanced by meals of redemption offered by Jesus and Aslan. The events Aslan is involved in before his death on the Table and his transformation into a meal mirror the experiences of Jesus in his transformation into the bread and wine of the Last Supper/Crucifixion. At his meal, Jesus appears aware of his upcoming death: "I will not drink again from the fruit of the vine until the day I drink it new in the kingdom of God."[112] Aslan also gives hints before his death that he would not be there at the battle the next day: "I can give you no promise of that."[113] Even the meal that Aslan's followers have is referred to as "Supper,"[114] subtly connecting it to the Last Supper meal. The shearing of Aslan, while his enemies are "jeering at him"[115] becomes a counterpart to Jesus being "stripped ... and mocked."[116] They are both restrained: Jesus "was crucified,"[117] while Aslan was muzzled and tied to the Stone Table. The parallels between the numerous experiences of the two Christ figures serve to connect their deaths as transformation into redemptive meals.

Food, although connected to betrayal, is also a means of redemption, as the creator of the meal shapes the inherent nature of the meal itself. Here is where the true counterpart of these false gods is revealed, for the false gods give only in order to take more from the person they have given to. Turkish Delight is given by the Witch so that she can obtain the entire set of children, while the chief priests of the Sanhedrin give the thirty pieces of silver so they can take Jesus, whereas the true Gods of Narnia and Christianity, Aslan and Jesus, are the creators of life who give without heeding the consequences, giving without needing anything in return. As true Gods they have no need of human-bestowed benefits, but rather give to benefit humanity.

The Christian God is a triune God: God the Father, Jesus the Son, and the Holy Spirit. It is in these three forms that God interacts with the human world and divinity in its entirety. Aslan represents all three figures in the Trinity: in Aslan's sacrifice we see the actions of Jesus, and Aslan as the "son of the great Emperor-Beyond-the-sea"[118] connects God the Father. Even the Spirit is represented when Aslan "breathed"[119] onto the animals to restore their lives; he was breathing out the "Holy Spirit" onto them, for in biblical Hebrew "ruach" and Greek "pneuma" can mean both "breath" and "spirit."[120] Therefore, his breath which brings the statues back to life is also the Holy Spirit bringing them to a new life after being "baptized with the Holy Spirit."[121] Aslan's relationship with food and with other characters implicitly involves the entire trinity, as he is not one but three. His divinity is proven through the mythologizing of the origins of the meal he provides after the battle: "[h]ow Aslan provided food for them all I don't know."[122] Food is dispensed by Aslan as easily as Jesus fed the five thousand, or God fed the Israelites in the desert, or the disciples were "fed" with the "gifts of the Holy Spirit."[123]

The redemptive qualities of food emerge not only through Jesus or Aslan giving food to their followers, but also through their most important action of transforming themselves into food. In Christianity, the Last Supper is an important meal not only because it was the last meal Jesus shared with his disciples, but also because it was a symbol of his coming death, transforming his body and blood into wine and bread. Similarly, Aslan is also transformed into a meal during his death at the Stone Table. Jesus transforms his flesh and blood into the bread and wine he shares with his companions, while Aslan becomes a figurative meal because the evil characters kill him on the Stone Table. Jesus enacted a meal where he "took bread ... broke it ... [and said to his followers] this is my body" and took the "cup ... the blood of the covenant."[124] This meal predicts and presages his death on the cross, allowing his followers to share in the divine meal. His body is transformed into bread which is broken and blood which is poured out. Crucifixion, while being a profane action of death, becomes sacred because Jesus experiences and transforms it. Aslan's death combines the Last Supper and the Crucifixion in his own death at the Stone

Table. He both dies and becomes a meal at the same time. The placing of his body on a table as well as the particular instrument of death, a knife, indicate the meal-like quality of his death and "consumption" by the evil characters who profanely feast as much on his "despair"[125] as much as on his actual flesh. However, the transformation of Aslan into food through death is also a sacred act which ultimately saves all of Narnia. This is reminiscent of the crucifixion of Jesus, which despite being a profane action of a political prisoner being killed in a brutal manner is also a sacred action through which Jesus sacrifices himself for all, "the Sinless who suffers for the Sinful."[126] These transformations identify the redemptive possibilities implicit within Christianity.

In this action of killing and consuming, the Witch becomes aligned to Satan, so that Aslan on the Table and "Christ on the cross opened … [themselves] to the Enemy's uttermost attack and that Satan thought the Son, cut off from the Father, surely could not stand on his own."[127] However, as the resurrection of Christ leaves Satan "weaponless and empty handed,"[128] so Aslan's rising from death also leads to the Witch's destruction. Her table of death "was broken into two pieces,"[129] her creatures of stone "are given new life,"[130] and ultimately Aslan killed the Witch herself. Her meal of death and destruction with the killing of Aslan has become a new meal of life that brings redemption. Jesus dies as the "scriptures must be fulfilled," and the "Son of Man is delivered into the hands of sinners."[131] But he also dies to redeem, showing forgiveness as embodied in his commandment, "Love one another as I have loved you."[132] His death for all indicates the true standard of loving others beyond self. Aslan also goes willingly to his death at the hands of the Witch in order to save "the betrayer."[133] Edmund does not die the lonely hanging death of Judas for his betrayal. Instead this text opens the possibility of forgiveness for betrayal and also the possibility of redemption. Aslan engages in the action of ransom, becoming the meal to replace Edmund so that he is spared, for in Hebrew "ransom" means not to pay money for someone's life, but "to act the part of a kinsman."[134] He lives the idea of loving someone, as a family member, by taking his place. "Aslan's own sacrifice for the sake of [one person,] Edmund,"[135] represents the idea of caring for all people through the medium of caring for an individual. The unholy death that he experiences becomes sacred and holy, because he submits to it willingly, for "when a willing victim who had committed no treachery was killed in a traitor's stead, the Table would crack and death itself would start working backwards."[136] The meals of Aslan and Jesus as they are killed and symbolically consumed begin as unholy events, but become redemptive actions where the meal itself celebrates the idea of love, and giving self for another supersedes notions of betrayal.

Conclusion

Food in Narnia plays an important role in how characters are perceived: both their portrayal of gender roles in food preparation and the nationality of the food that they consume are signifiers of personality and propensity to good or evil. Good characters are allied with British food and following traditional gender roles. Part of their positive representation is due to how they conform to these personality signifiers. Equally, the evil characters are shaped by the food that they eat, or offer. Frequently, they eat food identified as foreign, which leads to them being identified as "other." Their inability to conform to gender stereotypes also legitimizes their negative representations. Important ideas about religion are also communicated through the medium of food, creating a reimagination of the Last Supper and the Passion within the Narnian landscape. In this context, food is identified as a source of betrayal when it is offered by false gods promising only obsession, just as redemption can emerge when a true God willingly transforms into a meal, saving and redeeming their respective worlds. Food draws us into Narnia but ultimately takes us beyond a fairy-tale world to better understand our own context.

Notes

1. Thomas M. Wilson (ed.), *European Studies 22: Food, Drink and Identity in Europe* (New York: Rodopi, 2006): 14.
2. Susanne Kubal, *Word of Mouth: Food and Fiction after Freud* (New York: Routledge, 2002): 3.
3. Allison James, "How British Is British Food?" in Patricia Caplan (ed.), *Food, Health and Identity* (London: Routledge, 1997): 73.
4. Ann Alston, *The Family in English Children's Literature* (New York: Routledge, 2008): 106.
5. Richard Jones, "The New Look—and Taste—of British Cuisine," *The Virginia Quarterly Review* 79(2) (2003): 209–32, at 209.
6. James: 80.
7. Lee Joliffe, "Tea and Hospitality: More Than a Cuppa," *International Journal of Contemporary Hospitality Management* 18(2) (2006): 164–8, at 164.
8. Judy Rosenbaum, "Critical Approaches to Food in Children's Literature (Review)," *Children's Literature Association Quarterly* 34(3) (2009): 297–9, at 297.

9. Harold Bloom (ed.), *C.S. Lewis: Bloom's Modern Critical Views* (New York: Infobase, 2006): 18.
10. C.S. Lewis, *The Lion, the Witch and the Wardrobe. The Complete Chronicles of Narnia* (New York: HarperCollins, 2000): 98.
11. *The Lion, the Witch and the Wardrobe*: 94–5.
12. *Ibid.*: 96.
13. *Ibid.*: 95.
14. *Ibid.*: 101.
15. *Ibid.*: 101.
16. *Ibid.*: 78.
17. *Ibid.*: 79.
18. Joliffe: 164.
19. *The Lion, the Witch and the Wardrobe*: 79.
20. *Ibid.*: 81.
21. Bloom: 18.
22. *The Lion, the Witch and the Wardrobe*: 81.
23. Wilson: 12.
24. *The Lion, the Witch and the Wardrobe*: 81.
25. *Ibid.*: 81.
26. Stephen Mennell, *All Manners of Food Eating and Taste in England and France from Middle Ages to the Present* (Oxford: Basil Blackwell, 1985): 240.
27. *The Lion, the Witch and the Wardrobe*: 98.
28. *Ibid.*: 102.
29. Susan Rowland, "*Literature and the Shaman: Jung, Trauma Stories and New Origin Stories in The Lion, the Witch and the Wardrobe by C. S. Lewis,*" *Journal of Jungian Scholarly Studies* 5(1) (2009): 1–13, at 11.
30. Rowland: 11.
31. *Ibid.*: 11.
32. Wilson: 32.
33. Rosenbaum: 297.
34. Kara Keeling and Scott Pollard (eds.), *Critical Approaches to Food in Children's Literature* (New York: Routledge, 2009): 113.
35. *The Lion, the Witch and the Wardrobe*: 83.
36. Alston: 106.
37. *The Lion, the Witch and the Wardrobe*: 84.
38. *Ibid.*: 76.
39. *Ibid.*: 84.
40. *Ibid.*: 86.
41. C. Neil Robinson, "Good and Evil in Popular Children's Fantasy Fiction: How Archetypes Become Stereotypes That Cultivate the Next Generation of Sun Readers," *English in Education* 37(2) (2003): 29–36, at 30.
42. *The Lion, the Witch and the Wardrobe*: 86.
43. *Ibid.*: 86.
44. Rowland: 11.
45. *The Lion, the Witch and the Wardrobe*: 86.

46. Donald E. Glover, *C. S. Lewis: The Art of Enchantment* (Athens: Ohio University Press, 1981): 139.
47. Glover: 140.
48. *The Lion, the Witch and the Wardrobe*: 109.
49. Glover: 140.
50. *The Lion, the Witch and the Wardrobe*: 100.
51. *Ibid.*: 110.
52. *Ibid.*: 81.
53. Kubal: 54.
54. *The Lion, the Witch and the Wardrobe*: 111.
55. *Ibid.*: 130.
56. Mary Anne Schofield, *Cooking by the Book: Food in Literature and Culture,* (Bowling Green, OH: Bowling Green State University Popular Press, 1989): 143.
57. Bloom: 149.
58. Mariana Ferrarelli, "Children's Literature and Gender: A Critical Approach," *Critical Literacy: Theories and Practises* 1(1) (2007): 63–8, at 65.
59. *The Lion, the Witch and the Wardrobe*: 109.
60. *Ibid.*: 79.
61. *Ibid.*: 79.
62. Ananya Kabir, "Abuses of Authority: English Literature, Colonial Pedagogy, and Shakespeare in Manju Kapur's Difficult Daughters," *The Upstart Crow* 21 (2001): 127–38, at 127.
63. Wilson: 36.
64. *Ibid.*: 36.
65. *The Lion, the Witch and the Wardrobe*: 97.
66. Peter Schwenger, *Phallic Critiques: Masculinity and Twentieth Century Literature* (London: Routledge & Kegan Paul, 1985): 98.
67. Alston: 108.
68. Bloom: 152.
69. *The Lion, the Witch and the Wardrobe*: 97.
70. *Ibid.*: 98.
71. *Ibid.*: 98.
72. Glover: 138–9.
73. *The Lion, the Witch and the Wardrobe*: 86.
74. Wilson: 36.
75. Schofield: 139.
76. Rowland: 10.
77. *The Lion, the Witch and the Wardrobe*: 76.
78. *Ibid.*: 86.
79. Alston: 108.
80. *Ibid.*: 114–15.
81. Rowland: 12.
82. *The Lion, the Witch and the Wardrobe*: 86.
83. *Ibid.*: 117.
84. *Ibid.*: 117.

85. Bloom: 93.
86. Kubal: 72.
87. Bloom: 154.
88. Kubal: 74.
89. *The Lion, the Witch and the Wardrobe*: 86.
90. *Ibid.*: 81.
91. Bloom: 97.
92. *Ibid.*: 18.
93. Luke 8:21.
94. *The Lion, the Witch and the Wardrobe*: 76, 93.
95. John 12:4–6.
96. *Ibid.*
97. Matthew 27:3.
98. Bloom: 86.
99. John 13:18.
100. *Ibid.*
101. John 13:27.
102. David Downing, *Into the Wardrobe: C. S. Lewis and the Narnia Chronicles* (San Francisco, CA: Jossey-Bass 2005): 95.
103. *The Lion, the Witch and the Wardrobe*: 94.
104. Downing: 93.
105. Matthew 26:14.
106. Vernon K. Robbins, *Exploring the Texture of Texts: A Guide to Socio-rhetorical Interpretation* (Valley Forge, PA: Trinity Press International, 1996): 26.
107. Arthur A. Just, *The Ongoing Feast: Table Fellowship and Eschatology at Emmaus* (Collegeville, PA: Pueblo, 1993): 131.
108. Matthew 26:59.
109. Matthew 27:3.
110. John 4:11–13.
111. Matthew 27:5.
112. Mark 14:25.
113. *The Lion, the Witch and the Wardrobe*: 120.
114. *Ibid.*: 120.
115. *Ibid.*: 122.
116. Matthew 27:28–9.
117. Matthew 27:35.
118. *The Lion, the Witch and the Wardrobe*: 100.
119. *Ibid.*: 126.
120. Downing: 71.
121. Acts 1:5.
122. *The Lion, the Witch and the Wardrobe*: 131.
123. Hebrews 2:4.
124. Mark 14:22–4.
125. *The Lion, the Witch and the Wardrobe*: 123.
126. Downing: 78.

127. *Ibid.*: 79.
128. *Ibid.*: 79.
129. *The Lion, the Witch and the Wardrobe*: 125.
130. Peter J. Schakel, *Reading with the Heart: The Way into Narnia* (Grand Rapids, MI: Eerdmans, 1979): 30.
131. Mark 14:49, 41.
132. John 13:34.
133. Glover: 139.
134. Downing: 79.
135. *Ibid.*: 77.
136. *The Lion, the Witch and the Wardrobe*: 125.

2

Scapegoating and Collective Violence in *The Lion, the Witch and the Wardrobe*

Melody Green

In the 1970s, the anthropological philosopher René Girard presented his theory of the scapegoat mechanism, a theory that explained how social groups control violence with an internal system of ritual and social behavior. At the time, he saw this model repeated throughout history, mythology, and literature, but the ability of Girard's theories to explain recognizable patterns of human violence have led to their increasing popularity since the attacks of September 11, 2001. Intriguingly, the scapegoat mechanism that Girard recognized is not only at work in C. S. Lewis's *The Lion, the Witch and the Wardrobe*, but it shapes the structure and outline of the story. While this book was first written shortly after World War II, over the years it has been adapted into film and radio plays, most of which have repeated the scapegoating model. In 2005, however, Disney released *The Chronicles of Narnia: The Lion, the Witch and the Wardrobe*, which appears, in places, to be less comfortable with this model than the earlier adaptations. An understanding of the implications of the most recent adaptation and its relationship to the scapegoating model must begin in an understanding of what the scapegoating model is and how it works in Lewis's text.

According to Girard, the scapegoat mechanism is the way that societies control their violent tendencies. This method is outlined in several texts, including *Things Hidden Since the Foundation of the World*, *Violence and the Sacred*, and *The Scapegoat*.[1] The scapegoat mechanism begins, he explains, in what he calls "mimetic desire." Girard argues that all human behavior is learned, and thus desire is also a learned thing. Desire itself is, therefore, imitative. Mimetic conflict occurs when two rivals desire the same thing. Because these mutual desires converge on the same object, conflict ensues. This conflict heightens and spreads to others until there is a social crisis, at which time a victim is blamed, a sacrifice made, and everything returns to a state of calm for a while. In *The Scapegoat*, Girard explains that this cycle is repeated until a sacrifice is made that causes everyone caught up in the sacrificial system to recognize that the violence is not outside of themselves, but rather inside.[2] This, then, leads to the ending of the system of sacrifices.

Initial conflict

In *The Lion, the Witch and the Wardrobe*, the initial conflict occurs between Aslan and the White Witch: they both desire to rule the land of Narnia. Their mimetic conflict began at the creation of Narnia, when the Witch was present to observe Aslan's creation of a new world. She saw his power; she wanted it for herself. While the mimetic conflict between Aslan and the Witch begins in *The Magician's Nephew*, *The Lion, the Witch and the Wardrobe* tells the story of the ending of this system of violence. The fact that this is the story not only of one sacrifice, but of a whole sacrificial system, is made clear by the Witch at the point when she intends to sacrifice Edmund. She explains to her dwarvish servant that the Stone Table is the correct location for sacrifices of this sort, pointing out that they have never been performed anywhere else. Clearly, sacrifices in this conflict have occurred before. The dwarf reminds her, however, that Aslan has chosen this spot as a rallying point for his army, possibly for the very purpose of preventing these sacrifices from occurring.[3] This is not accidental on Aslan's part; he knows the purpose of the Stone Table, and recognizes its importance in the cyclical struggle for power in which he and the Witch have been caught.

In *The Lion, the Witch and the Wardrobe*, the mimetic conflict is explained by two characters, Mr. Tumnus and Mr. Beaver. Tumnus tells Lucy about a glorious past in which there were parties that, at times, touched on the bacchanal.[4] This is a past in which, though Lucy does not know it yet, Aslan ruled Narnia. Now, however, the White Witch rules, and the land is covered with snow: it is a perpetual winter that is never alleviated by the hope and joy that is associated with Christmas.[5] The mimetic rivalry has expanded past just the Lion and the Witch. Over time, all Narnians appear to have aligned themselves with one or the other of the rivals. Both Mr. Beaver and Mr. Tumnus explain that even the trees cannot be trusted, because some are on "her" side.[6] In the comfort of his home, Mr. Beaver explains the conflict to the children, explaining not only that the conflict exists, but also how their arrival, along with that of Aslan, upsets the balance of power.

Escalation of conflict

In the scapegoat model, the society in which mimetic conflict has caused polarization sees a sharp escalation of the conflict when something upsets the stability of the current social order. In *The Scapegoat*, Girard explains that this could be caused by outside forces or internal ones; a natural disaster or a political upset could equally be the cause of the escalated conflict.[7] In Narnia, this occurs with the arrival of the children and the return of Aslan. According to an ancient prophecy, four children are supposed to rule in Narnia, so their presence escalates the crisis; for those who believe the prophecy, their empowerment means the Witch's downfall.

In Girard's model, however, as the conflict escalates, the differences between the rivals disappear. He explains in *The Scapegoat* that the perceived problem is not that the two sides are so different, but that they are perceived as not being different enough: those on one side of the conflict feel that those on the other side no longer respect differences, or they are not behaving in the way that is expected.[8] This leads to heightened conflict, as the differences that defined groups disappear and the boundaries between sides become blurred. This disappearance of differences is shown in Narnia again through the guidance of Mr. Beaver and Mr. Tumnus. All trees cannot be trusted because there is no way to visually tell the difference between the ones that are on Aslan's side and the ones that are on the Witch's side. Mr. Beaver also tells the children that they cannot trust any creature who looks, acts, or sounds human, but is not.[9] According to Mr. Beaver, those who fit this description are all on the Witch's side. Mrs. Beaver does speak up for dwarves, some of whom her husband grudgingly allows to be on their side, but his conviction of lost boundaries keeps Mr. Beaver from reflecting on the simple fact that many others who are loyal to Aslan fit this same description. At the Stone Table, he and the children meet many creatures on Aslan's side, including various creatures that appear to be half human, or partially human, or humanoid in appearance. This includes centaurs, man-headed bulls, bull-headed men, and tree-women who look more human than tree. Mr. Tumnus, a half-human, half-goat, was at first on the Witch's side, but after meeting Lucy he changes sides. Tumnus realizes that he has much in common with the child who looks not unlike several other creatures he knows. In realizing this, the mimetic conflict has not disappeared for Mr. Tumnus; instead, he makes a conscious choice to do the one thing that others caught up in these rivalries fear. Mr. Beaver's apparent bigotry is a fear of the dissolution of differences; Mr. Tumnus is punished for making a choice that makes the differences less clear. In *Violence and the Sacred*, Girard explains that this loss of difference threatens the social order, the foundations of culture, and even individual identities. It is this fear that propels those caught up in the scapegoat mechanism to choose a victim.[10]

Loss of differentiation

Violence and the Sacred also argues that not only does the difference between rival groups disappear, but also the differences between the original rivals, as well. The rivals caught up in the mimetic conflict become a "monstrous double"—the differences between the rivals disappear, and while previously only one had appeared to be a monster, now both have elements of monstrosity. Before the arrival of the children in Narnia, Aslan was defined by his followers as the rightful leader who happened to be absent, while the Witch was the unrightful leader who was fearfully present. Aslan's return immediately removes part of the divide between himself and the Witch. Tumnus has explained to Lucy that once there were glorious summers when Aslan ruled, but the Witch's rule is marked by winter. With Aslan's return the winter disappears, thus signifying the beginning of a shift in power. With both the Lion's and the Witch's right to rule in question, another difference has dissolved. Then, when Aslan and the Witch meet at the Stone Table, Aslan appears to betray his own followers by agreeing with the Witch that there is a need for a blood sacrifice.

Social agreement

This agreement leads to the next step in the scapegoating mechanism: what began as a rivalry between two people turns into communal unease, which then leads to "collective violence"—the social agreement that someone must die in order to make everything better. In agreeing on the need for a sacrifice, each member of the communities involved engages in the act of collective violence. Even if they do nothing themselves, they are now a part of the community that is going to perform a sacrifice: they have all become complicit.

In *The Scapegoat*, Girard explains that the victim is chosen because of something that marks him as different from the rest of the community.

This could be power or a lack of power, health or illness, wealth or lack of wealth. Often, the chosen victim is someone from a foreign land. The determining factor is simply that there is still a noticeable difference between the individual chosen, and those who are doing the choosing.[11] It is not enough, however, that this victim is different: the scapegoat is accused of a crime that strikes against the very fabric of society, and is then blamed for the subsquent social upheaval.[12]

In *The Lion, the Witch and the Wardrobe*, while all four children are foreigners and can therefore be blamed for the social upheaval, one particular child stands out. Edmund is not only a non-Narnian Son of Adam, but he is also guilty of a crime that strikes against the very foundation of society: he betrayed his family to an enemy who wished to destroy them. At the Stone Table, Aslan and the White Witch agree that Edmund is the ideal victim. This agreement starts when the Witch announces his victimization: by declaring him a "traitor," the Witch points out that he is the ideal sacrifice. Aslan's response does not dispute the claim that she makes, only her purpose in making that claim. Their conversation goes on to reveal that Aslan and the Witch agree that Edmund's betrayal endangered not only his own family, but all of Narnia.[13]

This reflects another aspect of the scapegoat model: in primitive societies, such guilt is viewed as a contagion—the non-guilty members of the society will "catch" the guilt and ultimately their society will be destroyed unless a sacrifice is made.[14] This guilt will make its presence known through violence. Girard further explains that the outbreak of violence that the scapegoat function serves to control is often described in terms of fire, floods, and storms, as well as physical acts of aggression and brutality.[15] In Narnia, this is quite literal. After Aslan agrees that Edmund is guilty, the Witch points out that "'unless I have blood as the Law says, all Narnia will be overturned and perish in fire and water.'"[16] Aslan again agrees with her that her statement about Narnia is true, and he agrees with what she claims needs to be done in order to solve the problem. This is the sacrificial mechanism at work. In Narnia, this structure has its own name: the Deep Magic. The Witch has earlier made it clear that this has been done before, showing that what is going to happen is not an aberration, but a part of a socially approved ritual behavior that exists to control the violence in their society.

Exchange of victim

This introduction of Deep Magic brings the reader to the next step in the process: while it is vital for the accusation of a crime to have occurred, for the sake of the violence-containing aspect of this function it is important that the sacrificial victim be innocent. If the sacrificial victim were guilty, then this would simply be revenge, instead of sacrifice. Because a crime against the very fabric of culture has been committed (or at least, an accusation has been made), the whole community must be involved in the act that repels the violence, but if the truly guilty one is killed, then only the injured parties are involved. This innocent victim is called the "scapegoat." Even though Aslan agrees that someone must die in order to maintain peace in Narnia, he is also aware that allowing the Witch to kill the boy would not solve any problems: the Witch would still be in power, Aslan would be revealed as powerless, and the mimetic conflict would, for the time being, appear to be over, with the Witch having the clear upper hand.

It is at this point that the collective nature of violence comes into play. The community, aware that a crime has been committed, converges on an innocent victim, placing the blame on him. This is the next step in the scapegoat function. When mimetic rivalry has escalated into mimetic conflict and someone has been blamed for it, a substitute victim is chosen. The substitute victim is chosen for the same reasons as the initial person accused: in other words, the actual victim is chosen because of anything that marks him as different from the rest of the community. This victim could be an animal or a human; it does not matter. The one thing that does matter is that this innocent victim become something sacred.

In Narnia, after the Witch and Aslan have publicly agreed that a sacrifice must occur, Aslan tells his people to "fall back" while he and the Witch talk alone.[17] This is important, because there is no way that Aslan's followers would agree to the bargain he is about to make with the Witch. But it is vital that the selection of a victim is collective. In requiring everyone but himself and the Witch to move, Aslan asks his followers to trust his ability to solve the problem. In their obedience, Aslan's followers physically show their agreement to give up their own voice, silently declaring that Aslan has the right to make this choice for them. Before the Lion asks everyone to step back, Susan, one of the outsiders to the community caught up in this system, asks if there is a way to work against the Emperor's magic. Aslan makes it clear that there is none, and no one asks any other questions. Instead, they all, including Susan, obey his command. Allowing Aslan to represent them in this choice makes the Narnians a part of the exchange between the Witch and the Lion: their obedience demonstrates their complicity in the sacrifice that will occur. Aslan's followers do not at this point know this, but in stepping back instead of asking for an explanation or demanding their right to be part of the negotiation they make themselves guilty of Aslan's death.

This allegiance is also shown when Aslan returns from the conversation with the Witch. In the book, he says to his followers, "'You can all come back. ... I have settled the matter. She has renounced her claim on your brother's blood.'"[18] He again commands them to move, and they again demonstrate their agreement by moving. No one stops; no one even asks what the agreement is. They simply accept what they do not know. At the same time, it is not accidental that Aslan refers to Edmund as their sibling even though he is speaking to all of his followers, not just the other three children. Aslan is signifying Edmund's rightful place in the community: he is no longer their chosen victim, but one of them.

While Aslan's followers become involved in the collective violence through their obedience and silence, the Witch's followers are much more directly involved. Those on the side of the White Witch engage in the physical sacrifice itself, obeying her commands to tie Aslan, beat him, muzzle him, and shave him, before she performs the final, murderous act. Both sides must agree on the selection of the victim and be collectively involved; in this case, both sides are—one subtly, and one in a quite straightforward manner.

Aslan as victim

The selection of Aslan as the scapegoat is quite appropriate. In *Violence and the Sacred*, Girard shows that in many cultures, the sacrificial victim is considered a "mythic or divine creature who is the incarnation of violence," and is sometimes viewed as a sacred king, while at other times viewed as a monster.[19] Aslan embodies both of these. His nature as the sacred king is declared by Mr. Beaver, when he first explains to the children that they will meet Aslan. Lucy asks if they are going to meet a human. Mr. Beaver answers with a list of names for Aslan: the King of the Wood, the Son of the Emperor-Beyond-the-Sea, and the King of Beasts.[20]

In making this declaration, Mr. Beaver affirms the suitability of Aslan for the role of sacrificial substitute. The Emperor-Beyond-the-Sea is a supernatural character referred to throughout the Narnia books, but he is never met. He is the god of the Narnians, and is much more distant than Aslan. As the son of the Emperor, Aslan is also a deity. He is, therefore, the sacred king that must be sacrificed. At the same time that Mr. Beaver declares Aslan's sacred nature, he also declares Aslan's monstrous side. Aslan is the King of the Beasts. As such, he is the monster that must die. Girard points out that, at times, these royal victims are called "the lion" or "the leopard," named after not simply abstract monsters such as the minotaur of Greek myth, but very real monsters that have attacked humans.[21] But unlike the sacrificial victims of primitive societies that have been called "the lion," Aslan truly is such a creature. By his very nature, he is a monster. In other books in the Narnia series, Aslan's monstrosity is also addressed. In *The Silver Chair*, Jill Pole asks if Aslan eats little girls. He responds: "I have swallowed up girls and boys, women and men, kings and emperors."[22] Mr. Beaver, however, describes the paradox that is the scapegoat: he is not "safe," because he is a monster, but he is "good," because of his innocence and his basic nature.[23]

In the typical acting out of the collective murder that alleviates the mimetic crisis, the social crisis is, for a while, relieved. But eventually, the societal stress builds up again and another sacrifice must be made. This is dealt with in many ancient societies by ritual sacrifices that occur at prescribed times. These systematic sacrifices, Girard argues in *The Scapegoat*, end only when a victim is chosen whose death causes the very people who were complicit in the sacrifice to realize that the violence is not something outside of themselves that they are trying to prevent, but something inside themselves, instead.[24] Realizing the violence inherent in themselves then puts an end to the sacrificial system.

In *The Lion, the Witch and the Wardrobe*, the Witch believes she has caught a bigger prize than Edmund when Aslan chooses to trade places with the child. She and her followers believe that because Aslan is her rival in the mimetic conflict, his death will give her a permanent victory. She explains her understanding of this to Aslan in the moment before she kills him: "Understand that you have given me Narnia forever, you have lost your own life and you have not saved his."[25]

Ending the system

Girard explains in *The Scapegoat* that systems of sacrifice come to an end when the community realizes that their scapegoat is not only an innocent victim, but a victim who deliberately chose his or her own victimization for the sake of the community. This, then, causes the community to realize that the violence they are trying to control is not outside of themselves, but rather inside. Recognizing the violence in themselves leads them to abandon the sacrificial structure. According to Girard, this is the role played by the Christ of the

Gospel narratives: by allowing himself to be punished for crimes he did not commit, he forces others to see the violence in themselves, thus bringing about an end to a sacrificial system.

Aslan shows his agreement with the sacrificial system by agreeing with the Witch that these rules had been put in place at the very beginning of time. His response to the Witch's insistence that she must have blood also shows his complicity with the scapegoat model. His complicity in his own victimization becomes clear at his death, and, even more importantly, after his resurrection. His willingness to allow his own death is witnessed by Lucy and Susan who watch his torture from a nearby hiding place. They watch Aslan as he knowingly and willingly approaches the Stone Table that is surrounded by his enemies, then watch as he is bound, beaten, shaved, muzzled, and killed, all the while making no move to save himself or stop his tormentors. After his return to life, Aslan explains to the girls that this, too, is a part of the Emperor's magic. He has a name not only for the sacrificial system, but for the way that the system can be brought to an end: "'Deeper Magic from Before the Dawn of Time.'"[26] This magical rule says that "'When a willing victim who had committed no treachery" died in the place of another, the system of sacrifice symbolized by the Stone Table would end.[27] Aslan made his choice to be killed, knowing that his death would not only save Edmund and Narnia, but end a sacrificial system. Even though he never uses the word "scapegoat," Aslan understands the nature of this system of exchange, and how it can be brought to an end. The ending of this cycle of violence is signified by the breaking of the Stone Table. In *The Scapegoat*, Girard points out that in order for the victim to be able to offer the benefits of his death to his persecutors, they must believe that he has come back to life and is, in some way, immortal.[28] Aslan permanently ends the scapegoating system that he has been engaged in not only by agreeing with his torturers that he must die, but also by coming back to life, breaking the Table, and leading his followers into a final, decisive battle. Aslan is able to extend his life to the statues in the White Witch's castle not only because he has returned to life himself and is sacred, but because death has no permanent hold on him. Releasing the statues leads to the final victory in battle, a victory that would not have happened if Aslan had not died and then returned to life.

Adaptations

While this story is violent, its continual popularity is evidenced by the fact that it has remained in print for over 60 years, and that it has been retold in multiple films and radio dramatizations. As a general rule, these retellings tend to follow the same sacrificial structure as the book, with a few apparently small exceptions. The most notable change in these adaptations is the role of collective violence in the victimization of Aslan. While the BBC and Focus on the Family radio dramatizations keep this aspect of the story, the films seem less willing to embrace the collective guilt involved in Aslan's death. At the critical moment in the 1967 BBC television series, Aslan tells everyone to fall back; he and the Witch walk offstage while no one else moves. The same thing occurs in the 1979 feature-length animated film: Aslan tells his followers to fall back, but they stand still while he and the Witch walk away. When they are done discussing, he returns but the Witch continues to stand on the spot where the decision was made. In the 1988 BBC television series, Aslan tells his followers to wait while he and the Witch discuss the issue, and then the two walk away while everyone stays in one place. Instead of commanding them to move, he commands them to stand still—a much easier action. Finally, in the 2005 Disney film *Narnia: The Lion, the Witch and the Wardrobe*, Aslan and the Witch hold a conversation between them that does not involve anyone else's agreement or obedience. Aslan and the Witch discuss Edmund's betrayal and its consequences in front of everyone, but while in the text they are interrupted by Mr. Beaver, Susan, and a bull with a human head, in this film they are interrupted only once. This interruption is undertaken by Peter, who says nothing at all during this scene in any other film version of the story. At the point when Aslan and the Witch agree to hold a more private conversation, Aslan says nothing to his followers at all. Instead, he declares to the Witch that they need to continue the conversation alone. The Lion never asks in any way for the agreement of his followers; their agreement with what is going to happen simply does not matter. The two rivals then enter a tent to make their deal, removing their conversation from the others visually as well as physically.[29]

All four film interpretations may well simply show Aslan and the Witch moving instead of the Narnians because it is easier to move two characters than it is to move a whole crowd, but a reason something happens is not always the same thing as what it means, or how it can be interpreted. In the case of these films, moving two characters instead of a whole crowd means that the collective aspect of Aslan's death is weakened or removed. In the first three films, Aslan does still give a command, but he does not bother to give his followers the chance to obey. In the fourth, their compliance is not required: this is a deal strictly between him and the Witch, and no one else is involved.

Aslan never gives his followers the chance to show their willingness to agree, because their compliance is not required. In the book, no one stands by Aslan and disagrees, but in the films, no one is even given the chance to. They have thus been removed from the equation; the violence here is not collective, even though the whole community needs a death for their continued existence. This could have something to do with the post-9/11 society in which the last film was created: in a world in which people choose themselves as well as people they have never met to be sacrificial victims for their own beliefs, the collective nature of such events may appear to be lost.

Ultimately, this reluctance to embrace the collective nature of the violence in the scapegoating system revealed in *The Lion, the Witch and the Wardrobe* reflects the difference between the values and expectations of the post-World War II British culture in which the book was written, and the later cultures in which the movies were made. With the horrors of the war in which entire cultural groups were scapegoated still fresh in cultural memory, Lewis's original text easily embraces the collective nature of violence. Just one generation later, however, retellings of the story reflect a shift that had already begun. Collective responsibility gives way to individual responsibility; Aslan's agreement with the Witch becomes increasingly more an agreement between the two leaders; responsibility is theirs alone. Aslan's army is relieved from any personal involvement in the death of a victim that they did not knowingly choose. At the same time, however, this shift in responsibility also increases the helplessness of Aslan's followers. They did not choose the victim; they would certainly not have chosen this specific victim if they had been allowed a choice. This helplessness is more pronounced in the 2005 film. In this, the followers of Aslan simply stand by while he and the Witch talk without them, then remove their conversation elsewhere. This essentially leaves Aslan's followers playing the role of children about whom adults are making an important decision, instead of as members of a community who have agreed to allow one person to make the decision for all.

Another sign of the shift away from collective violence is Aslan's response when he returns from the conversation with the Witch. In Lewis's text, he announces that everyone can return because the Witch has agreed to give up her "claim" on "your brother's blood."[30] In stating this, the Lion not only talks to the children, but points out that Edmund has been returned to the community as a whole. This reinforces the point that everyone, not just the two who worked out the details, is involved in this exchange. With the exception of the second BBC television series, the films interpret this statement differently. In the 1967 film, Aslan still refers to Edmund in familial terms when he announces that the Witch no longer desires his blood, but he faces the children, not his followers, while doing so. Thus his other followers are visually removed from the conversation. It is no longer the community, but the individual family that matters here. Aslan does the same thing in the 1979 animated film, in which only the four human children are shown on the screen as he speaks. This agreement with the Witch does not, at this point, appear to have anything to do with saving everyone from destruction. It is strictly about the children, not about the society. In this scene, the 2005 film again moves the selection of the scapegoat further from the Girardian model: instead of referring to Edmund as a family member or as a member of the community, Aslan uses the term "Son of Adam," which is used in the book to signify the non-Narnian nature of the children. Edmund is not reinstated as a member of the community, nor is his relationship to the other children reinforced. He is not even named; he has been objectified and is now completely out of the equation.

Downplaying the role of the community in the scapegoat function as it occurs in these films reflects a discomfort in contemporary culture not only with group responsibility, but with the scapegoat function itself. Unfortunately, denying one's own role in the system does not bring about the end of such cycles. Whether the original conflict involves control of land or a simple object, the only way to end such cycles is to recognize the innocence of one's victim, the violence in oneself, and the futility of the system itself.

Notes

1. René Girard, *Things Hidden Since the Foundation of the World*, trans. Stephen Bann and Michael Metteer (Stanford, CA: Stanford University Press, 1987); Girard, *Violence and the Sacred*, trans. Patrick Gregory (New York: Athlone Press, 2005); Girard, *The Scapegoat*, trans. Yvonne Freccero (Baltimore, MD: Johns Hopkins University Press, 1986).
2. Girard (1986): 166–7.
3. C. S. Lewis, *The Lion, the Witch and the Wardrobe* (New York: HarperCollins, 1950): 109.
4. *The Lion, the Witch and the Wardrobe*: 20–1.
5. *Ibid.*: 44.
6. *Ibid.*: 25, 66.
7. René Girard, *The Scapegoat*, trans. Yvonne Freccero (Baltimore, MD: Johns Hopkins University Press, 1986): 12.
8. Girard (1986): 22.
9. *The Lion, the Witch and the Wardrobe*: 79.

10. René Girard, *Violence and the Sacred*, trans. Patrick Gregory (Baltimore, MD: Johns Hopkins University Press, 1979): 49–51.
11. Girard (1986): 18.
12. *Ibid.*: 15.
13. *The Lion, the Witch and the Wardrobe*: 130.
14. Girard (1979): 26–8.
15. *Ibid.*: 31.
16. *The Lion, the Witch and the Wardrobe*: 142.
17. *Ibid.*: 115.
18. *Ibid.*: 115.
19. Girard (1979): 251–2.
20. *The Lion, the Witch and the Wardrobe*: 79.
21. Girard (1979): 252.
22. C. S. Lewis, *The Silver Chair* (New York: HarperCollins, 1953): 17.
23. *The Lion, the Witch and the Wardrobe*: 77.
24. Girard (1986): 155–6.
25. *Ibid.*: 125–6.
26. *Ibid.*: 150.
27. *Ibid.*: 133.
28. Girard (1986): 44.
29. *The Lion, the Witch and the Wardrobe*, directed by Pamela Lonsdale (BBC, 1967) [on YouTube, accessed December 20, 2010]; *The Lion, the Witch and the Wardrobe*, directed by Bill Melendez (Children's Television Workshop, 1979) [on DVD]; *The Chronicles of Narnia: The Lion, the Witch and the Wardrobe*, directed by Marilyn Fox (BBC, 1988) [on DVD]; *The Chronicles of Narnia: The Lion, the Witch and the Wardrobe*, directed by Andrew Adamson (Disney, 2005) [on DVD].
30. *The Lion, the Witch and the Wardrobe*: 132.

Part II
Applications and Implications

3

Moving Beyond "All That Rot": Redeeming Education in *The Chronicles of Narnia*[1]

Keith Dorwick

Throughout *The Chronicles of Narnia* series,[2] learning in classrooms in Narnia and on Earth is often disparaged in ways that range from the comedic to the horrific. In spite of C. S. Lewis's lifelong career as a teacher and scholar, the traditional pedagogical enterprise is usually, if not always, pictured as oppressive and stultifying. Indeed, references to formal classroom instruction found in the pages of the *Chronicles* are so negative that a reader begins to wonder how anyone learned anything at all in school, whether here on Earth or in Narnia.[3] However, in certain cases, education can be used to bring the children of Narnia that much closer to Christ, both in his form of Aslan in Narnia's world and as Christ in ours. My title, then, is a pun: I mean that education must be redeemed in order to be instructive, and that some forms of education are redemptive.

If that is so, then what does count as a good education? Successful learning, in the context of the *Chronicles*, is a matter of becoming no less than what Thomas à Kempis famously called the *Imitatio Christi*—the Imitation of Christ—in his work of that title.[4] From that perspective, rote learning is a hindrance, one of the "childish things" that won't be needed, as St. Paul put it.[5] Aslan himself makes the end of schooling one mark of Paradise: "The term is over: the holidays have begun."[6] If one wishes to educate the heart and spirit, one must meet Aslan and use him as a model for life's decision making. Then, Lewis would argue, we can make right decisions. Throughout the series, Aslan sets the children various tasks, and then, in a private discussion afterwards, helps them to interpret and to learn from those experiences.

True learning, then, consists of experiential learning: "Experiential education, fraught with ill-structured problems [such as the finding of an enchanted prince, the task Jill faces in the thicker, confusing air of Narnia],[7] relies on a process of discovery and evaluation for knowledge development or skill acquisition. This is intentional, as the skills we teach (leadership, decision making, problem solving, etc.) cannot be bound or defined by either purely right or purely wrong answers."[8]

Partially, the negative references to classroom instruction are biographical. Lewis's horrific experiences in school have been well documented (both by himself and by his biographers), and a short recollection in a letter written by his brother Warren about the school they attended together may be sufficient to make the case:

> In spite of [the Headmaster, the Reverend Robert] Capon's policy of terror, the school was slack and inefficient, and the timetable, if such it could be called, ridiculous. When not saying lessons, the boys spent the whole of school working out sums on slates; of this endless arithmetic, there was little or no supervision. Of the remaining subjects, English and Latin consisted, the first solely and the second mainly, of grammar. History was a ceaseless circuit of the late Middle Ages; Geography was a meaningless list of rivers, towns, imports and exports.[9]

Lewis's biographers identify the school in question as Wynward School, known as "Belsen" in Lewis's 1955 autobiography, *Surprised by Joy*[10]; the pseudonym for his school is perhaps an echo of the German concentration camp Bergen-Belsen, founded in 1940.[11] According to Roger Lancelyn Green and Walter Hooper, Lewis's father Albert "seems to have chosen the very worst" of "all the schools in the British Isles." Indeed, Capon was the subject of a court trial for brutality toward one of his charges, a matter that was settled "out of court and against the defendant."[12] This early awful experience left its marks on Lewis's writings: it is not just the boys at Wynward who have difficulties with arithmetic. In *The Magician's Nephew*, Digory and Polly run afoul of Digory's Uncle Andrew and become trapped in his attic study due to a difficulty in figuring out the number of steps required to get to the empty house past Digory's and Polly's: "When they had measured the attic they had to get a pencil and do the sum. They both got different answers to it at first and even when they agreed I am not sure they got it right."[13]

Though other connections could be made here between the kind of lessons taught to the two Lewis boys, I shall move beyond the biographical and look at Lewis's most direct analysis of formal education. His *The Abolition of Man* is directly connected to the subject of this chapter; its daunting subtitle is "Reflections on Education with Special Reference to the Teaching of English in the Upper Forms of Schools."[14] This book, the printed version of a series of lectures he gave at the University of Durham in February 1943, details his oft-repeated belief that humanity itself depends on an objective system of knowing and facticity in which moral judgments not only should but must be made on the basis of that objective system:

> The occasion for Lewis to crush this fatal superstition of autonomous values creation arose in the midst of the tumult of World War II when the University of Durham invited Lewis to present the prestigious Riddell Memorial Lectures on February 24–26, 1943. These lectures were presented on the evenings of these three successive dates, and were published later that same year by Oxford University Press as *The Abolition of Man*.[15]

In the context of *The Abolition of Man* and *Mere Christianity*, first broadcast as a series of radio lectures from 1941 to 1944,[16] Lewis's apparent anti-educational stance in the *Chronicles* makes more sense. In these texts, and in others, Lewis is addressing the problem of "subjectivism."[17] In Lewis's thought, if there are no objective standards, no appeals to a commonly held standard, the appeal to a subjective morality can only come from our emotions and instincts.[18] For instance, Lewis points out that if morality is relative, "we no more could have blamed [the Nazis for the war] than for the color of their hair."[19]

In order to help his listeners understand the dangers of relativism, and its connection to Nature—by which Lewis means the world of the instincts unmediated by an entirely objective Natural Law—Lewis begins *The Abolition of Man* with a discussion of a textbook he calls "The Green Book." He analyzes this book in an attempt to show how widespread and pernicious subjectivism had become, and quotes the work of the authors to show how impossible it was—in their opinion—to make objective moral and critical judgments.[20] Perhaps we can understand the strength of his feeling about the state of English education in the 1950s if we read his epigraph for the opening section of *The Abolition of Man*, "Men without Chests." He quotes a fifteenth-century carol titled "Puer Nobis Nascitur." The translation Lewis used was by Percy Deamer and found in the readily available 1928 *Oxford Book of Carols*, a standard collection of hymns still used by Anglican music directors in its current edition:

> So he sent the word to slay
> and slew the little childer[21]

For Lewis, then, classroom instruction as practiced in his day was a metaphoric act of murder, equivalent to the killing of all children two years and younger in Bethlehem by the tyrant King Herod, the subject of "Puer." I do not want to overstate Lewis's case; he was merely quoting the carol as an epigraph. Nevertheless, such a strong and pointed choice certainly indicates that he felt the kind of education taught in texts like the Green Book was entirely damaging to students.

Instead, there is a central moral ground, defined by Lewis as "the *Tao*," the basis and foundation of all thought systems because it is nothing less than the foundation of all thought:

> It is the reality beyond all predicates, the abyss that was before the Creator Himself. It is Nature, it is the Way, it is the Road. It is the Way in which the universe goes on, the Way in which things everlastingly emerge, stilly and tranquilly, into space and time. It is also the Way which every man should tread in imitation of that cosmic and supercosmic progression, conforming all activities to that great exemplar ... It is the doctrine of objective values, the belief that certain attitudes are really true, and others really false, to the kind of thing the universe is and the kind of things we are.[22]

Without teaching the Tao, there is a deadening of the human spirit that will produce "men without chests."[23] It is this deadly form of schooling that he seems to be consciously attacking in the negative portrayals found in the *Chronicles*.

Lewis begins with an appeal to our innate sense of justice. "What interests me [about the way in which people argue] is that the man who makes [arguments about the way we ought to be treated by others] is not merely saying that the other man's behaviour does not happen to please him. He is appealing to some other kind of behaviour which he expects the other man to know about."[24] If we don't accept that, we will learn how not to be human any more, and most of us will be in subjection to a ruling elite. In contrast, the *Chronicles* are a picture of what education ought to be.

Bad schools make bad students

When Lucy peeks at the books in Mr. Tumnus's personal library in *The Lion, the Witch and the Wardrobe*, we know that he is a faun of no little learning: one wall of Mr. Tumnus's cave holds "a shelf full of books [with] titles like *The Life and Letters of Silenus* or *Nymphs and Their Ways* or *Men, Monks and Gamekeepers; A Study in Popular Legend or Is Man a Myth?*"[25] Clearly, these are not the Narnian equivalent of mysteries or other cheap novels; clearly, too, these are mirror images of real-world academic and popular texts. For instance, a quick search showed that my university library holds a copy of Carol Rose's *Giants, Monsters, And Dragons: An Encyclopedia of Folklore, Legend, And Myth* and Alan K. Bowman's *Life and Letters on the Roman Frontier: Vindolanda and Its People.*[26] What is myth to Tumnus is real to us; what is real to us (including our own selves) is myth in Tumnus's world, since the human race has long died out in Narnia under the White Witch's iron yoke. If this catalogue of scholarly works is anything more than just a parody of academic titles, then the sting comes from Mr. Tumnus's role as one of the many traitors in the *Chronicles*. His books about men would be on the reading list of every "bad Faun" who is "in the pay of the White Witch." After all, his particular job is to be on the lookout for Sons of Adam and Daughters of Eve who might have wandered in from our world, exactly as Lucy herself has done, and turn them over to the White Witch.[27] One has to know one's enemies.

The next reference to the educational achievements of fauns in Narnia is seemingly far less pointed. It is (mostly) a gentle-natured joke on Lewis's part that makes Mr. Tumnus remark that if he had "worked harder at geography when I was a little Faun," he would know the "far land of Spare Oom" and "the bright city of War Drobe," his malapropisms for Lucy's description of her arrival from "the wardrobe in the spare room."[28] These mistakes poke fun at both Mr. Tumnus and at geography in the same moment that it makes Lucy herself—a very normal little girl to Lewis's readers at this point of the *Chronicles*—a mystical figure from another universe, as, in fact, she is to the inhabitants of Lewis's imaginary country. But in fact, as a Daughter of Eve, she is much more than that, at least potentially: "If we let Him—for we can prevent Him if we choose—He will make the feeblest and filthiest of us into a god or goddess, a dazzling, radiant, immortal creature, pulsating all through with such energy and joy and wisdom and love as we cannot now imagine ..."[29] This is, for Lewis, the goal of every Christian and the very real possibility that faces all humans. Of course, it works the other way around as well—if that kind of glorification does not occur, the alternative is that we become a "hellish creature."[30]

But it takes baby steps to start on the path to hell, and, for Lewis, an education that absolves itself of moral choices and of any real possibility for actually knowing anything real is its gateway. This is one reason Lewis resists rote learning. Polly Plummer, the heroine of

The Magician's Nephew, remarks that it is a good thing that the lands between the great river and the Western Waste have no populace. This, after all, means that no one will have to learn history, which is represented (by Polly) as merely dates that must be memorized:

> "I wish we had someone to tell us what all those places are," said Digory.
>
> "I don't suppose they're anywhere yet," said Polly. "I mean, there's no one there, and nothing happening. The world only began today."
>
> "No, but people will get there," said Digory. "And then they'll have histories, you know."
>
> "Well, it's a jolly good thing they haven't now," said Polly. "Because nobody can be made to learn it. Battles and dates and all that rot."[31]

"Battles and dates and all that rot" pretty well sums up the attitude toward education, at least on this playful level. Polly's reductionist view of education is shared by many of the characters in the seven novels, and is perhaps little different than that felt by many children in our world.

History and geography—lacking as they do references to mythological creatures and the dangers of Faeryland—do not fare well in the world Lewis has created. Eustace finds himself turned into a dragon in *The Voyage of the Dawn Treader* because he doesn't know enough not to sleep on a dragon's hoard: "Eustace had read only the wrong books. They had a lot to say about exports and imports and governments and drains, but they were weak on dragons."[32] And drains are specifically identified with a prosaic quotidian approach to mystery that is immediately condemned by Digory as something only a grown-up would say. Polly and Digory think the empty house in their row is empty because of pirates or smugglers; Polly reports that her "Daddy thought it must be the drains." Digory (rightfully) throws that explanation out of court: "Pooh! Grown-ups are always thinking of uninteresting explanations,"[33] thus making the process of taking the magic out of the world a conscious act of anti-creation. Grown-ups have to work at ways of making the world dull.

But being grown-up is not only uninteresting; for Lewis, it is damnable. As many critics—including both Neil Gaiman and Philip Pullman—have noted, Susan so wants to be an adult that she is no longer a friend of Narnia. Jill tells us of Susan's choice: "She's interested in nothing nowadays except nylons and lipstick and invitations. She always was a jolly sight too keen on being grown-up."[34] As Pullman put it, "Susan, like Cinderella, is undergoing a transition from one phase of her life to another. Lewis didn't approve of that. He didn't like women in general, or sexuality at all, at least at the stage in his life when he wrote the Narnia books. He was frightened and appalled at the notion of wanting to grow up."[35]

Gaiman's short story in which the grown-up Susan is now a retired professor of children's literature forces its readers to confront the harsh realities of Susan's life after the train wreck that killed Peter, Edmund, Lucy, Digory, and Polly: "My younger brother was decapitated, you know. A god who would punish me for liking nylons and parties by making me walk through that school dining room, with the flies, to identify Ed, well ... he's enjoying himself a bit too much, isn't he? Like a cat, getting the last ounce of enjoyment out of a mouse."[36] In short, Gaiman's Susan refuses to trade "further up and farther in"[37] for the reality of the train wreck that also took her parents' lives.

In Lewis's opinion, the thing most likely to cause young readers to lose faith in the non-factual (but true) is an educational system designed to kill imagination, curiosity, and the spirit. Thus, the *Chronicles* are full of dark, even savage, renditions of what it is to be in school, as in *Prince Caspian*: "The first house they came to was a school, a girls' school, where a lot of Narnian girls, with their hair done very tight and ugly tight collars round their necks and thick tickly stockings on their legs, were having a History lesson." When one of the students tells her class that she sees "a LION" outside the school, her instructor Miss Prizzle threatens her with an "order-mark" because of her insistence that she has seen a lion. Ultimately, she escapes the threat of not one, but "two order-marks," one for "talking nonsense" and one, the text implies, for not bowing to the teacher's authority immediately, only because the rest of the schoolgirls ("mostly dumpy, prim little girls with fat legs") and Miss Prizzle herself flee when the classroom is magically transformed back into a Narnia redeemed by Aslan and turned into a forest glade. In short order we visit a second classroom, where a "tired-looking girl was teaching arithmetic to a number of boys who looked very much like pigs" who are turned into pigs—complete with a Greek pig call by Bacchus himself—in order to let her join the procession and be with Aslan.[38]

Still, teaching in *Prince Caspian* can be a mixed bag. While the history taught under Miraz is "duller than the truest History you ever read"[39] because it is, to reverse Lewis's famous distinction, "factual but not true," the history taught by Dr. Cornelius in private sessions is both true and factual, with details of the Old Narnia that excite the young Caspian. When Dr. Cornelius suggest they turn from history to grammar, Caspian wants to continue the history lesson ("Oh, please, not yet"), and then gets very excited when he realizes "it was like in the [old] stories." Thus, even characters who ought to like formal education are ambivalent about it: the half-dwarf Dr. Cornelius speaks well of formal education of princes, but turns to grammar only as a means of defusing Caspian's questions about his uncle Miraz's usurpation of the throne: "Will your Royal Highness be pleased to open Pulverulentus Siccus at the fourth page of his *Grammatical garden of the Arbour of Accidence pleasantlie open'd to Tender Wits*?" "After that," Lewis's narrator adds, "it was all nouns and verbs till lunchtime, but I don't think Caspian learned much."[40] Grammar, of course, is a standard part of the classical education, part of the trivium, but here is it used as a way of deadening the excitement and interest of an engaged student, almost as a soporific. Certainly the narrative frames the teaching of grammar as a safe subject, one suitable for the quelling of curiosity about a potentially deadly subject for Caspian.

In *The Voyage of the Dawn Treader*, Coriakin is the Magician who oversees the Dufflepuds, creatures with one foot who move about by jumping and who have turned themselves invisible, inadvertently catching both Coriakin and Aslan in their spell.[41] Aslan asks him if he "grow[s] weary … of ruling such foolish subjects as I have given you here?" Coriakin responds that he wishes for the day when "they can be governed by wisdom instead of this rough magic."[42] His is a supervisory role over them and he is their caretaker, but, like many good teachers, he hopes to be made obsolete. He would no doubt like to see subjects stand on their own feet and be responsible citizens, rather than "planting boiled potatoes to save cooking them when they were dug up."[43] However, his teaching assignment is a jail sentence. We find out when we meet Ramadu (a retired star) in a subsequent chapter that Coriakin has been given oversight of the Dufflepuds as a punishment: "He might have shone for thousands of years more in the Southern winter sky if all had gone well." To the extent that Coriakin fills a teacherly role, he does so only because he is atoning for the "faults a star can commit."[44]

On Lewis's Earth, schools fare badly as well. I am speaking here of Experiment House, the school that is almost a parody of bad pedagogy. Its sins are innumerable. It is Experiment House that has caused Eustace to become what Edmund calls a "record stinker."[45] Though it is not named in *The Voyage of the Dawn Treader*, Eustace's curriculum is a prime example of the education that deadens our souls and causes a loss of our own humanity: "Eustace Clarence liked animals, especially beetles, if they were dead and pinned on a card. He liked books if they were books of information and had pictures of grain elevators or of fat foreign children doing exercises in model schools."[46] Geography as a discipline is beneath contempt for Lewis: nothing seems to have put him off so much as did the study of other countries than England. Drawing from his memories of geography as a child, rote memorization of lists could apparently turn out nothing but fussy, small-minded people. Worse, Eustace is, as a direct result of his education, a bully ("there are dozens of ways to give people a bad time if they are only visitors in your own home"[47]).

He is also sneaky and a cheat: when the *Dawn Treader* is becalmed and water needs to be rationed, he steals down to get some water, only to run into Reepicheep, the most valiant of the Talking Mice of Narnia, who, too small to otherwise help with the ship, has set himself to guard duty. Eustace is not able to see the justice of having everyone take short rations. Instead, he sees privilege as his right. As he writes in his journal, "A horrible day. Woke up in the night knowing I was feverish and must have a drink of water. Heaven knows I'm the last person to try to get any unfair advantage but I never dreamed that this water-rationing would be meant to apply to a sick man."[48] He is consistently cruel to those he sees as less powerful than he is, as when he twirls Reepicheep around by his tail only to find out that Reepicheep is not above using his sword's flat edge to whip him into shape: "'Then take that,' said Reepicheep, 'and that—to teach you manners—and the respect due a knight—and a Mouse—and a Mouse's tail.'" The narrator adds that since Eustace "(of course) was at a school where they didn't have corporal punishment, ... the sensation was quite new to him."[49]

Experiment House is far too modern for such old-fashioned ideas as "spare the rod and spoil the child." It is no surprise that Eustace Clarence Scrubb's parents would choose such a place. They were, after all, "very up-to-date and advanced people. They were vegetarians, non-smokers and tee-totallers and wore a special kind of underclothes. In their house there was very little furniture and very few clothes on beds and the windows were always open."[50] Once again, the curriculum of joylessness and the rejection of physical pleasure is a first step toward damnation, due to what might be called a pinched soul.[51] No wonder Experiment House is such a bleak place.[52]

Given its concern about proper education—and its strong critique of the English educational system—*The Silver Chair* is squarely in the tradition of such school novels as *Tom Brown's Schooldays*. Though the locale of *The Silver Chair* ranges from the heights of Aslan's mountains to the castle at Cair Paravel at the mouth of the great river to the wild lands north of Narnia, and takes the form of a quest, it also takes place within a few moments of Earth's time and a single location: the back of the school gym at Experiment House on a rainy English day. Moreover, its narrative is concerned entirely with what one does and does not know and how one is to learn what one ought to do. It opens with Jill Pole crying her eyes out; she is hiding behind the school gym at Experiment House which continues to be a source of the narrator's great scorn: "I shall say as little as possible about Jill's school, which is not a pleasant subject." The narrator then goes on to say quite a bit, including a dig at the very sanity of its teachers and especially its principal. After noting that Experiment House is coeducational, "what used to be a 'mixed' school," the narrator adds that "some said it was not nearly as mixed as the minds of the people that ran it. ... All sorts of things, horrid things, went on which at an ordinary school would have been found out and stopped in half a term; but at this school they weren't. ... [If] you knew the right things to say to the Head, the main result was that you became rather a favourite than otherwise."[53] And we soon find out that Experiment House is decidedly anti-Christian in an aside from the narrator: "When I was at school one would have said, 'I swear by the Bible.' But Bibles were not encouraged at Experiment House."[54]

Against this bad teaching—in which children run free and develop bad characters as a result—the school bullies are taught some character by being walloped by Jill, Caspian, and Eustace in full court dress, making it clear that everything is subject to Aslan/Christ, even the bodies of both Narnians and earthlings. Filled with Aslan's strength, and at his direction, the boys use the flat of their swords and Jill a riding switch to cane the gang who have come to bully them. When the bullies see the three figures in "glittering clothes" and "colorful things," carrying "weapons in their hand," "all the meanness, conceit, cruelty, and sneakishness almost disappeared in one single expression of terror. For they saw the wall fallen down, and a lion as large as a young elephant lying in the gap." This terrifying vision is enough to scare them into rushing to the Head. Her subsequent hysterical report (Lewis has his narrator go out of his way to note that the Head is a woman) is enough to cause her to lose her job, though she ends up in Parliament, "where she lived happily ever after." More importantly, her account caused "about ten people to be expelled."[55]

Not sparing the rod: direct knowledge of Aslan by Aslan

Leviticus's ancient exchange "An eye for an eye, a tooth for a tooth" is definitely operant in Narnia. Certainly we see it in *The Horse and His Boy*. Both Shasta and Aravis receive wounds from Aslan. "'I'll never do anything nasty to a cat as long as I live,' said Shasta, half to the cat and half to himself. 'I did once, you know. I threw stones at a half-starved mangy old stray.'" At this, Aslan (then in the shape of a large cat) turns round and scratches him.[56]

But a scratch for a scratch is made even more pointed later in the text with Aravis's encounter with Aslan: "The lion [Aslan, though we don't know it yet] rose on its hind legs, larger than you would have believed a lion could be, and jabbed at Aravis with its right paw. Shasta could see all the terrible claws extended. Aravis screamed and reeled in the saddle. The lion was tearing her shoulders."[57] The wounds are very specifically described by another character, the Hermit of the Southern March: "though they are smart they are no more serious than if they had been the cuts of a whip. It must have been a very strange lion; for instead of catching you out of the saddle and getting his teeth into you, he has only drawn his claws across your back. Ten scratches: sore, but not deep or dangerous."[58] On a first reading, one thinks it is merely an encounter with a feral lion in the desert, but when Aravis and Aslan talk, he identifies himself and tells her why he attacked her:

> "It was I who wounded you .... I am the only lion you met in all your journeyings. Do you know why I tore you? ... The scratches on your back, tear for tear, blood for blood, were equal to the stripes laid on the back of your stepmother's slave because of the drugged sleep you cast upon her. You needed to know what it felt like."[59]

That is what Lewis is trying to tell his readers. For him, true learning in Narnia— rather than a reliance on personal judgments that will tear our hearts out—means that we need to hurt, really hurt, in order to feel repentance and be able to listen to Christ/Aslan in order that we can make right moral decisions. He says as much in *Mere Christianity*: "Christianity simply does not make sense until you have faced the fact [that we know there is a moral standard out there which we have failed to meet]. Christianity tells people to repent and promises them forgiveness. It therefore has nothing (as far as I know) to say to people who do not know they have anything to repent of and who do not feel they need any forgiveness."[60]

And who (with the exception of traitors such as Edmund) needs more forgiveness than Eustace, who managed to get himself turned into a dragon through greed? It is a teaching moment for him, as everyone agrees that "Eustace's character had been rather improved by being a dragon ... The pleasure (quite new to him) of being liked and, still more, of liking other people, was what kept Eustace from despair. For it was very dreary being a dragon."[61] Worse, Eustace has had to confront what everyone else has always known: "Poor Eustace realized more and more ... he had been an unmitigated nuisance and that now he was a greater nuisance still."[62] But repentance is not enough, though it is a necessary first step. It takes Aslan to make him human again. After Eustace has tried to peel off his dragon's hide three times, he realizes that only Aslan can do the job, and he lets Aslan tear it off with his claws. It hurts and it goes deep to Eustace's core: "The very first tear he made was so deep that I thought it had gone right into my heart. And when he began pulling the skin off, it hurt more than anything I've ever felt. The only thing that made me able to bear it was just the pleasure of feeling the stuff peel off."[63] He is then thrown naked into a pool (one of the strongest echoes of Christian baptism in any of the *Chronicles*) and healed. He concludes with a final summation: "I'd turned into a boy again,"[64] with its faint allusions to Pinocchio. As was true of Edmund, Aslan's tutoring turns humans back to their true selves.

Thus, corporal punishment from Aslan (whether dealt out directly or indirectly, as in the case of the caning at the end of *The Silver Chair*), works. It is, however horrible, a real experience grounded in the body. One has to feel Aslan's claws to learn what life is really about. That is the truest knowledge of all: that given by Aslan himself. For Lewis, education has to involve being out and about in the world and trying one's best to interpret and understand that experience. From this perspective, it is odd that *The Silver Chair* is a tale about the efficacy of rote learning and discipline as imposed by the most perfect teacher in the *Chronicles*, Aslan himself. Though otherwise in the *Chronicles* rote memorization is pictured as a way of tearing magic out of the world and is in and of itself bad, its importance in *The Silver Chair* drives the entire plot of the novel. For instance, had Jill kept the signs given to her by Aslan clear in her mind, she could have directed Eustace and Puddleglum under the old Giant's City, thus avoiding their narrow escape from being eaten by the Gentle Giants of Harfang.[65] But this rote memorization of a list comes complete with Aslan's instructions on how to keep it accurate: "remember, remember the signs. Say them to yourself when you wake in the morning, and when you lie down at night, and when you wake in the middle of the night. And whatever strange things may happen to you, let nothing turn your mind from following the signs."[66] This knowledge is not of imports and exports but the instructions on how to find the missing prince of Narnia straight from Aslan's mouth.

Though Aslan describes the rescue of Prince Rilian as "the task for which I called you and him [Eustace] here out of this world,"[67] there is also a bigger agenda: that the children might get to know his counterpart, Christ, in this world: "[in your world,] I have another name ... This was the very reason you were brought to Narnia, that by knowing me here for a little, you may know me better there."[68]

It is always the experiential education that focuses on the knowing and loving the person (or beast) of Aslan himself that is deeply valued in Narnia. Readers see this kind of learning operating in a comic mode when Bree (a Talking Horse of Narnia) is denying that Aslan could possibly be a real lion: he tells Aravis, in a parody of postmodern anti-incarnational theology, "'No doubt, when they speak of him as a Lion, they only mean he's as strong as a lion or ... as fierce as a lion. Why, ... if he was a lion he'd have four paws, and a tail and Whiskers.'"[69] At that moment, Aslan comes behind Bree and tickles him with one of his very real whiskers, giving Bree the fright of his life ("'Aie, ooh, ooh-hoo! Help!'") and what we might call a lesson in Narnian Real Presence. Once again, that physical experience—in this case, the tickling of a whisker—is glossed by Aslan, with echoes of Thomas putting his hand into Christ's wound before believing in the Resurrection: "'Do not dare not to dare. Touch me. Smell me. Here are my paws, here is my tail, these are my whiskers. I am a true Beast.'"[70] The false theology of a Christ that is not really human (that is, Docetism) is here transferred to affirm Aslan's real nature as a Beast who is also the Son of the Emperor-Beyond-the-Sea. As the four Pevensies learn in *The Lion, the Witch and the Wardrobe*,

> Wrong will be right, when Aslan comes in sight,
> At the sound of his roar, sorrow will be no more,
> When he bares his teeth, winter meets its death,
> And when he shakes his mane, we shall have spring again.

Here, it is clear that academic exegesis of "an old rhyme" cannot be trusted. Though the rhyme's subject is clearly a lion, Mrs. Beaver immediately adds, "'You'll understand when you see him.'" Though Mr. Beaver gives away the game ("'Don't you know who is King of the Beasts? Aslan is a lion – the Lion, the great Lion'") in his next speech, experience is the only sure guide. Ultimately, the children will have to see Aslan to know him.[71]

This double-edged real world (as it were) learning experience is also central to our reading of *The Voyage of the Dawn Treader*: for instance, Lucy's visit to the Magician's study in which she sees "moving pictures" that reference the Crucifixion ("a cup and a sword and a tree and a green hill") and highlight moral questions in the Magician's spell book[72]; while a reference to Sidney's definition of poetry, "a speaking picture, with this end,—to teach and delight,"[73] is also a reference to medieval traditions of stained glass and of icons. These works of art were nothing less than Biblical teachings translated (not reduced) to pictures that teach: "The term Poor Man's Bible refers to various forms of Christian art (paintings, carvings, mosaics, and stained glass) that were used primarily in churches and cathedrals to illustrate the teachings of the Bible. These art forms were very popular in the Middle Ages and were intended to educate the largely illiterate population about Christianity."[74]

In what is clearly modeled after a medieval manuscript, in Pauline Baynes's illustration,[75] Lucy sees, and therefore can say, the spell that lets one know what others are thinking of her. By doing so, she hears her friend Marjorie Preston deny her friendship to bully Ann Featherstone.[76] This upsets her deeply and earns her a rebuke from Aslan: "'Child,' he said, 'I think you have been eavesdropping.'" He affirms that Lucy will never be able to forget what she has heard.[77] Eavesdropping, whether magical or not, has its costs.

The stakes are higher yet with another spell, that which would "make beautiful her that uttereth beyond the lot of mortals." The teaching here is a warning for Lucy to turn away from vanity, but also from jealousy, and of wanting to be grown up too soon (always a sin for Lewis, as noted above). This represents real moral danger, that of Pride, which Lewis identified as the most dangerous sin in *Mere Christianity*.[78] And Aslan reacts and comes to her defense with a warning, a moving picture of a "great face of a lion, of The Lion, of Aslan himself, staring into hers. It was painted such a bright gold that it seemed to be coming towards her out of the page ... At any rate she knew the expression on his face quite well. He was growling and you could see most of his teeth."[79] Note the insistence that this is a matter of moral urgency: Lewis's narrator uses three references to Aslan, each more specific than the last, to ensure that neither Lucy nor his readers can deny they were warned; his image overwrites the text "there in the middle of the writing, where she felt quite sure there had been no picture before," so that Lucy might not cross beyond the border of humanity. What one cannot see, one cannot read, and one cannot speak.

So it goes throughout the *Chronicles*: while classroom instruction is always denigrated, the double pattern of experience and instruction is seen everywhere in the stories. Again and again, the characters are represented as doing the best they can to do the right thing and attempting to act like Aslan, and in failing—usually they fail—they are brought face to face with Aslan and corrected, sometimes gently, sometimes to the point of corporal punishment. Nothing else matters: Lewis is picturing his secondary world as nothing less than a school for Heaven. Against that background, the mere memorization of facts is nothing compared to the ontological task of becoming more and more like Christ. There is no other way to become fully human, in Lewis's theology, than learning how to become the *imitatio Christi*. The true education of Narnia is to sit at the very paws of Aslan himself, learning how to humble the self and be like Christ.

Notes

1. I presented a conference version of this paper under the title, "Mere Memorization: The Sad State of Formal Education in Lewis's Narnia," at the 2004 C. S. Lewis and the Inklings Conference at LeTorneau University. I'd like to thank two of my colleagues at the University of Louisiana at Lafayette for their help with this paper. Fellow Episcopalian Claiborne Rice first brought the Call for Papers for the Inklings Conference to my attention and has since refused to let this essay die an untimely death; and Jenny Geer helped me think through some of the issues involved. I also would like to thank my editors Michelle Ann Abate and Lance Weldy, as well as the anonymous reader of an early draft of this essay, for their helpful comments. I am particularly indebted to the anonymous reader for suggesting the use of *The Abolition of Man* and for noting that *The Silver Chair* is all about the need for rote learning, as well as other suggestions.
2. The edition of the *Chronicles* I am using is the first American edition of all seven of the novels gathered in the so-called preferred order in one volume by HarperCollins: C. S. Lewis, *The Chronicles of Narnia*, with illustrations by Pauline Baynes (New York, 2001), originally published in Great Britain by Collins in 1998. I chose it for its ubiquity, if not always for its accuracy. Obvious typos have been silently emended after consulting other editions of the *Chronicles* including first editions where I could locate them.
3. The few examples of one-to-one instruction by characters specifically identified as teachers—such as the impromptu tutorial held by Professor Kirke in his study for Peter and Susan on the subject of Lucy's potential insanity in *The Lion, the Witch and the Wardrobe* (New York: HarperCollins, 2001): 130–2, and the conversations between Dr. Cornelius and the young Caspian in the towers of his uncle's castle in *Prince Caspian* (New York: HarperCollins, 2001): 336–45—are apparent exceptions to this rule. It is classroom instruction with rows of chairs and a teacher giving out discipline at the front of the room that bothers Lewis so.
4. Thomas à Kempis, *Imitation of Christ*, Holiness Data Ministry Digital Edition, May 17, 1995: http://wesley.nnu.edu/wesleyctr/books/1201-1300/HDM1212.pdf (accessed July 10, 2011).

5. I Corinthians 13:11.

6. C. S. Lewis, *The Last Battle* (New York: HarperCollins, 2001): 767.

7. C. S. Lewis, *The Silver Chair* (New York: HarperCollins, 2001).

8. Rachel Collins et al., "Black-and-White Thinkers and Colorful Problems: Intellectual Differentiation in Experiential Education," *Journal of Experiential Education* 33(4) (2011): n.p.

9. Roger Lancelyn Green and Walter Hooper, *C. S. Lewis: A Biography* (New York: HarperCollins, 2003): 8.

10. *Ibid.*: 7; C. S. Lewis, *Surprised by Joy: The Shape of My Early Life* (Boston, MA: Houghton Mifflin Harcourt, 1995): 23.

11. "Bergen-Belsen." *Holocaust Museum*. United States Holocaust Memorial Museum, January 6, 2011: www.ushmm.org/museum/exhibit/online/dp/camp1.htm (accessed February 13, 2011.).

12. Green and Hooper: 7.

13. C. S. Lewis, *The Magician's Nephew* (New York: HarperCollins, 2001): 14.

14. C. S. Lewis, *The Abolition of Man* (New York: Macmillan, 1973): n.p.

15. David Naugle, "Education and The Abolition of Man," in *C. S. Lewis: Original Work On and About C. S. Lewis*. HarperOne, June 16, 2009: http://cslewis.com/ (accessed February 12, 2011). The copyright date of *The Abolition of Man* is 1947, but, as Naugle correctly notes, both the lectures and the first publication of *The Abolition of Man* were in 1943.

16. C. S. Lewis, *Mere Christianity* (San Francisco, CA: HarperCollins, 2001); Walter Hooper, *C. S. Lewis: A Complete Guide to His Life and Works* (New York: HarperOne, 1998): 123–4.

17. Hooper: 313.

18. *The Abolition of Man*: 78.

19. *The Abolition of Man*: 53; *Mere Christianity*: 5.

20. *The Abolition of Man*: ch. 1.

21. Douglas D. Anderson, *The Hymns and Carols of Christmas*, 1996–2001: www.hymnsandcarolsofchristmas.com (accessed February 13, 2011).

22. *The Abolition of Man*: 28–9.

23. *Ibid.*: 35.

24. *Mere Christianity*: 3.

25. *The Lion, the Witch and the Wardrobe*: 116.

26. Alan K. Bowman, *Life and Letters on the Roman Frontier: Vindolanda and Its People* (New York: Taylor and Francis, 1998); Carol Rose, *Giants, Monsters, And Dragons: An Encyclopedia Of Folklore, Legend, And Myth* (New York: W. W. Norton, 2001).

27. *The Lion, the Witch and the Wardrobe*: 117–19.

28. *Ibid.*: 115–16.

29. *Mere Christianity*: 205–6.

30. *Ibid.*: 120.

31. *The Magician's Nephew*: 86.

32. C. S. Lewis, *The Voyage of the Dawn Treader* (New York: HarperCollins, 2001): 464.

33. *The Magician's Nephew*: 13–14.
34. *The Last Battle*: 741.
35. Philip Pullman, "Narnia's Darkside," *Guardian*, October 1, 1998. Reprinted in *The Cumberland River Lamp Post*, September 2, 2001. Ed. Richard James. At: www.crlamppost.org/darkside.htm (accessed February 13, 2011).
36. Neil Gaiman, *Fragile Things: Short Fictions and Wonders* (New York: William Morrow, 2006): 187.
37. *The Last Battle*: 762.
38. *Prince Caspian*: 408–9.
39. *Ibid.*: 408.
40. *Ibid.*: 336–7 (emphasis in original).
41. *The Voyage of the Dawn Treader*: 485–505.
42. *Ibid.*: 499.
43. *Ibid.*: 501.
44. *Ibid.*: 522.
45. *The Voyage of the Dawn Treader*: 426.
46. *Ibid.*: 425.
47. *Ibid.*: 425.
48. *Ibid.*: 457.
49. *Ibid.*: 437.
50. *Ibid.*: 425.
51. Lewis's *The Great Divorce* (New York: HarperOne, 2001) is the greatest proof text for Lewis's concern with lacking a generosity of spirit. In it, the plot consistently damns its characters merely for being petty.
52. Throughout, I am assuming that both Eustace and Edmund attended Experiment House, though it is only named as such in *The Silver Chair*.
53. *The Silver Chair*: 549.
54. *Ibid.*: 551.
55. *Ibid.*: 662–3.
56. *The Horse and His Boy*: 247.
57. *Ibid.*: 271.
58. *Ibid.*: 274.
59. *Ibid.*: 299.
60. *Mere Christianity*: 31.
61. *The Voyage of the Dawn Treader*: 471.
62. *Ibid.*: 472.
63. *Ibid.*: 474–5.
64. *Ibid.*: 475.
65. *The Silver Chair*: 596–611.
66. *Ibid.*: 559–60.
67. *Ibid.*: 558.
68. *Ibid.*: 540.
69. *The Horse and His Boy*: 298.
70. *Ibid.*: 299.

71. *The Lion, the Witch and the Wardrobe*: 146.
72. *The Voyage of the Dawn Treader*: 495–6.
73. Sir Philip Sidney, *An Apology for Poetry or The Defence of Poesy*, ed. Geoffrey Shepherd (London: Manchester University Press, 1965): 120.
74. "Poor Man's Bible." *The New World Encyclopedia*: www.new worldencyclopedia.org/entry/Poor_Man%27s_Bibleonline (accessed July 2011).
75. *The Voyage of the Dawn Treader*: 492.
76. *Ibid.*: 496.
77. *Ibid.*: 498.
78. Lewis dedicates an entire chapter (Chapter 8 of Book 3, "The Great Sin") to this issue.
79. *The Voyage of the Dawn Treader*: 496.

4

War and the Liminal Space: Situating *The Lion, the Witch and the Wardrobe* in the Twentieth-Century Narrative of Trauma and Survival

Nanette Norris

In 1920, Eglantyne Jebb, founder of the Save the Children Fund, said, "It is the children who pay the highest price for our short sighted economic policy, our political blunders, our wars." In reference to the latter of the three negative phenomena, the twentieth century was possibly the most belligerent in history, with three world-changing wars:[1] the impact of these and other traumas upon the survivors is still a young field of study. For World War II alone, deaths are estimated at between 50 and 70 million.[2] In England, where C. S. Lewis spent World War II and where *The Chronicles of Narnia* begin their adventures, over 60,000 civilians are thought to have died in air raids. What place can a children's story possibly have in the narrative of trauma and survival? This essay argues that *The Lion, the Witch and the Wardrobe*[3] responds to trauma and dislocation in England during World War II with the provision of an imaginative, liminal space in which problems can be safely confronted through those which are analogous to the real world, thereby providing a measure of articulation and subsequent healing for the victim of trauma and betrayal. Further, because this literature is unattached to a particular time and place, it remains available for all children who suffer possible trauma.

Liminal: lying between two defined spaces without belonging to either of them. This could mean the wardrobe, which is the threshold into Narnia; the ability to pass into Narnia is particular to the child: I have not been able to make the back of *my* wardrobe disappear for many years, but as a child, my imagination took me on this journey. It can also mean Narnia itself, in which case we must query the spaces which surround this literary world—where is Narnia in historical or in psychological time? Narnia first came into being for readers because of war. On one side of it is the reality of children being moved out of London into the country, because incoming bombs had made their homes unsafe. On the other side, the children emerge from the liminal space as heroes in their own right, having grappled with morality, terror, and death, and having been prepared to view the world with hope for the future. *The Lion, the Witch and the Wardrobe* occupies the space of the survivor's memory, for whom war and conflict destroy one world and build another.

The Lion, the Witch and the Wardrobe speaks to trauma and recovery because of a complex framing. It speaks to trauma because it is framed as a war narrative, both in the historical time in which the novel was written and in Narnia time. It speaks to survival because the protagonists are imaged as children (who signify, at their most basic level, hope for the future). It also speaks to survival in the frame of the fantasy genre, in which the rules of life-as-we-know-it are suspended, opening possibilities for alternative actions and outcomes.

The early twentieth century saw the development of the investigation of trauma through the rise of psychology as a defined area of study; this paralleled a developing understanding of childhood as a separate and unique phase of life. Trauma studies intensified following World War II and the Holocaust, and the Holocaust continues to inform such studies, as well as those of individual and cultural memory. Literature which deals with trauma—and our interpretation of this literature—has changed since the days of Bruno Bettelheim and his discussion of the importance of violence in fairy tales[4] in that, with our growing sensibility of childhood, we have become invested in the innocence of childhood and the innocence of the experiences of children: we feel that children should not have to undergo danger, grief, betrayal, or any of the myriad negative experiences that, we believe, can cause trauma and scarring. On the other hand, acknowledging the role of childhood as a preparation for the sometimes intensely difficult and dangerous adult experience, many people feel that children should be exposed to hard truths, such as knowledge of the Holocaust, in the relatively controlled environment of narrative. One thinks of *The Devil's Arithmetic* (by Jane Yolen) or *If I Should Die before I Wake* (by Han Nolan). As Kenneth Kidd observes, "Presumably the exposure model became necessary because we no longer have the luxury of denying evil or postponing the child's confrontation with such."[5] In her review of Kidd's essay, Hamida Bosmajian notes how Kidd calls texts like *Arithmetic* "a misuse of identity politics via fairy tale magic into another world, claiming all the while direct confrontation with evil."[6] Kidd sees "pop-psychoanalysis" as having appropriated the fairy tale: "the wounded-but-resilient (inner) child of pop-psychoanalysis enable[s] a poetics of popular transmission and transference, whose major genre is the fairy tale. Through the fairy tale, people tell stories about challenge and survival, hardship and hope."[7] Kidd speaks of "children's literature of atrocity"[8] as though it were a modern-day invention (in fact, Postman and others believe childhood itself is the modern invention[9]) and criticizes what he calls the "traumatized but resilient child"[10] he sees as a trope in contemporary children's trauma literature, as well as the "utopian trauma theory,"[11] which posits that trauma literature can help in the production of a happy ending for the reader. He acknowledges the benefits of some children's trauma literature:

> Children's literature, of course, has been very usefully understood as therapeutic and testimonial. Certain genres seem to function much like the dreamwork as Freud described it, at once acknowledging but distorting or screening trauma. Drawing upon Freud, Bruno Bettelheim famously suggested that fairy tales help children work through both painful experiences and everyday psychic trouble. And fairy tale motifs surface in other kinds of texts about war and especially the Holocaust. Thus Donald Haase, among others, examines "the fairy tale's potential as an emotional survival strategy" in and around Holocaust narrative.[12]

However, his preference is for "an engaging model of children's literature as trauma testimony—one that is necessarily imperfect but that reckons with the difficulty of memory and narration."[13]

Seen in this light, *The Lion, the Witch and the Wardrobe* as a trauma or exposure narrative is too obviously upbeat and utopic about how it presents and deals with the trauma. And although Kidd takes umbrage with the utilitarian project of somehow persuading the young reader into understanding trauma by vicarious experience, he nonetheless would prefer a similar, if more nuanced, *raison d'être* for the literature.

C. S. Lewis wrote before the advent of trauma studies and directly on the heels of two world wars. *The Chronicles of Narnia* do not claim a direct confrontation with the evils of human war except insofar as the children step from a world which is actively confronting Hitler into a world in which a Witch has already taken control, where the evils of war quickly become the evils of human nature, anthropomorphized. Nonetheless, there is no denying of evil or postponing of the child's confrontation: throughout *The Chronicles of Narnia*, the fantasy world is hyper-realistic in its confrontation of potentially traumatic events, from betrayal to shame to murder.[14] The exposure might be seen as somewhat mitigated or buffered by the placement of the narrative into the liminal space, out of time and place. However, research into memory and the remembrance of trauma suggests that it is more our *desire* to buffer the experience that leads us to speak of the liminal space as buffering: memory operates in a manner similar to *The Chronicles of Narnia* narrative, in dissembling experience and recreating a newly ordered narrative with which to make sense of the (potentially traumatic) experience.

In fact, memory studies show that "our concepts of time are neither universally given entities nor epistemological preconditions of experience but outcomes of symbolic constructions, constructions that are by their very nature cultural and historical," and that "[n]arrative discourse is our most advanced way to shape complex temporal experiences, including remembering."[15] In other words, the very nature of experience is shaped by culture and history, and even the act of remembering takes place within the confines of language and narrative discourse.

Trauma studies have revealed complex reactions to trauma, central to which is the operation of memory.[16] In memory, time shifts, objects become displaced, and painful truths manifest in metaphors. Interviews with Holocaust survivors have elicited feelings of incredulity, as though life has been lived in an out-of-body experience, as well as guilt at having survived when so many did not. Victor Frankl writes about the after-war experiences of many survivors as being like emerging too quickly from a deep dive, where the release of pressure is dangerous and results in the bends.[17] If *The Chronicles of Narnia* partake of "identity politics" as Kidd suggests of other exposure narratives, it is rather to be a part of this process of gradual normalization which implicates the survivor in the success of the survival.

Studies also show that "[w]hen a parent or other powerful figure violates a fundamental ethic of human relationships, victims may need to remain unaware of the trauma not to reduce suffering but rather to promote survival"[18]; and, moreover, that an experience that one might presume to be traumatic may not be interpreted as such by the person concerned, at the time, or not until much later when the experience has been processed and situated in a narrative (cultural and historical) context.[19]

This suggests that a potentially traumatic experience, firstly, can be repressed and available only to symbolic language, as Bruno

Bettelheim suggested. Secondly, the narrative discourse of the fairy story or fantasy tale enables articulation of the repressed material, at arm's length. Thirdly, the narrative of the fantasy tale serves to give order and meaning to the (denied) experience. It does not deny the potentially traumatic elements, such as betrayal and violence, but it does enable a positive outcome, so that, as the experience enters into symbolic construction, the identity construction is positive (King and Queen) rather than negative (Victim).

Finally, as Jacqueline Rose has pointed out, the genre of children's literature is especially problematic in that there are no children in children's literature, but rather figures of the adult desire for the experience of childhood, and there is no child *behind* the story, a child for whom the narrative is created and of whose reception of the narrative we can be sure.[20] Katharine Smith adds:

> Alternately, because children are imagined as innocent, they are also figured as the survivors of trauma, those who can offer adults spiritual advice in how to triumph over pain through simple, honest, essential values like love, trust, hope, and perseverance. (Child healers, of course, are a Romantic construct and pervade children's literature.) This dualistic configuration recalls the work of Perry Nodelman[21] and Jacqueline Rose, and creates another version of the child as "other" by proposing both child fragility and strength. Like many constructions of childhood, the dualistic depiction of the child experiencing trauma is also deeply invested in allaying adult anxieties. If the child is victim, she must turn to adults; if the child is savior, she surpasses adults and her core values— her core identity— remain safe and somewhat untouched by historical event. Either way, the adult is somewhat reassured about the damage that trauma can do to the "innocent" child.[22]

Lewis and the war years

The death of King Edward and the onset of World War I mark a revolution in thinking that is still in the process of being assessed. It involved notions of identity, individuality, and democracy, as well as previously unthinkable metaphysical concepts which paved the way for the ubiquitous "virtual reality" of our own time.[23] The short period of peace between the two world wars was darkened by economic depression: the years 1914–45 placed heavy strain upon the imaginative wonder so evident in the prewar Edwardian literature.[24]

The Chronicles of Narnia are one of the first imaginative offerings for children after the onset of war in 1914. Interestingly enough, Lewis grew up during the Edwardian period, with all the imaginative development that implies. Gary Tandy writes that "Lewis demonstrated in his own personality and habits an embattled posture toward the outside world," seeing himself as one "of a small band of determined survivors fighting against forces in the outside world."[25] *The Chronicles of Narnia* show, for one thing, that he fought against the tide that would swamp the imagination in ultra-realism, and, for another, that he believed children have the capacity to overcome the horrors to which they are subjected in the outside world—that they, too, are survivors.

Sheila Egoff argues that children's literature post-1920 is dominated by what she terms the "problem" novel.[26] *The Chronicles of Narnia* straddle the divide between "imagination" and "problem," with the emphasis falling on imagination, and "problem" occurring within the liminal context of the fantasy story itself. Originally conceived in 1939[27] (although written between 1949 and 1954), *The Lion, the Witch and the Wardrobe* opens with Peter, Susan, Edmund, and Lucy being evacuated from London to the country house of Professor Digory Kirke. That is all that we hear of the war, but it is enough to situate the story as part of the ongoing problem of war: dislocation and trauma. Children were moved out of London in 1939,[28] 1940, and 1944, so we can date this detail fairly accurately. Lewis could have changed this point; he could have taken it out. The book was published in 1950, after the war, and at the time that he wrote it he did not realize he would write another book, a return to Narnia. It would seem that he wanted the war to inform it.

Born in 1889, in Belfast, Lewis was raised in Ireland. In 1917, he volunteered with the British army, and was commissioned as an officer with the Third Battalion, Somerset Light Infantry, with whom he went to the Somme Valley in France. He was wounded in April 1918, by a British shell falling short of its mark. Wyndham Lewis, in his *Blasting and Bombardiering*, writes that "war, art, civil war, strikes and coup d'états dovetail into each other."[29] So it is with Lewis: the long reach of war coloured his youth, his coming-of-age, his maturity, and, of course, his art. In this sense, the work becomes "a trip to a stricken area …[,] an area of [the] past which requires a little retrospective attention."[30] *The Chronicles of Narnia* were begun during World War II, with the writing continuing well after. Having experienced World War I first hand, Lewis certainly would have been disturbed by the years that anticipated World War II. As a thinker and an artist, it is clear that he could not remain silent about the impact of the trauma of war on psychological development.

He seems to be saying that each one of us is faced with serious moral decisions in our lives. Certainly, his own life is evidence that he was required to make tough moral decisions. As a young man, an Irish boy, joining the British force was in itself a difficult decision to make. Allegiance to Britain was by no means a given: the issue of Home Rule had been hotly debated for many years prior to the war.[31] After the war, having lost his own mother when he was a boy, and having made a promise to a friend, "Paddy" Moore, who was killed in action in France, Lewis lived with, and cared for, Paddy's mother, Jane. However deep their relationship became as time went on, the decision to stand up to the promise he made in the trenches must have involved the young Lewis in a moral struggle at first. His personal theological debate of those same years is well known.

Operation Pied Piper: the effects of evacuation on children

The Lion, the Witch and the Wardrobe opens with a very brief mention of the wartime experience that caused Peter, Susan, Edmund, and Lucy to find themselves in an old country mansion owned by "an old Professor," run by a housekeeper, and without their parents: "This story is about something that happened to them when they were sent away from London during the war because of the air-raids."[32] Peter says, "We've fallen on our feet," and that is the last mention of the war. However, the war informs the text metaphorically. The evacuation to which these few lines refer was code-named "Operation Pied Piper," and was utterly unique in its scope. On September 1, 1939, "1,473,391 children and adults from the crowded cities of Britain [were moved] to the relative safety of the countryside."[33] Some 826,959 unaccompanied children[34] were collected at assembly points and filled into waiting trains *regardless* of their destinations, the result of which was evacuees not arriving in the numbers expected at the stations, siblings separated, and any number of ill-suited and never-vetted (many press-ganged) host homes receiving active children to look after.[35] Thus, when Peter says they have "fallen on their feet," he indeed means it could have been a lot worse, given the experience of many other children.

The evacuation plans seem to have been underlined by a willful "double-think": on one hand, "[p]ropaganda played on the fears of parents and argued that children would be healthier and stronger in the country. Mothers in particular were portrayed as being irresponsible if they did not consent to the evacuation of their children."[36] The idea that soldiers would fight better if they thought their children were safe seems also to have played a role. On the other hand, "[e]vacuation was not simply about moving civilians from dangerous areas to places of relative safety; it was about the dispersal of population, and meeting essential wartime demands. The evacuation of children liberated more women to work in munitions factories."[37] Some children were evacuated to "known danger areas,"[38] and others were shipped overseas, to Canada and the United States, as part of an evacuation which "became known as the 'useless mouths' policy."[39] In other words, as Penny Elaine Starns and Martin L. Parsons have argued, the evacuation was never a simple moving of children "out of harm's way," but a conscious and concerted effort to free up human and other resources for the war effort.

It was an effort that required unprecedented and forceful propaganda in order to ensure the cooperation of the people, and a massive betrayal, a violation on the largest scale of "a fundamental ethic of human relationships." Those in power betrayed parents and children alike, through separation, and those they betrayed were the weakest and most vulnerable of the society, the 'useless mouths.' The parents betrayed their children, by cooperating with the decisions of those in power and allowing their children to be put in such potentially traumatic circumstances. "According to recent research, which is based on the oral history testimonies of over 500 evacuees, at least 15 percent of these children were subjected to sexual abuse and a further 20 percent to physical and mental abuse."[40]

> They were used as political pawns, advertising campaigns, farm laborers, domestic servants, and collectors of poison plants. They were abused by some host parents, village workers, priests, and in some cases even teachers. They were subjected to radical changes in their culture and surroundings, inadequate diet, education, and medical care, accompanied by social exclusion and scapegoating.[41]

It remains a question as to how much of this potential for trauma was known or realized at the time. "The first ever evacuation of unaccompanied children took place after Guernica was bombed and destroyed on 26 April, 1937."[42] Four thousand "half-starved Basque children" were taken in by the British at that time, housed in tent camps, and eventually dispersed throughout England. After *Kristallnacht* (1938), Britain agreed to accept 10,000 children without visas: "On arrival in Britain the children were housed in camps where on Sundays the 'cattle market' took place. They were herded together in a large hall and prospective hosts arrived to look them over and choose which, if any, to take home. Most wanted only young children, so the sweet and small ones were picked first."[43] When the same techniques were used for the dispersal of children throughout the United Kingdom in 1939, there must have been a sense of familiarity for the people and communities involved.

Starns and Parsons point out that historians have debated the evacuation process in terms of social class structures (the evacuees from the city were regarded as being of a different, and usually lower, class than their country hosts), and "[c]onventional accounts of evacuation history have portrayed the British government as one which initiated evacuation schemes merely in order to protect children from the horrors of war."[44] Reports of potential traumatic effects of the evacuation began to appear while the evacuations were ongoing,[45] but much less was known about trauma at that time as compared to nowadays.

Trauma of betrayal and loss in *The Lion, the Witch and the Wardrobe*

Betrayal

In "The Tropes of Trauma," Hamida Bosmajian reminds us that,

> What does emerge are patterns of fantasy displacements and compensations over and against the sites of murder. The child under fire is at that moment at the site where trauma brands the human being; the child in the shadow of war is the survivor for whom the war will always be the subtext to everything termed normal and to everything that is displaced into and heightened by fantasy, for every oral history, every narrative, poem, or graphic work of art about trauma is, in one way or another, an ordering of traumatic experience, a bandaging or dressing of the wound or, in time, the scar.[46]

In the shadow of war, Peter, Susan, Edmund, and Lucy—and all who identify with these fictional characters—have their experience articulated for them in the fantasy of the narrative, enabling an "ordering of traumatic experience." Trauma in the novel is encapsulated in two categories: betrayal and loss. Betrayal is the most fundamental of traumatic events. In *The Lion, the Witch and the Wardrobe* there are three essential forms of betrayals, which I will categorize according to the potential *power* relation:[47] intimate, acquaintance or arm's length, and corporate. Each is equally capable of producing fatal results, but arguably *intimate* betrayals cause the most emotional fall-out. In the narrative, the most intimate betrayal is figured in the real-life betrayal by the children's family, which is clarified by Edmund accusing Susan of "[t]rying to talk like Mother."[48] That she is unsuccessful in stepping into the shoes of her absent parent becomes evident in the escalation of the bad behavior of her sibling. The absent parents are the first betrayal, the effect of which informs the entire story but remains outside or beyond its scope—the elephant in the room or the signifier of absence, as Lacan would say.[49]

The series of personal betrayals executed by Edmund are possibly the most tragic because they are totally understandable on one level, as the spiteful behavior of a child: "And Edmund gave a very superior look as if he were far older than Lucy (there was really only a year's difference) then a little snigger and said, 'Oh, yes, Lucy and I have been playing – pretending that all her story about a country in the wardrobe is true.'"[50] These betrayals are deadly serious, though, because they mean life and death to his siblings:

> You mustn't think that even now Edmund was quite so bad that he actually wanted his brothers and sisters to be turned into stone. He did want Turkish Delight and to be a Prince (and later a King) and to pay Peter back for calling him a beast. As for what the Witch would do with the others, he didn't want her to be particularly nice to them – certainly not to put them on the same level as himself; but he managed to believe, or to pretend he believed, that she wouldn't do anything very bad to them.[51]

His treachery is potentially mitigated by his youth and his addiction (to Turkish Delight), and certainly the children become reconciled to him later, but Edmund is an example of the type of person who is motivated by petty personal gain at the expense of others: his betrayal is all the more serious because he is one of their nearest and dearest, he is family. In the Christian subtext of the story, he is Judas, and underscores just how *ordinary* and unremarkable betrayal can be— what Hannah Arendt was later to call "the banality of evil."[52]

The potential betrayal of Lucy by Mr. Tumnus is an example of arm's-length betrayal. He has no ties to Lucy and no obligation beyond *right action*. Lucy is awakened to the possibility of such betrayal, made wise by it, and certainly anxious for her own safety, but knowledge of this near-betrayal is received in a cooler manner than she later receives Edmund's lie.

Failure to betray is harshly punished: Mr. Tumnus receives no reward for letting Lucy leave Narnia: the Witch has him arrested for high treason, in one of the many ironies of the narrative in which doing the right thing falls foul of the controlling desires of those in power. One is reminded of the force of the propaganda in Britain which labeled as traitors families who were non-compliant with the evacuation plan.

The Witch's betrayal of Edmund—by luring him with Turkish Delight, by playing on his character weakness, and then abusing him once he no longer serves her purpose—is an example of corporate betrayal. The Witch represents an outside force with potentially much power but little to no personal feeling or connection. She is entirely self-involved and can be depended upon to use and abuse. Her connection with Edmund exists only for as long as she perceives him to be useful to her. Most revealing is the fact that Edmund is equally as anxious to use the Witch (to get Turkish Delight from her, and perhaps the title of Prince), underscoring the reciprocity of this relationship. When Edmund shows up without his siblings, he is at some level aware that he has let down his side of the bargain and opened himself to her maltreatment. In other words, the basis for this relationship between the individual and the (self-serving) state (or corporate body as represented by the Witch) is inherently flawed and likely to result in mutual betrayals.

I would argue that, when the children meet Aslan and become invested in him as savior, as protector, they enter into an intimate relationship with an otherwise arm's-length and possibly even corporate entity (he is the King, after all). The operant word here is *trust*—the children *trust* Aslan as they trusted their own parents, their own family members, their own society. When the Witch confronts Aslan with Edmund's treachery and the Deep Magic, and Aslan "[does] not deny it," Susan responds with a deep emotional reaction of bewilderment, fear, and a profound sense of powerlessness, as one betrayed: "'Oh, Aslan! … Can't we do something about the Deep Magic? Isn't there something you can work against it?'"[53] When Aslan talks to the Witch and enters into negotiations with her, "[i]t was a terrible time, this waiting and wondering."[54] We begin to see the children anxious, worrying, experiencing entirely adult concerns: "I've a most horrible feeling—as if something were hanging over us."[55] This is the "site where trauma brands the human being" as Bosmajian termed it—the emotional reaction to absolute and utter helplessness in the face of calamity. Aslan says nothing; he does not include or involve the children, or in any way prepare them for what is to come. They witness the Witch kill with a knife their only intimate relation, the one who at that point in time means everything to them: father, mother, friend, government. Not only did Aslan plan it and allow it; he said nothing, and allowed them to experience this potentially traumatizing act, an act that some may argue is the ultimate act of betrayal of innocence: murder.

And always, outside the frame and beyond the narrative, lies the betrayal of the war, of the parents who allowed the government to transport their children into the unknown and dangerous, who allowed their children's innocence, their children's childhoods, to be abruptly shortened in multiple experiences of betrayal.

The difference between *The Chronicles of Narnia* and other exposure narratives lies in the identity politics. A narrative such as Jane Yolen's *The Devil's Arithmetic*, which magically transports a modern-day Jewish child into a concentration camp and brings the character to the moment of her death by gassing, in the liminal/pseudo-historical space, before returning her to her family home,[56] is a conscious manipulation of shock witnessing in order to personalize and reiterate the traumatic branding. *The Chronicles of Narnia* evoke the potentially traumatic moment in a mythic space (not pseudo-historical), which enables a working-through, reordering, and articulating of the essence of the experience, toward a successful, non-traumatized outcome.

The concept is from Sigmund Freud's 1914 paper, "Remembering, Repeating and Working-Through," in which he first argued that the traumatized person will act out the repressed traumatic memory: "For instance, the patient does not say that he remembers that he used to be defiant and critical towards his parents' authority; instead, he behaves in that way to the doctor."[57] In these terms, when Edmund denies the pseudo-parental voice of his sister, and immediately after betrays his siblings, he is acting out the abjected trauma; his acting out points to betrayal as the site of traumatic branding, and most likely intimate betrayal, as he betrays those with whom he is intimate. The narrative enables this acting out to take place and to be worked through so that the troubled person can reintegrate into normal social relations without the burden of the trauma. Certainly, this is a psychoanalytic theory of which Lewis may have been aware.

Loss

Loss results in the second site of traumatic branding. As with betrayal, loss is experienced in ever-widening circles of relations, and, as with betrayal, loss is something against which we are absolutely powerless. First, the children lose their parents and the certitude that comes of being in a stable environment, their home. Next, they lose their confidence in one of their own, with the realization of Edmund's lies and betrayal. They are (dis)located to a new culture and environment. They lose their acquaintance, Mr. Tumnus. Their new guardians, Mr. and Mrs. Beaver, are placed in grave danger by harboring them: they are all obliged to move to less comfortable shelter in the cave, as the Beavers lose their home and the children lose their temporary shelter, reminiscent of the movements of Jews and others through Europe, fleeing from Hitler's atrocities. Again, the losses are intimate, then arm's length. In the narrative, the intimate loss, the one that is outside the frame of the narrative—the loss of parents and home—is the most traumatic and lies beyond articulation.

Why is this loss the most traumatic? It is never discussed in the narrative beyond the brief comment by Edmund that his sister is attempting to fill her mother's shoes, and therefore could easily be dismissed as unimportant. However, we know from trauma studies (and psychoanalysis concurs) that the breakup of the family unit upon which one depends is a basic marker for trauma. The key point is that one depends upon others, upon the group, upon the relationships, for one's well-being. Well-being is threatened by the breakup of this primary unit. In one sense, it lies outside the frame because it has been abjected—the narrative refuses to acknowledge it.[58] However, it also lies outside the frame because the characters are on the cusp. The narrative shows them going beyond the family unit, becoming mature, forming new relationships and taking charge of their own destinies: "It was strange to her to see Peter looking as he did now— his face was so pale and stern and he seemed so much older."[59]

Edmund suffers a corporate loss: the Witch alters in her behavior toward him. He (mis)places his trust in her on the basis of her superficial behavior: "'She was jolly nice to me, anyway, much nicer than they are. I expect she is the rightful Queen really. Anyway, she'll be better that that awful Aslan!' At least, that was the excuse he made in his own mind for what he was doing. It wasn't a very good excuse, however, for deep down inside him he really knew that the White Witch was bad and cruel."[60] His judgment is off; it is self-serving, and the consequences cause him to feel disillusionment, even shame. The Witch represents any regime which has the power to seduce supporters and then to do them wrong—this could be Germany under the Nazis or Britain in its attempt to fight the invasion. Edmund's acting out of the scenario of seduction and subsequent rejection, it can be argued, can be seen as a metaphoric transference of the sexual trauma some children were known to have experienced. Certainly, it responds to a Freudian reading. Edmund does not gain his sword—in Freudian terms, his phallus—until he returns to his family group and joins with Aslan.

The loss of Aslan, whose appearance was heralded with such high hopes ("*Wrong will be right, when Aslan comes in sight*"), is the greatest and most shocking loss in the narrative, and we know from the

Christian subtext that his death, his self-sacrifice, on the Stone Table not only fulfills the "deep magic from before the dawn of time" but parallels the murder of Christ, which is also the self-sacrifice of Christ, with the redemption which this act made possible, according to Christian theology. It raises the question at the heart of both exposure narratives and traumatic events alike: what is the purpose of suffering? The betrayals and the losses are all sufferings of one type and another, but the narrative makes no attempt to avoid them, just as life outside the narrative was replete with these experiences.[61]

Beyond betrayal and loss

Perhaps literature as a psychoanalytic tool is simply asking too much of a story. Perhaps *The Chronicles of Narnia* strike us as a tad naive in our complex, post-Holocaust society, where witnessing is privileged over storytelling. Suffice it to say, some very bad things were happening in Great Britain that are echoed in the land of Narnia. Let's not ask how the children of Great Britain got through the dislocation, the separation, the abandonment, the fear—this is the domain of interviewers and psychologists. How did Peter, Susan, Edmund, and Lucy come through?

The order of the narrative is such that before they witnessed the death of Aslan, Peter made his first kill. That's what it's called in the army, and that's what it was for Peter. It is an important detail: Peter got a sword and shield from Father Christmas, and when he heard Lucy's horn, and when Aslan said, "Back! Let the Prince win his spurs,"[62] he found himself in the awful position of having to defend his sister from the attack of "a huge grey beast," so he "plunge[d] his sword, as hard as he could, between the brute's forelegs into its heart."[63] Thus, even before Aslan's death and resurrection, the children were firmly implicated in the life-and-death struggle of the war, on the most personal level possible. In the fantasy world, Peter enacts the very adult job of fighting the enemy for the sake of saving his family, and it is a very contemporary, Germanic enemy. This scene in particular uses the discourse and imagery of anti-German propaganda, in which the "Hun" was depicted variously as a "mad brute,"[64] a wolf, and with beast-like visage, in the traditional German army field uniform, or *feldgrau*, which was grey.

There was no angst over whether they were old enough, mature enough, or whether they could or should remain shielded and innocent: the war enveloped them, in Narnia as in real life, and they were expected and prepared to do what needed to be done. Neither "economically useful" nor "emotionally priceless," in Patricia Pace's terms,[65] the children must "earn their spurs," earn the right to be Kings and Queens, to be rulers, to have power and influence in the adult world. Some people simply do not have the luxury of peace. I can remember my mother telling the story of how, when the air raid sounded, she would wake my brothers, who were aged two and three at the time, and hurry them to the kitchen where they would huddle under the steel table until the "all clear" sounded. They were in a village just outside of London. One night a shell demolished the house across the street. Just like that. You did what you had to do, and you behaved ethically and honorably. You kept your measure of civilization in the midst of the chaos and destruction, or tried to. That is the "moral" of the story, if you will. But I doubt if the story has lived this long and been this hugely popular solely because of its moral.

Death has no dominion

In Lewis's Christian terms, we come to grips with trauma and survival by not fearing death. In *Death So Noble*, Jonathan Vance writes that the "insistence on the immortality of the fallen was part of the consolatory act but, in a broader context, it was also part and parcel of making sense of the war. Having accepted that the war had been a crusade in defence of Christian principles, people simply could not conceive of [soldiers] descending into oblivion after fighting for a righteous cause."[66] Vance is speaking of the way in which World War I was memorialized, but the point applies equally to World War II: the fear of death was ubiquitous. Death is the betrayal of Life. The slaughter of World War I had severely shaken the foundations of faith; World War II continued this loss of belief. Death conflates the two traumas of betrayal and loss. But death is the one event which is conspicuously absent from the narrative. Not abjected, it is, rather, figured: the courtyard of the Witch's house, filled with stone beings, offers a powerful image of lifelessness and each of the statues memorializes a fallen soldier; the horror of this slaughter is realized in metaphor. The point is driven home in the description of the battle with the Witch when Peter notes that Edmund destroyed her wand.[67]

Having once disgraced himself by treachery, and having been seduced by the enemy previously, Edmund redeems his honor and his good name in battle, fighting intelligently and fearlessly, without a thought for his own safety. The narrative argues that traumatic fixation is not the only possible outcome of traumatic experience. The reward for such selfless action is immortality. Rather than show the deaths, with the exception of Aslan's death, the narrative chooses to show the resurrection, a remarkable afterlife about which there can be no fear.

Conclusion

The life-and-death problems of the land of Narnia are, in the end, remarkably similar to those of the real world. This essay has discussed the ways in which *The Lion, the Witch and the Wardrobe* imaged the traumas of World War II. However, unlike our contemporary children's trauma literature, whose project is often to create the memory of trauma, *The Lion, the Witch and the Wardrobe* offers a liminal space, which is neither of this world nor totally removed from it, in which the traumatic experience can be ordered, articulated, and can undergo a working-through which, trauma studies suggest, can be of sincere benefit for someone victimized by trauma. Furthermore, rather than the sense of loss and victimization so often seen in post-Holocaust works, the narrative reinscribes a sense of hegemony through prewar values of honor, duty, and fearlessness in the face of the enemy. Moreover, it privileges imagination over ultra-realism, believing that children have the innate capacity to overcome the horrors to which they are subjected in life.

Notes

1. "[T]he First World War of 1914–1918; the Second World War of 1939–1945; and the Cold War of 1946–1988. Indeed, various periods of the twentieth century were defined in terms of world-changing wars." Shireen T. Hunter, "Introduction," in Shireen T. Hunter (ed.), *Strategic Developments in Eurasia after 11 September* (London: Frank Cass, 2004): 1.
2. See Martin Gilbert, *The Second World War: A Complete History* (New York: Henry Holt, 1994).
3. C. S. Lewis, *The Lion, the Witch and the Wardrobe. The Chronicles of Narnia* (New York: HarperCollins, 2001). Subsequent reference will be to this edition. *The Lion, the Witch and the Wardrobe* is the second book in this volume; it was originally published separately by Geoffrey Bles, in 1950, and was the first of the *Chronicles* to be written and published.
4. Bruno Bettleheim, *Uses of Enchantment* [1975] (New York: Vintage, 2010).
5. Kenneth Kidd, "*A* is for Auschwitz: Psychoanalysis, Trauma Theory, and the 'Children's Literature of Atrocity,'" *Children's Literature* 33 (2005): 120–49, at 120–1. Reprinted in *Under Fire: Childhood in the Shadow of War*, ed. Elizabeth Goodenough and Andrea Immel (Detroit, MI: Wayne State University Press, 2008).

6. Hamida Bosmajian, "The Tropes of Trauma," *Children's Literature* 37 (2009): 297.
7. Kidd: 132.
8. *Ibid.*: 121.
9. Neil Postman, *The Disappearance of Childhood* (New York: Random House, 1994).
10. Kidd: 131.
11. *Ibid.*: 126.
12. *Ibid.*: 122. The Donald Haase citation is from "Children, War, and the Imaginative Space of Fairy Tales," *The Lion and the Unicorn* 24(3) (2000): 360.
13. *Ibid.*: 144.
14. This applies to the entire *Chronicles of Narnia*, although only *The Lion, the Witch and the Wardrobe* specifically focuses on issues of war.
15. Jens Brockmeier, "Stories to Remember Narrative and the Time of Memory," *StoryWorlds: A Journal of Narrative Studies* 1 (2009): 118.
16. See Ana Douglass and Thomas A. Vogler (eds.), *Witness and Memory: The Discourse of Trauma* (New York: Routledge, 2003). See also Cathy Caruth, *Unclaimed Experience: Trauma, Narrative, and History* (Baltimore, MD: Johns Hopkins University Press, 1996); Dylan Trigg, "The Place of Trauma: Memory, Hauntings, and the Temporality of Ruins," *Memory Studies* 2(1) (2009): 88: "in Cathy Caruth's account of trauma as an 'unclaimed experience,' we can sense the displacement of the traumatized body, therefore, as a phenomenon marked by an experience that literally overwhelms the relation between place, time, and embodiment."
17. Victor E. Frankl, *Man's Search for Meaning* [1959] (New York: Pocket Books, 1997).
18. Jennifer J. Freyd, "Betrayal Trauma: Traumatic Amnesia as an Adaptive Response to Childhood Abuse," *Ethics and Behavior* 4(4) (1994): 307.
19. Susan Clancey, *The Trauma Myth* (New York: Basics, 2009).
20. Jacqueline Rose, *The Case of Peter Pan or The Impossibility of Children's Fiction* (London: Macmillan, 1984).
21. Perry Nodelman, "The Other: Orientalism, Colonialism, and Children's Literature," *Children's Literature Association Quarterly* 17(1) (1992): 29–35.
22. Katharine Capshaw Smith, "Forum: Trauma and Children's Literature," *Children's Literature* 33 (2005): 116.
23. See my *Attack on all Fronts: The Culture of Twentieth Century War* (forthcoming from Fisher Imprints).
24. We think of *Alice in Wonderland*, *Black Beauty*, *Peter Pan*, and many other classics of the so-called "Golden Age" of children's fiction.
25. Gary L. Tandy, *The Rhetoric of Certitude: C. S. Lewis's Nonfiction Prose* (Kent, OH: Kent State University Press, 2009): 4.
26. Sheila Egoff, "Which One's the Mockingbird? Children's Literature from 1920s to the Present," *Theory into Practice* 21(4) (1982): 239–46.
27. Roger Lancelyn Green and Walter Hooper, *C. S. Lewis: A Biography* (New York: Harvest, 2002): 302–7.

28. There were three waves of evacuation: 1939, 1940, and 1944, but children were constantly on the move throughout England during these years.

29. Wyndam Lewis, *Blasting and Bombardiering* (Los Angeles, CA: University of California Press, 1967): 4.

30. *Ibid.*: 6.

31. Catherine Switzer, "Unionist Popular Culture and Rolls of Honour in the North of Ireland During the First World War," in Nanette Norris (ed.), *Unionist Popular Culture and Rolls of Honour in the North of Ireland During the First World War and other Diverse Essays* (Lewiston, NY: Edwin Mellen, 2011): 12.

32. *The Lion, the Witch and the Wardrobe*: 111.

33. John Welshman, *Churchill's Children: The Evacuee Experience in Wartime Britain* (Oxford: Oxford University Press, 2010): 43.

34. *Ibid.*: 46.

35. Penny Elaine Starns and Martin L. Parsons, "Against Their Will: The Use and Abuse of British Children during the Second World War," in James Marten (ed.), *Children and War* (New York: New York University Press, 2002): 267.

36. *Ibid.*: 268.

37. *Ibid.*: 268.

38. *Ibid.*: 267.

39. *Ibid.*: 268.

40. *Ibid.*: 272. See John Macnicol, "The Effect of the Evacuation of Schoolchildren on Official Attitudes to State Intervention," in Harold L. Smith (ed.), *War and Social Change: British Society in the Second World War* (Manchester: Manchester University Press, 1986); Martin L. Parsons, *I'll Take That One: Dispelling the Myths of Civilian Evacuation, 1939–1945* (Cambridge: Beckett Karlson, 1998).

41. *Ibid.*: 276.

42. Jessica Mann, *Out of Harm's Way: The Wartime Evacuation of Children from Britain* (London: Headline, 2005): 18.

43. *Ibid.*: 21.

44. Starns and Parsons: 266.

45. See Enid M. John, "A Study of the Effects of Evacuation and Air Raids on Children of Pre-School Age," *British Journal of Educational Psychology* 11(2) (1941): 173–82; W. Mary Burbury, "Effects of Evacuation and of Air Raids on City Children," *British Medical Journal* 8(2) (1941): 660–2; Frank Bodman, "Child Psychiatry in War-Time Britain," *Journal of Educational Psychology* 35(5) (1944): 293–301; Anna Freud and Dorothy T. Burlingham, *War and Children* [1943] (Westport, CN: Greenwood, 1973).

46. Bosmajian: 299.

47. See Michel Foucault, "The Subject and Power" [1982], in *The Essential Foucault*, ed. Paul Rabinow and Niklas Rose (New York: New Press, 2003): 126–44. Foucault is looking at what legitimates power, and how objectification through power turns human beings into subjects.

48. *The Lion, the Witch and the Wardrobe*: 111.
49. Jacques Lacan, "French Freud" (translation of "La Lettre Volée," trans. Jeffrey Mehlman), *Yale French Studies* 48 (1972): 39–72.
50. *The Lion, the Witch and the Wardrobe*: 129.
51. *Ibid*.: 131.
52. Hannah Arendt, *Eichmann in Jerusalem: A Report on the Banality of Evil* [1963] (New York: Penguin Classics, 1994).
53. *The Lion, the Witch and the Wardrobe*: 176.
54. *Ibid*.: 176.
55. *Ibid*.: 178.
56. Jane Yolen, *The Devil's Arithmetic* [1988] (New York: Puffin, 1990).
57. Sigmund Freud, "Further Recommendations in the Technique of Psycho-Analysis: Recollection, Repetition, and Working-Through," *Collected Papers Vol. II*, trans. Joan Riviere [1914] (London: Hogarth, 1949): 150.
58. See Julia Kristeva, *Powers of Horror: An Essay on Abjection* (Columbia, NY: Columbia University Press, 1982).
59. *The Lion, the Witch and the Wardrobe*: 192.
60. *Ibid*.: 152.
61. C. S. Lewis, *The Problem of Pain* (New York: Macmillan, 1944).
62. *Ibid*.: 170.
63. *Ibid*.: 170.
64. "Destroy This Mad Brute," US World War II propaganda poster.
65. Patricia Pace, "All Our Lost Children: Trauma and Testimony in the Performance of Childhood," *Text and Performance Quarterly* 18 (1998): 233–47.
66. Jonathan F. Vance, *Death So Noble* (Vancouver, BC: UBC Press, 1997): 44.
67. *The Lion, the Witch and the Wardrobe*: 192.

5

C. S. Lewis's Manifold Mythopoeics: Toward a Reconsideration of Eschatological Time in the Construction of *The Chronicles of Narnia*

Joseph Michael Sommers

In his essay, "On Three Ways Of Writing for Children," C. S. Lewis defines his children's writings as "fantasy," a "sub-species" of children's literature distinguishable from the fairy tale in ways that he does not go on to define.[1] He does provide us with some hints, however, to distinguish the fairy story as something far different from what he constructs as fantasy. For Lewis, not all children's literature is (nor should be) fantasy, but for "modern children," fantasy suits their needs better than the fairy story.[2] For me, Lewis's contention brings about an obvious question of why "modern children" in his post–World War II period *necessitated* fantasy. What, from Lewis's construction of the fantastic (and its difference from the fairy tale), provides his audience with something "modern children need"?

This essay will explore Lewis's answer, specifically how his fantasy differs from that of the fairy story in matters of time and space. In Bakhtinian terms, we call that concept "the chronotope." Explaining that term is not simple. However, at its core, the chronotope is literally an examination, as the name self-reflexively indicates, of the construction and use of time (*chronos*) and space (*topos*) within a text, the time and space surrounding the text, and how this comingling of time crafts the "form-shaping ideology" of the genre of the text itself.[3] My conclusions hold that fantasy, for Lewis, allowed the post–World War II child to "escape" from a reality caught up in the national boundaries of the folk into fairy tales during a time of crisis where an escape from reality is necessitated. In "On Three Ways," Lewis asserts that "we run to [the fairy story] from the disappointments and humiliations of the real world; it sends us back to the real world undivinely discontented."[4] What makes the journey into fantasy so satisfying for him comes in its "emptying of the actual world," where the child can abandon his or her reality, for one with a "new dimension of depth"[5] absent of the horrors of the child's reality. Of particular interest will be *The Chronicles of Narnia* as both a constructed time, place, and destination as well as Lewis's attempt to escape the reality of his own time and place. Narnia will be shown to be Lewis's eschatological take on how a child might escape Lewis's contemporary moment—a time and place he held a particular animosity toward. And while much has been made of J. R. R. Tolkien's accusations of Lewis's alleged allegorizing of the Christian Bible to create shoddily composed children's stories based on the tenets of his own conversion, I will argue Lewis's side: *The Chronicles of Narnia* are not only not allegorical, but they are, in fact, only *broadly* Christian.[6] Lewis, in an effort to escape the reality of his time and place, invoked a great many myths, histories, and realities of times and places in the past (not merely Christian ones) in order to create his new world alongside the one in which he lived. As such, M. M. Bakhtin's concept of the chronotope will help illuminate Lewis's interests in collapsing mythic time, adventure time, folkloric time, and chivalric time. In doing so, he amalgamated a great many mythologies into a reading of Christian myth *analogous* to modern times, yet not *allegorically* connected to the stories as they were told before. The end result of this collapse of so many uses and types of time is that Lewis's fantasy bends the cyclical mythic time into linear, teleological, eschatological time pointing toward a very definite end to a child's reality and escape into a fantasy.

Critical debate on *The Chronicles of Narnia*, let alone on Lewis's intents and portents, usually have the same point of genesis: Tolkien's remarks on the *Chronicles* as being "allegory, a literary form [Tolkien] never enjoyed."[7] Tolkien's indignation with the work was likely tied to the notion that Lewis, a relatively new convert to Christianity after years of a strict atheism,[8] had the audacity to allegorically connect Christian tenets with "*Nymphs and their Ways* [and] *the Love-Life of a Faun*."[9] As Tolkien likely could not believe that Lewis would dare mar a story connected with Christ with mythological antecedents dealing with ribaldry, Bacchic subject matter and so on, he once asked Roger Green, "Doesn't [Lewis] know what he is talking about?"[10] Walter Hooper attests that Tolkien's indignation had much to do with the fact that he believed that this allegorical construction of Christian concepts was "too hastily written and contain[-ed] too many inconsistencies."[11] I must wonder, however, that if Lewis were to affirm his faith by writing an allegory set in time contemporaneous with his own, why, then, would he get so many of the "facts" wrong, let alone mix in so much pagan mythology as to render the work as faulty allegory? Lewis was considered to be an academic and a scholar of the first order; why then would he compose such a shoddily cobbled allegory? My answer is that he simply did not.

This, too, is a point of some major critical debate. To this day, critics align themselves with Tolkien and, more recently, with Philip Pullman who has taken up Tolkien's arguments with greater vigor. Chad Wriglesworth flatly calls the writing "allegory" even while acknowledging that "Lewis gathers and grafts ... images into a new state of being, reshaping pagan signs and medieval lore into an imaginative and highly accessible Christian context."[12] David Holbrook, too, believes that if we are to examine Lewis as a writer within the Christian tradition, then "Aslan seems too full of magic."[13] In no way am I arguing that Lewis tries to write something *non*-Christian in his *Chronicles*. To the contrary, I believe Lewis attempts to reexamine his time and place in the world around him *vis-à-vis* revisiting Christianity by examining concurrent and predating mythologies. That he chooses to represent the idea of escape from his own moment as escape from the mortal coil points to how Christianity's eschatological perspective brings him relief.

This idea of a re-mythologization of Christianity within a modern filter has been picked up individually by Mark Freshwater and Michael Nelson. Freshwater claims that it is Lewis's childhood reading experience of George MacDonald's *Phantastes* that fueled his imagination toward being able "to create modern myth .... MacDonald was the first modern writer to show [Lewis] that this was possible."[14] He goes so far as to connect this idea of Lewis's reimagination with his actual conversion experience itself, stating that "Lewis had begun to abandon his religious beliefs ... because he didn't think Christianity had much connection with the unhappy world around him."[15] A young Lewis, in a 1916 letter to Arthur Greeves, confirms this:

> I think that I believe in no religion. There is absolutely no proof for any of them, and from a philosophical standpoint, Christianity is not even the best. All religions, that is, all *mythologies* to give them their proper name, are merely man's own invention—Christ as much as Loki ... and so Christianity came into being—one mythology among many, but the one we happen to have been brought up in.[16]

Lewis would, of course, alter that trajectory, but, as Michael Nelson asserts, not as much as critics often claim: "To Lewis, belief in God was the only intellectually honest position he could take: 'I am an empirical Theist. I have arrived at God by induction.'"[17] Nelson asserts that Lewis's famous paradox of Jesus being realized as a "true myth"[18] came by way of collapsing his youthful mythological precepts concerning religion and his empirical eye: "The Christian story of the dying god, in other words, lay at the exact intersection of myth and history ... 'myth had become fact.'"[19]

Dependent upon definition: what is Lewis's concept of allegory?

Lewis has actually explicitly stated that *Narnia* is not allegorical, at least in the way he understood allegory. In a letter dated June 8, 1960, to a little girl named Patricia, Lewis answers the question of *Narnia's* allegorical ties with little equivocation:

> I'm not exactly "representing" the real (Christian) story in symbols. I'm more saying "Suppose there were a world like Narnia and it needed rescuing and the Son of God (or the 'Great Emperor oversea' [sic.]) went to redeem *it*, as he came to redeem ours[;] what might it, in that world, all have been like?" ...
>
> 1) The creation of Narnia is the Son of God creating *a* world (not specially *our* world.)
> 2) Jadis plucking the apple is, like Adam's sin, an act of disobedience, but it doesn't fill the same place in her life as his plucking did in his. She was already fallen (very much so) before she ate it.[20]

Although I only provide two examples from this letter here, Lewis goes on to list five further differences between *Narnia* and any biblical construct. It is not meant to be an exhaustive list, but only to illustrate the point that Lewis never foresaw what he was doing as strict allegory as he understood it.

Lewis preferred to imagine what he was doing as "retelling."[21] Allegory, to him, was something far different than retelling. To extrapolate further and contextualize this discussion within *The Chronicles of Narnia*, in a letter dated December 29, 1958, Lewis explains how, under his terminologies, Aslan is in no way allegorical in connection with the figure of Jesus Christ:

> If Aslan represented the immaterial Deity, he would be an allegorical figure. In reality however he is an invention giving an imaginary answer

to the question, What might [Jesus] Christ become like if there really were a world like Narnia and He chose to be incarnate and die and rise again in *that* world as He actually has done in ours? This is not allegory at all. ... Allegory and such supposals differ because they mix the real and the *unreal* [emphasis mine] in different ways. Bunyan's picture of Giant Despair does not start from supposal at all. It is not a supposition but a fact that despair can capture and imprison a human soul. What is unreal (fictional) is the giant, the castle and the dungeon. The incarnation of Christ in another world in mere supposal: but *granted* the supposition, He would have been a physical object in that world as He was in Palestine, and His death on the Stone Table would have been a physical event no less than his death on Calvary.[22]

Many points arise from this letter, but one in particular demands attention here. It has already been critically established that Lewis had Bunyan's *The Pilgrim's Progress*, Milton's *Paradise Lost* and *Paradise Regained*, and Spenser's *Faerie Queene* in the back of his mind as he began his *Narnia* set. As he notes, though, where he differs from those authors in regard to construction of his tale comes in the idea of including fictions, the "unreal," into his story in an effort to create something new, something analogous to the story of Christ and not allegorical to it. The unreal Lewis sought to include, as Nelson points out, are the many classical mythologies which permeated his own childhood reading experiences. And Lewis did not limit himself to the study of classical mythologies of the Norse, Celts, Greeks, Romans, and other heathen cosmologies, but also readily included Gnostic Christian mythology with his portrayal of Jadis being a descendant of Adam's first wife (in the apocryphal sense), "her they called Lilith."[23]

The end result of this erudition becomes realized in what Lewis himself coined as his own "mythopoeics."[24] In a letter written to T. S. Eliot, Lewis asserts some doctrine of his faith in mythopoeics: "The connection ... is that they are all concerned with *story*, or if you will *mythopoeia*."[25] Lewis's assertion is that the narrative, freed from dogmatic instruction or overt pedantry, could teach, fundamentally speaking, all that one would be required to know, free from the inter-polation of a body concerned with politics.[26] Lewis explores the idea when he writes to Arthur Greeves in 1930, stating: "I am still inclined to think that you can only get what you call 'Christ' out of the Gospels by picking & choosing & slurring over a good deal ... Of course the trouble of writing about it is that the words inevitably mean more than one intends."[27] Authors who Lewis viewed to have slurred, so to speak, in order to create were all roughly labeled by him as "mystics," people who wrote in "quasi-theosophical, semi-astrological" ways.[28] In fact, as

Lewis considered the sacred act of prayer in 1944's *Beyond Personality*, he, somewhat playfully, included it under the chapter heading of "Let's Pretend."[29] "Pretending," in many ways, is how children attempt to orient themselves to the discourses of adulthood; therefore, "pretending" in prayer is a manner by which the adult comes to orient him or herself to some sort of spiritual life. Mythopoeics play into this pretending; it was through his friendship with Greeves and Tolkien that Lewis discovered the capacity and possibility for the idea of "myth" and "truth" to blur by way of examining the similarities of the Jesus Christ "myth" to similar ones in Greek (Dionysus), Roman (Bacchus), Norse (Balder), and other pantheons.[30] His conclusions were a strange alchemy of negative capability, story, history, truth, and fact. Wilson writes:

> He stopped short of understanding Christianity [the religion] because when he thought about that, he laid aside the receptive imagination with which he allowed himself to appreciate myth and became rigidly narrow and empiricist. He should understand that "the story of Christ" is simply *true myth*: a myth working on us in the same way as the others, but with this tremendous difference that it *really happened*.[31]

In short, Lewis's ultimate acceptance of the capacity to be religious came *vis-à-vis* abandoning hope in organized religion and regaining faith in the capacity to tell (many) stories appreciated for their spiritual value and, often, their historical value as well.

Toward a chronotopal examination of *The Chronicles of Narnia*

In the December 29, 1958 letter to Mrs. Hook, Lewis dismissed the allegorical argument of *The Chronicles of Narnia* by asking the simple question of what might happen if Jesus had been born in *another* world not similar to our own (presuming such other worlds could exist). It is an important element to both his argument concerning *Narnia* as well as my own because it brings up specific matters indigenous both to Narnia and Lewis's own time and place in history: the fantastic land's connections to the world of the real that it is constructed against. I choose my words here quite deliberately as I would easily contend that Lewis constructs Narnia, chronotopally speaking, as an antidote to the times he lived. He writes in *Miracles*:

> The Christians say that God has done miracles. The modern world, even when it believes in God, and even when it has seen the defencelessness of Nature, does not. It thinks God would not do that sort of thing. Have

we any reason for supporting that the modern world is right? I agree that the sort of God conceived by the popular "religion" of our own times would almost certainly work no miracles. The question is whether that popular religion is at all likely to be true.[32]

The animosity toward his time period drips off each of Lewis's words. Besides the obvious cultural antecedents of both world wars,[33,34] Lewis "despised" what he perceived as the degraded virtues of a people connected with the modern period in which he lived: "modernism, evolutionism, materialism and historicism with the traditional Christian verities."[35] In many ways, Lewis connected these ideas, celebrated as they gained potency in an increasingly industrialized, urban twentieth century, with a declining capacity to embrace religion free of ideological precepts. In response, Lewis sought refuge in another world not marred by its own history. In effect, Lewis culled out the best pieces of other worlds, literally, in his estimation, the best places and times which reflected his ideals, to create his own world. At the very least, Lewis took elements of our reality and its imagination to create his world from the best thoughts and little pockets of time and space that he believed had been considered.

Lewis turned to mythologies. As many biographers have pointed out, Lewis's secular youth spent under the tutelage of W. T. Kirkpatrick helped cement a fondness for mythology that had been fostered since he first began to read.[36] From the *Aeneid*, to Frazer's *Golden Bough*, to British faerie myth, to the Egyptians' resurrection myths of Osiris, to the "Irish [myths] better still [and] the Norse best of all," Lewis explored a greater canon of mythos than anything resembling a typical British educational experience.[37] His correspondence with Greeves is littered with deep consternation about the relevancy and possibilities for fact and truth contained within the great many myths of humankind. He writes that, within mythology, "Anything MAY exist … Whenever any new light can be got as to such matters, I will be glad to welcome it … [Y]ou see most legends have a kernel of fact in them somewhere."[38] Here, Lewis shows an open-minded approach to myth alongside a thorough optimism that, within myth, some answers to that which troubled him and his spiritual dearth, not to mention his present historical moment, might be found.

What Lewis did with *The Chronicles of Narnia* was to create a portal out of our own agreed-upon historical reality into a reality of his own construction, created out of the different realities he had become familiar with as a child. As the criticism exposes, and as he rightly claimed, it is a universe governed by Christian precepts, but not exclusively. In fact, in creating an alternative universe, he does not set it contemporaneous with his time. Actually, he establishes the place as far from his reality as possible in a time equally separate from a modernity that he reviled. Therefore, it is not, in the manner that Wriglesworth suggests, "allegory" or "fairy tale"; if anything, Lewis wanted to get as far away as possible from the real and the local that the fairy tale would have cemented him to. What Narnia really is, for Lewis anyway, is "fantastic," "marvelous," and "uncanny," far from anything anyone contemporaneous with Lewis would have known or understood children's fiction to be.[39]

With his animosity toward all things he saw as contemporary and the attitudinal change it represented regarding children and the imagination, Lewis felt that there was no better solution than to pull his universe and its cosmology from the time and place he wished it to be as a method of a more romantic escape for his audience.[40] In lieu of a world divided and frightened by wars of an abominable nature, he sought refuge for his audience in a time *analogous* but not allegorical—a time and place where he felt war and fighting had rules, reason, and rationality—a civility not known or understood in the twentieth century. He based, constructed, and laid his universe in a time of chivalry and order to combat and escape[41] from what the world of the two world wars appeared as to him.

For example, Maria Nikolajeva notes that "magic," both a fundamental element of fairy tale and also clearly in the vein of the Nesbitian style that Lewis picks up when he constructs Narnia, loses its familiar, supernatural valences of the fairy tale and begins to "create a tension between the marvelous and the everyday."[42] There are several instances in *The Chronicles of Narnia* where this is apparent: the ubiquitous "lamppost" growing like anything otherwise natural and organic in Narnia's infancy;[43] the Pevensie girls preparing lunch and eating with the Beavers as they would, perhaps, with their own parents;[44] and when we first meet Eustace, as Edmund and Lucy become absorbed (literally) by the painting of the *Dawn Treader*, the event is treated by Eustace as some sort of everyday silly prank pulled on him by the Pevensies, even though he has clearly been brought through a portal into a new world.[45] My point is that part of Lewis's fundamental framework for Narnia and for those who may enter into it and return to it is that they must be young enough and filled with enough imagination and will to resist "reality"; they must be willing and able to accept a fantastic reality built upon disparate, impossible cosmologies.[46] These cosmologies merge within the alternative fantastic reality Lewis creates. This explains why the children are outlawed from Narnia as they age—notably Susan, who is completely exiled from Narnia, and Narnian afterlife, as she has "grown–up" too concerned with "nylons and lipstick and invitations."[47] Often mischaracterized as some sort of anti-feminist or poorly gendered stance against a real-life adversary of Lewis,[48] it is considerably more likely that, as Aslan allowed Digory, Polly and the others into Narnia later, Susan would be welcomed back to the Narnian afterlife as soon as she parted ways with the adult convictions that barred her in the first place. An excellent example of this idea exists whereby the children can only "see" Aslan as they begin to *accept* his possibility of reality in *Prince Caspian*. Lucy, who sees him first, declares: "'*I* saw you all right. They wouldn't believe me.'"[49] Aslan later tells her that the others will indeed "see" him but "'not at first … it depends.'"[50] What it depends upon is whether or not the children, now a year older and worldlier, are willing to once again accept Aslan into their reality as they did when they first journeyed through the wardrobe. Lewis mitigates such contradictions through a conflation of taking magic, legends, mythologies, histories, and so forth, and filtering them all through a sieve of his imagination to create a guiding theological ideology to his fantastic world that is viable, sustainable, and consistent with the rules of reality. As he wrote:

> Myth is the isthmus which connects the peninsular world of thought with the vast continent we really belong to. … it was through almost believing in the gods that I came to believe in God … To declare Christianity true was not to declare all other religions false. Rather, Christianity was true because it was the answer to two vital questions: "Where has religion reached its true maturity? Where, if anywhere, have the hints of all Paganism been fulfilled?"[51]

Of course, his paganism is our mythopoeics, but the case is deliberately laid out: it is only through a reconstruction and reorganization of a plural past that Lewis feels that he can construct a future, forgoing the present he exists within.

Entering *The Chronicles of Narnia* through Bakhtin's chronotope

In order to rectify, or at least deal with, that plurality, I turn to Bakhtin. Folklore and fairy tales, by Bakhtin's admittedly complicated definition, are matter of "national and local" discourse.[52] Myth, lyric, and the epic all occupy a verbal form, which, by their heritage and nature, preserves national time and halts dialogue by instilling in a reader some sense of the past in the present moment of reading.[53] In this act of preservation, the folk and fairy tale seem to operate much as Bakhtin constructs the epic, where the world presented is one of a "national heroic past" that is "absolute" and part of a "national tradition."[54] And yet, in his later *"Bildungsroman"* essay, Bakhtin asserts: "The folksong, the folktale … and the saga were above all a new and powerful means of humanizing and intensifying one's native space. With folklore there burst into literature a new, powerful and extremely productive wave of *national-historical time* that exerted an immense … and productive influence on literature."[55] He goes on to state that "folklore is in general saturated with time … Time in folklore, the fullness of time in it, the folkloric *future* … [,] all these are very important and fundamental problems."[56] This idea would appear to be contradictory; how can something preserve a national past and yet allow for future, even concurrent, embellishment that may detract from the nationally accepted discourses? To be more concrete, how can folklore preserve national traditions and yet invoke a sense of looking forward into the future of the folk? At the heart of these questions is an implied friction between the arbiters of a preservational nationalist discourse, that being a government or other regulatory body (like the church), and the oppressed folk seeking evolution[57] as they look toward a future that represents possibility and change to them.

While fairy-tale time exists proudly "once upon a time," it can also be a time of *"collective* life," which Bakhtin marks as folkloric, or fairy-tale, time, replete with *"productive growth"* in a "time maximally tensed towards the future."[58] Yet, it is also married with a publicized "historicization" of private affairs, "food, drink, copulation, birth and death" as "common affairs," while also being wed to a "new context of magical significance."[59] This magical significance, for Bakhtin, deals with rituals—and in this new sense of time and place "the rituals and everyday life are tightly interwoven with each other … Ideological reflection [the word, the symbolization] acquires the force of magic."[60] What he is describing here is not allegory, but a symphony of the everyday and the symbols which create a differential between the common and the fantastic in an effort to unravel the piety of the sacred and force it into an area of *"ritualistic parody."*[61] Thus, Bakhtin states: "The elements of the matrix (which had in its ancient form encompassed a great deal) are, as before, tightly bound up with each other, but they are interpreted in a ritualistic *and* magical way, and differentiated on the one hand from communal production, and on the other hand from individual everyday life [as] analogous phenomena."[62] Correspondingly,

Lewis's fantasies exist in a very real, discernable time and place, which have a direct connection to specific times and places in our historic reality. But, as Bakhtin illustrates, "the gross realities of the ancient pre-class context ... are dissociated from each other, and undergo ... a sharp hierarchical reinterpretation."[63] Thus, as Lewis borrows and applies discordant historical, theological, and mythological tropes and figures to his world, he does so in an effort to juxtapose this world with the one he chooses to escape. However, they are specifically targeted by and connected to the contextual moment of the time of composition. In effect, Lewis utilizes elements of religion—the biblical stories themselves devoid of that which he conceives of as political, or having Bakhtin's problem of an "absolute past"—and re-envisions them as one of many mythologies which allow him to bring the past into the present, operating in folkloric time toward a better future. Further, this future timescape is still connected directly, by specific points, to present time.

Two particular incidents in *The Chronicles of Narnia* illustrate this point: the analogy between the War for Narnia and World War II in the first volume,[64] *The Lion, the Witch and the Wardrobe,* and the parallel between the destruction of Narnia and the death of the Penvensies and their extended family during the British Railway Disaster of 1949. *The Lion, the Witch and the Wardrobe* begins thus: "This story is about something that happened to [the Pevensie children] when they were sent away from London during the war because of the air-raids."[65] We can extrapolate from history that the date of the setting of this incident exists somewhere between June and October 1940 in the second major evacuations during the most extensive bombing of British towns by the German Luftwaffe. Lewis himself had hosted children when he lived at the Kilns in 1939.[66] That same year, he composed a variation of the initial lines of the book's first words: "This book is about four children ... They all had to go away from London suddenly because of the Air Raids, and because Father, who was in the Army, had gone off to the war and Mother was doing some kind of war work."[67] The differences are minor but significant. Both versions indicate a direct correlation between the story being told, concerning a war for Narnia, and the history that surrounds its composition. Likewise, in revision, Lewis deemphasizes the parent's position as the center of the audience's concern: it is not important to worry about Mother and Father Pevensie, both of whom are working with the war effort which threaten their children. Rather, the focus should be set upon the children's escape from the dangers of the here and now and the potentiality they will find in their future away from the present. Similarly, in *The Last Battle,* set nine years (Earth time) later at the apocalyptic end of Narnia, the Pevensies (save Susan) are all welcomed back into Aslan's afterlife. The Pevensies believed that the "railway carriage" they were on was in some sort of accident, which opened a portal to Narnia.[68] In fact, Aslan tells them: "Have you not guessed? ... There *was* a real railway accident .... [Y]our father and mother and all of you are—as they used to call it in the Shadowlands—dead. The term is over: the holidays have begun. The dream is ended: this is the morning."[69] The differences between the reality and the analogues set in the fantasy of Narnia are of direct concern for me, and will be addressed shortly, but, for now, the point concerns the couching of Lewis's fantasy within the boundaries of an absolute past of history. He makes operative use of that past by interpolating a set of secondary histories, mythologies, and adventures in an effort to create a secondary world with which his protagonists, the Pevensies and their family, can escape what Colin Manlove called the "tendenc[ies] in modern life"—becoming part of the modern moment—even if their escape leads ultimately to an ahistorical end.[70]

Lewis actually collapses the notions of the magical realm with historical periodicity through a sieve of mythologies to give us a place, period, and time that the Pevensie children and their extended family escape from reality. The realm is created by both Aslan and Lewis; Lewis is working out of a moment that existed both historically and, in a sense, historiographically. He includes the history of many histories and mythologies in creating a new time and place for his world to exist. It is this conflation that lies at the heart of this investigation. For it is within Lewis's construction of a religious fantasy through mythopoeics that we find him shoving mythic time (which, as Nikolajeva notes, is cyclical[71]) against eschatological time (which is teleological, and leads, not to an absolute *past*, but to an "absolute end" which, given its Christian precursors, is "utopian"[72]). He resolved the two through a parallel, analogous response to the history of the author's sense of reality. In essence, what Lewis accomplishes is to allow his audience (whom he creates to associate with and join the Pevensie children) to escape the realities of the present moment by entering into a fantasy which allows both mythic time and adventure time to coexist simultaneously, but is bound to the rules of an ultimately religious, or eschatological, cosmology.

The outreach into Narnia: considering the existence of contradictory time

I have already discussed Lewis's disdain for his contemporaneous historical moment within the composition of *The Chronicles of Narnia*.

The precedents of that moment, whether they be seen through a theological, personal, or historical context, do not mitigate the fact that Lewis viewed his current moment as one of separation between the self and God (in however many plural forms). That he set the first published account of the Pevensie children's sojourns in Narnia within the historical context of the London evacuations of children following attacks on the city in World War II seems to cement a solid argument for a foundation of escape from a possible death by the German Luftwaffe. But this does pose the question: if Lewis's construction of Narnian time seems to work on the principles of eschatological time—that is, if the children escape our reality due to a fear of imminent death at the hands of war to enter into a world where they become closer to an incarnation of God, yet are set along a course toward an equally imminent death due to being placed in the line of fire of *another* war—why go on the journey in the first place? What is the difference in Lewis's eyes between dying in the reality he saw personally in the trenches of World War I and close at hand during World War II, versus dying in a world with witches, anthropomorphized animals, magic, and magical adventure? The answer lies within the morality of the culture(s) in which Lewis grounds his universe.

Lewis borrowed elements of mythologies and histories which distinctly mark Narnia: Tumnus, a faun, has works of Silenus on his shelf, denoting Greek and Roman mythological influences[73]; Jadis is described as being descendent from Lilith, a figure from apocryphal Christian mythology[74]; Aslan is constructed as God-like, in the Judeo-Christian sense, and Christ-like[75] as well as parallel to Adonis or Osiris[76] (Nelson goes as far as to extrapolate that Aslan also contains fragments of the Norse myth's Balder whose death, like Aslan's, triggered Ragnarok, a literal read of the biblical Apocalypse). Classical examples of borrowed mythos abound; often left out of the discussion, however, is Lewis's construction of Narnia itself as an inherently medieval society built upon a chivalric code of honor which guides and governs the land itself.

Wriglesworth notes that Lewis constructs his Narnian texts as might a "medieval compiler … reshaping pagan signs and medieval lore into an imaginative and highly accessible Christian context."[77] Cair Paravel, for example, is modeled after an idyllic medieval castle replete with grand throne rooms, treasure chambers, and a "Great Hall … with ivory roof[,] and [on] the west hall hung with peacocks' feathers."[78]; the Pevensies, upon receiving presents from Father Christmas, engage in a battle with Jadis's forces for the four thrones of Narnia marked by Arthurian-styled flourishes, and—after Peter slays a wolf—Aslan takes Peter's sword and essentially knights him. Lewis writes: "'Hand [the sword] to me and kneel, Son of Adam,' said Aslan. And when Peter had done so he struck him with the flat of the blade and said, 'Rise up, Sir Peter Wolf's-Bane. And, whatever happens, never forget to wipe your sword.'"[79] Even Narnia's revival from Jadis's one hundred years of winter seems to pay homage to the Arthurian legend[80] of the Fisher King where the land ails as the king ails and becomes more fertile as he heals. As Aslan approaches, eternal winter without Christmas finally gives way to Christmas and, eventually, spring as Narnia thaws and becomes fecund. Jonathan Himes notes that Lewis's fascination with the medieval extended to the Norse culture as well, *vis-à-vis* the works of William Morris. Lewis's construction of the End Times was one where "Morris conceived of heroic societies in the upper stages of barbarism for the romances he wrote."[81] Himes suggests that Lewis's interests in the North, particularly Morris's stories, might mitigate suggestions that Lewis was interested in stories which dealt with the good "overcoming evil" since Morris was neither Christian nor interested in such "pathos and dignity."[82]

And yet, I would suggest that Lewis borrowed as might a medievalist, and from the medieval period specifically, due to what he perceived as that period's interest in pathos and dignity. As Paul Fussell notes, no one who served in World War I could see the barbarism shown there and not be inspired toward considerations of "regeneration," rebirth, and "hope."[83] I would suggest that Lewis invokes the chivalric time of the medieval period in an effort to provide children with an escape from the barbarism of World War II and provide them with a fantasy world which, while mirroring the world surrounding them, had some sort of code or order about it. His order, of course, is Christianity's control, and his code is chivalry. Lewis writes, "Christendom has made two efforts to deal with the evil of war—chivalry and pacifism. Neither succeeded. But I doubt whether chivalry has such an unbroken record of failure as pacifism."[84] Chivalry then—both the "heavy cavalry" of King Arthur and the common courtesy of "giving a woman a seat in a train"—is the differential structure between the wars of the twentieth century and those contained within the medieval period.[85]

I have made mention of Arthurian romance, but I have not addressed Lewis's connection, or infatuation, with the King Arthur story, particularly Thomas Malory's interpretation. Malory's construction of knights and knighthood fascinated Lewis's sense of decorum concerning warcraft. Within the construct of this warrior of the

Middle Ages, Lewis seemed to find something with which he could rectify the idea of combat that haunted him from seeing and feeling first hand the results of World War I. In 1940's "The Necessity of Chivalry," he writes, "The knight is a man of blood and iron, a man familiar with the sight of smashed faces and the ragged stumps of lopped-off limbs; he is also a demure, almost a maidenlike, guest in hall, a gentle, modest, unobtrusive man."[86] The knight, then, represents some compromise between the need and necessity of war and an order or civility to it. For Lewis, humility and civility were qualities lacking in the contemporary battlefield—elements which rendered modern war as the stuff of savagery:

> What, you may ask, is the relevance of this idea to the modern world? It is terribly relevant ... [T]he medieval ideal brought together two things which have no natural tendency to gravitate towards one another. It brought them together for that very reason. It taught humility and forbearance to the great warrior because everyone knew by experience how much he usually needed that lesson. It demanded valour of the urbane and modest man because everyone knew that he was as likely as not to be a milksop.[87]

The difference for Lewis was that chivalry, the by-product and guidance of medieval warfare, might produce "hope" in a modern age where war did not seem to have any.

As such, it is fair to suggest that Lewis modeled Narnia, the time and place itself, to some extent or another on medieval precursors. More to the point, attuning Narnia somewhat ahistorically to Lewis's contemporary time and yet analogously setting it to what Bakhtin called the time of "chivalric romance"[88] allowed him to construct a world built not only around virtuous adventures, but one where "time and space themselves become miraculous. ... as in the fairy tale, hours may be extended and days compressed; time itself may be bewitched ... . time can become like dreams, and so dreams themselves take on new functions and influence events."[89] What this brings to our discussion is manifold but still causal: (1) Lewis chose a particular blend of types of time (epic, mythological, chivalric) to situate antipodally, yet analogously in time and place (contemporary England compared with a representation of a medieval England), to his current contemporary period. (2) His choices allow time and place, textually, to take on virtues particular to the stories that had previously held time, textually (such as the idea of knighthood and the code of chivalry being held textually within medieval texts), in particular ways that seem to arrest time. (3) By framing his stories within these overlapping sets of time,

Lewis creates an opportunity to manifest an idea of a textual time which is marked by contradictory forces (circular time and eschatological time) in his constructed cosmology, based upon its connections to the virtues of the opposing time. In other words, Lewis found a way to make mythic time linear by suggesting that to die in the service of Aslan (God) was superior to dying for a country fighting a godless conflict in World War II. Lewis presents Narnia not only as a world parallel to ours, but as an *alternative* to ours: one which can *end* his modern times as a destination since his mythopoeic/Christian hybrid world is timeless.

There are a few textual issues to unpack within that dense set of concepts. First, though not written in chronological order, *The Chronicles of Narnia*'s cosmological construction operates as a teleology, written from its alpha: "The Lion was pacing to and fro about that empty land and singing his new song ... And as he walked and sang, the valley grew green with grass,"[90] to its omega: "They all stood beside Aslan, on his right side, and looked through the open doorway. The bonfire had gone out. On the earth all was blackness. ... But when Aslan had roared yet again ... they heard the sound of the horn: high and terrible, yet of a strange and terrible beauty."[91] And with Father Time seemingly blowing the horn of Narnia's Ragnarok, old Narnia is obliterated and "new" Narnia is created. Strangely enough, although the new Narnia, which is essentially the Narnian afterlife, is created through the obliteration of old Narnia, it is a world which is almost exactly the same:

> "Those hills," said Lucy, "the nice woody ones and the blue ones behind—aren't those very like the southern border of Narnia?"
>
> "Like!" cried Edmund after a moment's silence. "Why, they're exactly like. Look, there's Mount Pire with his forked head, and there's the pass into Archenland and everything!"
>
> "And yet they're not like," said Lucy, "They're different. ... they're more ... more ... oh, I don't know..."
>
> "More like the real thing," said the Lord Digory softly.[92]

The new world is different, though. Aslan, by obliterating all connections with the "real" world through the destruction of old Narnia, has opened the door to a reality which is *still* Narnia, but is now the "real Narnia" which none of the Pevensie clan had been able to know since they had grown up.[93] It is important to remember Aslan's often uttered proviso to visitors to Narnia: as Peter tells the others of his private discussion with Aslan in *Prince Caspian*, "There were things [Aslan] wanted to say to Su and me because we're not coming back to Narnia … [W]e're getting too old."[94] Lewis constructs old Narnia as a place of age restriction where the passage of time, on the earthly plane, restricts the imagination and ages the body (remember that the Pevenies could age and remain in Narnia in *The Lion, the Witch, and the Wardrobe*) and affects the capacity to return to it. But, in new Narnia, a place without "a beginning and an end,"[95] all are welcomed because it is a *real* place that exists outside of time. The reason that new Narnia is timeless is that new Narnia represents Lewis's construct of the afterlife (where time, ostensibly, does not exist).

Thus, it is essential to our understanding of the complexity of Lewis's concept of fantastic escape time to acknowledge that, as Nikolajeva notes, when Lucy first enters Narnia, she does enter into mythic—or as Nikolajeva calls it "cyclical"—time where death is, indeed, "reversible."[96] As the *Chronicles* progress, however, death becomes increasingly more permanent a condition: the destruction of Narnia, the death of the Ape, Reepicheep et al., and so on. The mitigating factor of this move from mythic and adventure time to the linear time of eschatology is based upon divine judgment. In using a chivalric topos for Narnia, Lewis allows the elements of the chivalric to bleed, quite literally, into his vision for the world; what we end up with is a world created and governed by a figure outside of time in the Christian sense, as that is how Lewis views his chivalry, in a god figure called Aslan. And, like the Christian God, in the particular manner that distinguishes the Christian God from Dionysus, Father Christmas, Balder and others, Aslan judges the virtues and merits of those whom he allows into his timelessness after they die: "The creatures came rushing on [through the door]. But as they came right up to Aslan one or other of two things happened to each of them. They all looked straight in his face, I don't think they had any choice about that."[97] If Aslan finds fear and reproach, those beings are whipped into the void; if he finds love, they are welcomed into new Narnia. Aslan can choose whom he wishes to let into his kingdom; for example, Susan, whether it be because she has not died on the earthly plane or whether it be due to the fact that she has embraced more "earthly," grown-up things, is not welcome yet.

Perhaps Paul Karkainen sums up my point best: "Lewis did not write fantasy with instruction in mind, but he has, in fact, filled his books with characters and events which portray a *variety* of Christian truths."[98] It is in that variety that Lewis saw and articulated other myths that anticipated and developed the "true" myth of Christ.[99] And while what Lewis does in *The Chronicles of Narnia* does not further anticipate the idea of Christ, it would seem to be operating in that same manner of further developing the Christian mythology as part of the normal movement of time, place, and narrative. Doris Myers suggests that Lewis may have been attempting to show the power of illustrating how "the ordinary person" could become mythical.[100] That may very well be, but I would argue that Lewis tried specifically to provide the ordinary *child* a possibility to escape the extraordinarily negative events surrounding his or her life through the fantastic voyage through time and space into Narnia. It is a world which was, in many ways, as troubled as his own, but it was also a world where the author could control time and space in such a way as to make it a superior alternative to the world he himself inhabited.

Notes

1. Walter Hooper, *The Collected Letters of C. S. Lewis*, Vol. II (San Francisco: HarperCollins, 2004): 770.
2. *Ibid.*: 777.
3. M. M. Bakhtin, *The Dialogic Imagination* (Austin, TX: University of Texas Press, 1981): 250.
4. C. S. Lewis, "On Three Ways of Writing for Children," *The Chronicles of Narnia* (New York: HarperCollins, 2005): 774.
5. *Ibid.*: 775.
6. Which is to say that they are less enamored with religion, religious tenets, and religious ideology than they are with biblical narratives taken from the text.
7. A. N. Wilson, *C. S. Lewis: A Biography* (New York: W. W. Norton, 1990): 222.
8. Mark Freshwater, *C. S. Lewis And the Truth of Myth* (Lanham, MD: University Press of America, 1988): 18.
9. Walter Hooper, *C. S. Lewis: A Complete Guide to His Life and Works* (San Francisco, CA: HarperCollins, 1996): 402.
10. Hooper (2004): 1041.
11. Hooper (1996): 402.
12. Chad Wriglesworth, "Myth Maker, Unicorn Maker: C. S. Lewis and the Reshaping of Medieval Thought," *Mythlore* 25 (2006): 29–40, at 29.
13. David Holbrook, *The Skeleton in the Wardrobe* (Lewisburg, PA: Bucknell University Press, 1991): 11.
14. Freshwater: 17.
15. *Ibid.*: 18.
16. Walter Hooper, *They Stand Together* (London: Collins, 1979): 135.
17. Michael Nelson, "'One Mythology among Many': The Spiritual Odyssey of C. S. Lewis," *The Virginia Quarterly Review* 72 (1996): 619–33.
18. Wilson: 126.
19. Nelson: 626.

20. Lyle Dorsett, *C. S. Lewis: Letters to Children* (New York: Collier Books, 1988): 92–3.
21. Hooper (2004): 1042.
22. *Ibid.*: 424–5.
23. C. S. Lewis, *The Chronicles of Narnia: The Lion, the Witch and the Wardrobe* (New York: HarperCollins, 2005): 147.
24. Hooper (2004): 389.
25. *Ibid.*: 655.
26. Wilson: 122–3.
27. Hooper (1979): 331.
28. Wilson: 123.
29. C. S. Lewis, *Mere Christianity*, (San Francisco, CA: HarperCollins, 2001): 124.
30. Wilson: 126.
31. *Ibid.*: 126 (emphasis mine).
32. C. S. Lewis, *Miracles* (San Francisco, CA: HarperCollins, 2001): 129.
33. Kimberly Reynolds, *Modern Children's Literature* (New York: Palgrave, 2005): 47.
34. In Hooper's *C. S. Lewis: A Complete Guide to His Life and Works*: 122, he notes that World War I was particularly difficult for Lewis: he was both wounded in the Battle of Arras and lost a dear friend in Paddy Moore in 1918.
35. Lee Rossi, *The Politics of Fantasy: C. S. Lewis and J. R. R. Tolkien* (Ann Arbor, MI: UMI Research Press, 1984): 29.
36. Nelson.
37. *Ibid.*
38. Hooper (1979): 135–7.
39. Maria Nikolajeva, *Children's Literature Comes of Age* (New York: Garland, 1996): 70.
40. *Ibid.*: 71.
41. Without pressing this idea too much, take, for example, the Pevensies escaping the locality of London for the more idyllic and peaceful home of the Professor. They leave the dangers associated with bombings and air raids to go "to the house of an old Professor who lived in the heart of the country, ten miles from the nearest railway station and two miles from the nearest post office" (*The Lion, the Witch and the Wardrobe*: 111). Literally, they are cleaved from all of the trappings of the modern society and whisked away to an almost castle-like estate held by a beneficent lord of the "very large house" (111).
42. Nikolajeva: 71.
43. C. S. Lewis, *The Chronicles of Narnia: The Magician's Nephew* (New York: HarperCollins, 2005): 67.
44. *The Lion, the Witch and the Wardrobe*: 143.
45. C. S. Lewis, *The Chronicles of Narnia: The Voyage of the Dawn Treader* (New York: HarperCollins, 2005): 426–7.

46. How else can one explain the presence of Father Christmas (*The Lion, the Witch and the Wardrobe*:159), Bacchus, literally reveling during "the romp" upon Aslan's return in *Prince Caspian*, and, of course, the many instances of Aslan which occur in every volume of the set. All are, as Paul Ford notes, representations in different "mythologies" of Jesus, but all are concurrently displayed as independent figures existing simultaneously in the same fantastic reality; Paul Ford, *Companion to Narnia* (New York: HarperCollins, 1994): 110.

47. C. S. Lewis, *The Chronicles of Narnia: The Last Battle* (New York: HarperCollins, 2005): 741.

48. Wilson has suggested that Narnia might even be some sort of defensive response to a lost argument to Elizabeth Anscombe's rejection of Lewis's *Miracles* or even a particularly anti-female bent consistent with the purview of the Christian church (the list of anti-feminist reads of Lewis is exceedingly long); Wilson: 213–15.

49. C. S. Lewis, *The Chronicles of Narnia: Prince Caspian* (New York: HarperCollins, 2005): 380.

50. *Ibid.*: 381.

51. Qtd. in Nelson.

52. M. M. Bakhtin, *Speech Genres and Other Late Essays* (Austin, TX: University of Texas Press, 1986): 52.

53. Gary Morson and Caryl Emerson, *Mikhail Bakhtin: Creation of a Prosaics* (Stanford, CA: Stanford University Press, 1990): 452.

54. Bakhtin (1981): 13.

55. Bakhtin (1986): 52.

56. *Ibid.*: 52 (emphasis mine).

57. Or, possibly, revolution.

58. Bakhtin (1986): 206–7.

59. *Ibid.*: 209–12.

60. *Ibid.*: 212.

61. *Ibid.*: 212.

62. *Ibid.*: 212.

63. *Ibid.*: 213.

64. Historically speaking, it was the first published.

65. *The Lion, the Witch and the Wardrobe*: 111.

66. Hooper (1996): 401.

67. *The Lion, the Witch and the Wardrobe*: 402.

68. *The Last Battle*: 743.

69. *Ibid.*: 767.

70. Colin Manlove, *The Chronicles of Narnia: The Patterning of a Fantastic World* (New York: Twayne, 1993): 5.

71. Maria Nikolajeva, *From Mythic to Linear* (London: Scarecrow Press, 2000): 128.

72. Morson and Emerson: 398.

73. *The Lion, the Witch and the Wardrobe*: 116.

74. *Ibid.*: 147.
75. *Ibid.*: 146.
76. Lewis writes in *Miracles*, "Is not Christ simply another corn-king [like] Adonis, Osiris or another? ... From a certain point of view Christ is 'the same sort of thing' ... And that is just the puzzle" (181–2).
77. Wriglesworth: 29.
78. *The Lion, the Witch and the Wardrobe*: 193.
79. *Ibid.*: 171.
80. A quick survey of Lewis's letters in Hooper, specifically the essay "Tolkien's The Lord of the Rings," reminds us of his dedication to Malory, specifically *Morte d'Arthur*; Hooper (2004): 112.
81. Jonathan Himes, "World's End Imagery: How William Morris and C. S. Lewis Imagined the Medieval North," *Extrapolation* 44(3) (2003): 304–10, at 308.
82. *Ibid.*: 308.
83. Paul Fussell, *The Great War and Modern Memory* (London: Oxford University Press, 1975): 135.
84. Hooper (2004): 252.
85. C. S. Lewis. "The Necessity of Chivalry, " *The Window in the Garden Wall*: http://yourdailycslewis.blogspot.com/2005/08/necessity-of-chivalry.html (accessed December 17, 2011).
86. *Ibid.*
87. *Ibid.*
88. Bakhtin (1986): 151.
89. Morson and Emerson: 400.
90. *The Magician's Nephew*: 64.
91. *The Last Battle*: 749.
92. *Ibid.*: 753, 758–9.
93. *Ibid.*: 759.
94. *Prince Caspian*: 417.
95. *The Last Battle*: 759.
96. Nikolajeva (2000): 128.
97. *The Last Battle*: 751.
98. Paul Karkainen, *Narnia Explored* (Old Tappan, NJ: Fleming H. Revell, 1979): 7 (emphasis mine).
99. Freshwater: 42.
100. Doris Myers, *C. S. Lewis in Context* (Kent, OH: Kent State University Press, 1994): 187.

Part III
Adaptations and Mediations

6

The Author, the Movie, and the Marketing: *The Lion, the Witch and the Wardrobe* and Early Reader Adaptations

Rhonda Brock-Servais and Matthew B. Prickett

Narnia and the early reader

C. S. Lewis's *The Lion, the Witch and the Wardrobe* was adapted into film three times prior to a major motion picture release. This blockbuster film by Disney and Walden Media attracted families with young children and thus opened the story to audiences younger than those capable of reading the original text. With the release of the movie, publishers took advantage of this new market and released a number of textual adaptations for young readers. However, these are not adaptations of C. S. Lewis's *The Lion, the Witch and the Wardrobe*; rather they are adaptations of the Walden Media/Disney film *The Lion, the Witch and the Wardrobe* released in December 2005. Linda Hutcheon reminds us in *A Theory of Adaptation* that for an adaptation to be successful, it must reach "both knowing and unknowing audiences" of the source material.[1] As the source material is the 2005 film, rather than Lewis's 1950 novel, early readers meet the standard of contemporary family entertainment and marketing. Further, Hutcheon reminds us that "multiple versions of a story in fact exist laterally, not vertically."[2] As such, they are perfectly in keeping with contemporary expectations of their genre—the movie tie-in. While these texts are marketing tools—it would be impossible to argue they aren't—they also serve as examples of how the Narnia books have been figured and refigured for various cultural standards.

Several varieties of young reader adaptations of *The Lion, the Witch and the Wardrobe* exist. There are picture books, both in the traditional large size and in a smaller paperback format, "I Can Read!" books; and early chapter books, some with color and some with black and white illustrations. Each reading level is indiscriminately advertised in other level texts, along with toy books like the *Activity Book and Gel Pen* and the *Coloring and Activity Book with Magnets.* With the exception of Hiawyn Oram's retelling, illustrated by Tudor Humphrie, all illustrations are either photo stills from the 2005 film or illustrations drawn to recreate the look of the film, down to costuming and setting for particular scenes, done, for the most part, by Justin Sweet. Examination of the content reveals further characteristics that unite all the books, regardless of reading level.

These texts add elements to Lewis's story: a more thorough explanation of history, particularly of the World War II blitz on London and the consequent flight of children into the countryside, and explanations and commentary on the children's behavior, in general, and on Edmund's, in particular. Two books that make the most of the historical, primary-world setting the children leave from are *Edmund's Struggle* (a chapter book with photo illustration) and *Step into Narnia: A Journey through The Lion, the Witch and the Wardrobe* (a picture book without a narrative line, presenting itself as an informational work). In this text, there are two double spreads titled "This Side of the Wardrobe" and "Cheerio"—the latter, oddly, follows pages of "Horrible Henchmen" found in the land of Narnia and is found in the middle of the book. In the first spread, the audience is told that "Lucy, Edmund, Susan and Peter live in London when World War II begins. The Germans are dropping bombs on their city. For safety, the children are sent to live with the Professor in a big house in the country," thus explaining the context for the story.[3] This is considerably longer than Lewis's "[the children] were sent away from London during the war because of the air-raids."[4] The latter section, curiously, is more informational in nature and is actually unrelated to the tale. It defines the United Kingdom, highlights Big Ben, and explains the symbolism of the Union Jack: "it has three crosses, representing the three kingdoms that are united under one rule."[5] *Edmund's Struggle* spends its first three pages of "Chapter One: Edmund's Anger" showing the children's home life in London. The reader learns that Edmund is fascinated with the airplanes, that he has been upset since his father left to go and fight in the war, and that he barely missed being hurt by a falling bomb, but was saved by Peter. The text insists on imparting knowledge about the war and circumstances irrelevant to the story except to explore Edmund's state of mind: "Edmund felt that Peter was always being mean to him, calling him names and treating him like a little baby. *One day*, he thought to himself, *I'll show Peter that I can be grown-up too.*"[6] There is a continued focus in the following pages—describing the move to the countryside and the earliest time in the Professor's house—on Edmund's anger at and resentment of his siblings.

What becomes evident is the emphasis on the children's behavior, proper or not, especially in *Edmund and the White Witch*[7] and *Edmund's Struggle*, but also in all the books that feature only a portion of the plot. Lewis offers that Edmund "would be spiteful, and on this occasion he was spiteful."[8] This is presented without explanation or apology. However, the adapted books present a strange pairing: they simultaneously posit that Edmund is a troubled child who "had a way of finding trouble wherever he went," which leads him to greater troubles, while they also state baldly that he is under a spell of the White Witch.[9] Sometimes he is described as not listening to or rejecting the Beavers, thus seeming to make a choice in his actions. Other times this agency is then mitigated when he runs away: "He was not sure whether he was running or being dragged."[10] Finally, there is an outright denial of agency through the repetition of his unquenchable desire for the White Witch's Turkish Delight. Once he arrives at her castle, he is more interested in procuring more of it than in becoming King of Narnia or making his brother and sisters servants. Somehow he is both bewitched and naughty. The books are simultaneously dismissing the seriousness of Edmund's betrayal while also warning audiences against wrong feelings—anger, resentment—that could lead to a betrayal. C. S. Lewis himself commented on these elements in children's stories in his essay, "On Three Ways of Writing for Children." He rejects the "moral or didactic" approach, opining that it assumes "too superior an attitude" toward children and thus spoils the story.[11]

Narnia and the contemporary child reader

Clearly, the fantasy land of Narnia itself has always been part of the draw to the book and its following series. A further addition in these Walden Media adaptations is an emphasis on the escapism of the plot, as well as the beauty and wonder of Narnia. This strain runs directly contrary to the instructional one examined above, and is one Lewis would have approved of, for he said that escapist books help to add depth to the reader's real world.[12] The celebration of fantasy is most apparent in *The Quest for Aslan*,[13] *Step into Narnia*, *Welcome to Narnia*, and *The Creatures of Narnia*,[14] the last of which retells an abbreviated version of the story with an emphasis on the roles played by nonhuman characters. All of these are abundantly illustrated. *Step into Narnia* has been described briefly above: a picture book formatted to appear to be informational or encyclopedic, its categories include "Friends and Helpers," "Creature Features," "Battles," and "Powerful Magic." There is a determined focus on the illustrations in this text. *Welcome to Narnia* emphasizes the child characters' wonder even after they have become Kings and Queens: "the Pevensie family never dreamed of the adventures they would have and the many creatures they would meet."[15] *Creatures of Narnia* reads a bit like a fantasy bestiary: "Lots of curious and wonderful talking creatures live in Narnia. Some are good, but others are very, very bad."[16] There are detailed physical descriptions of fauns and dwarfs; beavers are associated with comfort and food, while wolves are associated with power and skill. Aslan, the true King of Narnia, is simply "a great and noble lion."[17] The great battle is related primarily in terms of which beings fought on which side: Cyclops, Minoboars, Harpies, and Giants vs. Unicorns, Centaurs, Gryphons, Fauns, and Satyrs.[18] The story ends with a direct address to the reader: "you will always remember [Narnia's] magical creatures." While Lewis would approve of the apparent escapism in general, this may, perhaps, go too far. He also wrote, "[W]e must meet children as equals."[19] Tolkien would agree; it is his opinion that "children as a class ... neither like fairy-stories more, nor understand them better than adults do."[20] In short, the texts seem to be assuming that what child readers will really be attracted to are the visualized creatures rather than the characters or the plot.

One expectation of books and a film that were released in 2005, and that are based on a tale originally published in 1950, is that there might be some revision to elements likely to make readers uncomfortable, such as the dated, stereotypical gender roles of the passive, mothering female and the active, independent male. By 2005, the spunky girl hero of a fantasy world was a commonplace character (see any novel by Tamora Pierce, Gail Carson Levine, or Phillip Pullman's *His Dark Materials* series), and the Lucy and Susan characters could easily have taken on a few of these traits. Instead, while Edmund "struggle[s]" and Peter has a "destiny," Lucy partakes of *Tea with Mr. Tumnus*.[21] This title is the only one to feature one of the female characters. Its focus is on the domestic space of Mr. Tumnus's home and the ritual of tea. Talk of the White Witch, the danger Narnia is in, in general, and the danger to Lucy, in particular, does not appear until the last few pages. Further, in the course of a 32-page early reader (from the I Can Read! series), Lucy has a total of three spoken lines, reducing her independence as a character. Either Mr. Tumnus is speaking or the narrator tells the reader what Lucy thinks or feels. The text is description heavy, of both the cozy cave and Mr. Tumnus himself, further reducing the importance of Lucy's character and shifting it onto the setting.

Gender typing is painfully obvious in *Step into Narnia*: the background to both the girls' biographical pages is pink. Lucy's includes flowers and pearls; it also features a diary entry in which she expresses a desire for togetherness with her siblings: "I want all of us to explore Narnia together."[22] Her "Favorite Thing" is "making friends," while her most "heroic moment" is "tending to the wounded after the final battle against the Witch."[23] Thus, Lucy's character is primarily defined by her empathy. On Susan's pages, her "Personality" is described as "mothering, sensible, kind."[24] There is also a maze, taking up half a page: the reader is asked to "help find the right path from Susan's horn to Peter's sword," emphasizing Susan's essential nature as a helper rather than a heroine.[25]

Finally, these adaptations eliminate elements of the overall story. First of all, the plot is consistently presented in pieces, with emphasis placed on one portion of the story alone (*Tea with Mr. Tumnus*, for example, or *Edmund and the White Witch*) or on a retelling that focuses on an individual (*Peter's Destiny*)[26] or on some other element, like *The Creatures of Narnia*. What is most notably missing in almost all the versions is Aslan's death and resurrection and the Christian allegory of the story. Several of the books that summarize the entire tale do not mention Aslan's death at all: "Aslan saw the bravery inside Peter. He asked Peter to help him lead the creatures of Narnia against the White Witch. They worked together and freed Narnia."[27] Others pass it over quickly:

> Then he quietly offered his own life to save Edmund's. … The Witch couldn't believe her luck! "Forget Edmund," she whispered to her dwarf and her hags. "Forget the children! Now I can kill the great Aslan, Power of all Good, without breath or roar … and rule forever! Tie him to the Table with a thousand ropes!' But as soon as Aslan was dead … the witch left ….[28]

Some have even briefer versions: "Aslan had secretly gone to the Witch's camp and sacrificed himself as a part of the agreement to free Edmund."[29] Aslan's sacrifice loses considerable importance in these stories because they have none of the allegory of Lewis's novel. It only becomes an important element when the story wants to draw parallels to the Christian ideals of salvation and redemption.

In Lewis's book much is made of Aslan's agreement with the Witch in the chapter "Deep Magic from the Dawn of Time," and the following chapter, "The Triumph of the Witch," which dwells on Aslan's suffering and death at the hands of evil through the devoted eyes of Lucy and Susan in order to sustain the allegory of Christ's passion. According to Lewis, stories should be straightforward about the fact that this is a world of "death, violence, wounds, adventure, heroism and cowardice and good and evil."[30] While these human characteristics all appear, with varying degrees of emphasis, the elimination of the symbolic elements—such as calling the children "Sons of Adam" and "Daughters of Eve" in the printed adaptations of the film, and a failure to evoke the importance of the children's faith in the powerful yet gentle Aslan—is rather ironic as the film was widely anticipated and then praised among Christian faithful. In his review of the film for *Christianity Today*, Jeffery Overstreet writes that mainstream critics cannot ignore the film simply because they see it as a "pending terrorist attack."[31] He reassures Christian audiences that sacrifice and redemption remain central to the plot and that "'The lion's share' of Lewis's meaningful story remains intact."[32] Of course, whether or not this film *is* Lewis's story remains an important question. Just four years before the release of the movie, HarperCollins was working to remarket Lewis's novels. With regard to that remarketing, one executive at HarperCollins addressed this issue in a memo in which he wrote that "we'll need to be able to give emphatic assurances that no attempt will be made to correlate the stories to Christian imagery/theology."[33]

Linda Hutcheon remarks that "multiple versions of a story in fact exist laterally, not vertically" and that faithfulness to an original is not the standard by which to judge an adaptation.[34] This theory of adaptation states rather clearly that this film is not Lewis's, nor should anyone expect it or its ancillaries to be. However, one might expect it to be associated with Lewis or to lead audience members back to the Lewis texts. In fact, of all the material examined, only one book, *Step into Narnia*, makes reference to the seven-book series. This is found on the final page with the art credits and again on the back cover. Most of the texts examined for this essay credit the film as being the source material, rather than the book. In some cases, when the book is mentioned, it appears rather far down on the list of people involved, including adaptor, illustrator, and screenplay writer. For instance, this is the first page of *The Creatures of Narnia*:

-The Chronicles of-
Narnia

The Lion, the Witch and the Wardrobe
The Creatures of Narnia
Adapted by Scout Driggs
Illustrated by Justin Sweet
Based on the Screenplay by Ann Peacock and Andrew Adamson
and Christopher Markus and Stephen McFeely
Based on the book by C. S. Lewis
Directed by Andrew Adamson

Clearly, the material referenced as the original text is the film rather than the book. Adherents of fidelity adaptation theory would, thus, count all this following material a failure, and question how it might provide an "afterlife" for Lewis's stories.[35] However, promoting C. S. Lewis is not the purpose of this material; recall that these are movie tie-ins, not stand-alone pieces in their own right. They expect the reader to have familiarity with the film and thus provide a way to relive and prolong the audience's experience with it or serve to introduce someone who is not familiar with it to the film to seek it out.

Movie tie-ins, especially, illustrate the complexities of adaptation. In *A Theory of Adaptation*, Linda Hutcheon reminds us that "adaptation is repetition, but repetition without replication," and that "there are manifestly many different possible intentions behind the act of adaptation: the urge to consume and erase the memory of the adapted text or to call it into question is as likely as the desire to pay tribute by copying."[36] These "many different possible intentions" are key to our reading of these texts. On the surface, they appear to be bastardized versions of the original. As an adaptation of an adaptation, these books are easy to dismiss as simply marketing tools used by a major company to advertise their most recent project. Hutcheon's discussion of intention is important to any discussion of adaptation. As she explores in her book, adaptation is doubly defined as a "product (an extensive particular transcoding) and as a process (as creative reinterpretation and palimpsestic intertextuality)."[37] By reading adaptations in such a manner, critics can look beyond fidelity readings—those which place the original texts and adaptations in a hierarchical structure of faithfulness—and look at the ways in which adaptations expand out from the original text. About process, Hutcheon further explains that "an emphasis on process allows us to expand the traditional focus of adaptation ... in order to consider as well relations among the major modes of engagement: that is, it permits us to think about how adaptations allow people to tell, show, or interact with stories."[38] The interaction between the source text and that adaptor is the most important. Without understanding why a text is adapted and the intentions behind adaptation, it becomes impossible to examine any aspect of the adapted material itself.

Marketing Narnia to new audiences

In producing *The Lion, the Witch and the Wardrobe*, Walden Media made a very lucrative and politically savvy move. While they did not advertise their intentions to create a Christian film, they also did not deny them. Though Disney's name is found on all the promotional materials linked to the movie, it is Walden Media that benefited the most from the success of the film, both in terms of money and of media attention. As a company that "specializes in entertainment for the whole family," Walden Media found success before the release of *The Lion, the Witch and the Wardrobe* with their family-oriented adaptations of several novels, including Jules Verne's classic *Around the World in 80 Days* and Louis Sachar's Newbery Award winning *Holes*.[39] While these films were financially successful and cemented Walden Media as a force within the family entertainment genre, it was *The Lion, the Witch and the Wardrobe* that brought the company and owner, billionaire and Christian conservative, Philip Anschutz, to international attention. As one of the richest men in the world, Anschutz made a name for himself as a philanthropist through contributing to several conservative organizations, including the Institute for American Values (which addresses issues of marriage and family) and Enough is Enough (an anti-pornography campaign). Anschutz's notoriety does not end with his charitable contributions. Along with Walden Media he also owns the Regal Entertainment Group, the largest movie theater chain in the United States, and he helped establish and fund the Discovery Institute, a Seattle-based think tank that promotes intelligent design. Given his ties to the Christian and conservative communities, it is no surprise that Anschutz would find Lewis's series, one of the most popular Christian allegories of the twentieth century, so appealing a target for adaptation.

While Anschutz has never explicitly claimed that he adapted Narnia to further any kind of Christian conservative agenda, shortly before and after the release of the film, critics were quick to accuse Walden Media, Anschutz, and even Disney of marketing specifically to Christian families. The review cited earlier from *Christianity Today* makes mention of secular critics who fear the film as if it were a "pending terrorist attack."[40] Nowhere was this criticism more prominent than in the *New York Times* between October and December of 2005, just before and after the movie's release and amassing of over

$700,000 in gross revenue. In his October 12 article, "Marketing of 'Narnia' Presents Challenge," Jeff Leeds writes that the marketing strategy for Narnia appears to be "aggressively courting Christian fans who can relate to the story's biblical allegory while trying not to disaffect secular fans."[41] He cites Narnia's music, which was released as a Christian pop album before the release of the film, as being typical of such marketing. He writes, "The 'Narnia' film arrives as the entertainment industry is taking notice of—and trying to profit from—what it views as the increasing influence of religiosity on American culture. Hollywood has been casting about for the next blockbuster on the order of last year's *Passion of the Christ*."[42] He goes on to explain that Disney, the company that also owns the record label, was not worried about alienating secular audiences because none of the Christian music would be used in any of the television advertising for the film, nor could it be found in the film itself.

Similar to Leeds, Charles McGrath also makes a point that the film's marketing strategy seems to lean heavily toward Christian audiences, but he does acknowledge that Disney and Walden Media "backed [themselves] into a corner" when taking on the Narnia project. In his November 13 article, "The Narnia Skirmish," McGrath writes, "If the studio plays down the Christian aspect of the story, it risks criticism from the religious right, the argument goes; if it is too upfront about the religious references, on the other hand, that could be toxic at the box office."[43] While McGrath does acknowledge the conundrum of trying to market to two different audiences, he still only mentions Disney's Christian music album with Narnia's name on it. Neither Leeds nor McGrath look past the Christian marketing and into the ways in which the film targeted more secular fans, or those unaware of the Christian elements of the story. Jessica Seigel's December 12 article, "The Lion, the Witch and the Metaphor," is slightly more balanced in its analysis of the film's marketing strategies. About the debate between Christian and secular fans of the series, she writes that "one side dismisses the hidden Jesus figure as silly or trivial, while the other insists the lion is Jesus in a story meant to proselytize. They're both wrong."[44] She argues that whether or not the film is being marketed to primarily Christian audiences does not diminish the fact that "parents today will not be innocent of the religious subtext, considering the drumbeat of news coverage."[45] She continues to explain that multiple interpretations of the film are possible and should be respected, but so should the surface-level entertainment value. The latter argument, as Seigel points out, was expressed by Lewis over 50 years ago in his essay "On Stories." She continues to evoke Lewis: "In his essay 'Sometimes Fairy Stories May Say Best What's to Be Said,' [Lewis] denounced as 'moonshine' the idea that he wrote the Narnia chronicles to proselytize the young. The lion Aslan, he wrote, bounded into his imagination from his experience as a Christian, coming to him naturally as should all good writing."[46] Seigel's argument that the book, and in turn the movie, can be appreciated by all audiences—knowing and unknowing—along with Leeds and McGrath's criticisms of marketing heavily to Christian families, reminds us that, to some degree, the Narnia series has always been positioned as a series that is defined by, and appeals to, multiple audiences. To argue whether or not the Christian allegorical subtexts of the film should be the primary focus is not new.

So, how exactly do the children's book adaptations and movie tie-ins fit in to this debate? The answer takes us back to the fact that these texts are marketing tools, no different from the Christian soundtrack that was released. As Hutcheon writes, "it is no surprise that economic motivation affects all stages of the adaptation process."[47] As marketing tools, the novels are meant to bring the reader of the adapted text to the movie or to prolong their experience of it. Such a strategy seems insulting to Lewis's original novels. As mentioned earlier, Lewis is often billed below the adapter, Disney, and Walden Media, and the movie. He is an afterthought. This is somewhat surprising considering that Walden Media has become one of the largest corporate supporters of education. With each new movie, they distribute educational materials to schools. As a company focused on family entertainment, Walden Media very much presents itself as encouraging critical thinking and a love of reading. According to Rachel Deahl in her 2006 article for *Publisher's Weekly*, Walden Media is unique in that "it's driven by two philanthropic ideals: to make kid-friendly movies that feature positive messages and to advance literacy."[48] Their dedication to children's literature is obvious in the number of films they have produced based on contemporary and classic children's book: Louis Sachar's *Holes* (2003), Kate DiCamillo's *Because of Winn-Dixie* (2005), Thomas Rockwell's *How To Eat Fried Worms* (2006), E. B. White's *Charlotte's Web* (2006), Susan Cooper's *The Dark is Rising* (2007, movie titled *The Seeker*), and Beverly Cleary's *Ramona and Beezus* (2010), to name just a few. Certainly, executives within the organization have stated publicly that the company is concerned about education and literacy. In her article, Deahl writes:

Debbie Kovacs, Walden's v-p of publishing, said that when the studio promoted *Holes*, one of its first big successes, to teachers and librarians, no one knew what the result would be. But after *Holes* became a hit, Kovacs said the company realized this marketing approach was a viable way to make money and to encourage reading in the process.[49]

Since then, as Deahl points out, Walden Media has formed close relationships with the American Library Association and literacy groups such as Reading Is Fundamental. These relationships have become vital in Walden's acquisition and promotion of certain film projects. Looking closely at some of the educational materials released along with the films, Walden Media's claim that they support children's literacy becomes questionable. One could even go so far as to say that they are invading a space that they do not belong in as an entertainment company.

Since Walden has made a foray into educational materials, one would expect an emphasis on Lewis; anything with the name "Narnia" on the cover is going to be haunted by Lewis's original series. But, as mentioned earlier, none of the movie tie-in novelizations make it easy for the reader to understand what exactly the source material is. Even the educational materials are centered on the movies. For example, in the Educator's Guide for *The Lion, the Witch and the Wardrobe*, the activities and information focus on the film. All the artwork in the 16-page booklet are pictures from the movie, and the introduction reads: "*The Chronicles of Narnia: The Lion, the Witch and the Wardrobe* is an epic film, set in a breathtaking world at the limits of imagination."[50] A later activity asks students to write a response to a piece of writing. Rather than an excerpt from the novel, students are given a page from the script. Nothing in this guide explicitly leads children, or instructors, to read the novels. While Walden Media may say publicly that their marketing and educational materials are meant to encourage children to read the books, the actual idea is an afterthought in the materials.

While the young reader texts and other movie tie-ins may lead a reader to the original C. S. Lewis series, however indirectly, and provide an "afterlife" for the original book, an analysis of these texts demonstrates that they are most concerned with the marketing and longevity of the Walden Media/Disney film and the success of the movies to come.[51] Cynics might look at all of this and dismiss such materials as being inferior or detrimental to Lewis's original text. But the movie tie-in books, and all other promotional materials, are cleverly and subversively successful for what they are—marketing. Walden Media has taken Lewis's text and appropriated it for its own purposes, as does any adapter. Hutcheon even addresses this issue when she writes, "The new film adaptation of C. S. Lewis's *The Chronicles of*

Narnia: The Lion, the Witch and the Wardrobe is accompanied by elaborate teaching aids, from lesson plans to web-based packages to materials for after-school clubs. Today, hardly a book or movie aimed at school-aged children does not have its own website, complete with advice and materials for teachers."[52] Perhaps Walden's Media's only fault in adapting Lewis's novel is that they were so successful at it.

Notes

1. Linda Hutcheon, *A Theory of Adaptation* (New York: Routledge, 2006): 121.
2. Hutcheon: 169.
3. E. J. Kirk, *Step into Narnia: A Journey Through* The Lion, the Witch and the Wardrobe (New York: HarperCollins, 2005): 6–7.
4. C. S. Lewis, *The Lion, the Witch and the Wardrobe* (New York: Macmillan, 1970): 1.
5. Kirk: 33.
6. Michael Flexer, *Edmund's Struggle: Under the Spell of the White Witch* (New York: HarperCollins, 2005): 3.
7. Scout Driggs, *Edmund and the White Witch* (New York: HarperCollins, 2005).
8. *The Lion, the Witch and the Wardrobe*: 23.
9. Jennifer Frantz, *Welcome to Narnia* (New York: HarperCollins, 2005): 16.
10. Flexer: 35.
11. C. S. Lewis, "On Three Ways of Writing for Children," in *Of Other Worlds: Essays and Stories*, ed. Walter Hooper (New York: Harcourt Brace, 1966): 33.
12. Lewis (1966): 29.
13. Jasmine Jones, *The Quest for Aslan* (New York: HarperCollins 2005).
14. Scout Driggs, *The Creatures of Narnia*, illus. Justin Sweet (New York: HarperCollins, 2005): 1.
15. Frantz: 28–9.
16. Driggs, *Creature of Narnia*: 1.
17. *Ibid.*: 15.
18. *Ibid.*: 20.
19. Lewis (1966): 34.
20. J. R. R. Tolkien, "On Fairy Stories," in *The Tolkien Reader* (New York: Ballantine, 1966): 2–84, at 3.
21. Jennifer Frantz, *Tea with Mr. Tumnus* (New York: HarperCollins, 2005).
22. Kirk: 13.
23. *Ibid.*: 12.
24. *Ibid.*: 16.
25. *Ibid.*: 17.
26. Craig Graham, *Peter's Destiny* (New York: HarperCollins, 2005).
27. Frantz, *Welcome to Narnia*: 26–7.

28. Hiawyn Oram, *The Lion, the Witch and the Wardrobe,* illus. Tudor Humphries, (New York: HarperCollins, 2004): 26, 28.
29. Flexer: 63.
30. Lewis (1966): 30.
31. Jeffrey Overstreet, "*The Chronicles of Narnia: The Lion, the Witch and the Wardrobe*", *Christianity Today*, December 9, 2005: www.christianitytoday. com/ct/movies/reviews/2005/lionwitchwardrobe.html (accessed December 17, 2011).
32. Overstreet.
33. Doreen Carvajal, "Marketing 'Narnia' Without a Christian Lion," *New York Times*, June 3, 2001: www.nytimes.com/2001/06/03/us/ marketing-narnia-without-a-christian-lion.html (accessed December 17, 2011).
34. Hutcheon: 169.
35. *Ibid.*: 176.
36. *Ibid.*: 7.
37. *Ibid.*: 22.
38. *Ibid.*
39. Walden Media, "About Walden Media": www.walden.com/company/ (accessed December 17, 2011).
40. Overstreet.
41. Jeff Leeds, "Marketing of 'Narnia' Presents Challenge", *New York Times*, October 12, 2005: www.nytimes.com/2005/10/12/movies/12narn. html (accessed December 17, 2011).
42. Leeds.
43. Charles McGrath, "The Narnia Skirmishes," *New York Times*, November 13, 2005: www.nytimes.com/2005/11/13/movies/13narnia.html (accessed December 17, 2011).
44. Jessica Seigel, "The Lion, the Witch and the Metaphor," *New York Times*, December 12, 2005: www.nytimes.com/2005/12/12/opinion/12seigel. html (accessed December 17, 2011).
45. Seigel.
46. *Ibid.*
47. Hutcheon: 88.
48. Rachel Deahl, "Walden Media Works to Make Movie-goers Readers," *Publisher's Weekly*, January 13, 2006: www.publishersweekly.com/pw/ print/20060116/17319-walden-media-works-to-make-moviegoers-readers-.html (accessed December 17, 2011).
49. Deahl.
50. Walden Media, "Educator's Guide": www.walden.com/book/the-chronicles-of-narnia-the-lion-the-witch-and-the-wardrobe-2/ (accessed December 17, 2011).
51. Hutcheon: 176.
52. *Ibid.*: 118.

7

The Lion, the Witch, and the Wii: Lewis's Theology in the Narnia Video Game

Aaron Clayton

Introduction

Concerns about whether or not *The Chronicles of Narnia* are truly an allegory remain contested, but even C. S. Lewis acknowledged that there is religious symbolism implicit within the series.[1] Although Lewis insisted that the Christian discourse embedded in the narrative was consequential on the storytelling and not deliberate, several theological concepts emerge: God's sovereignty, determinism, glory, and moral objectivity. While *The Chronicles of Narnia* are only one permutation of Lewis's mind (and as a creative source may not implicate his own theological disposition), the fact remains that theology is present within these texts. This chapter will examine how Lewis's theology as represented in *The Lion, the Witch and the Wardrobe*[2] translates into the video game of the same name,[3] which is directly based, not on the book, but on the 2005 Disney film.[4] The examination will reveal that because of the game's faithfulness to certain elements of the storyline in Lewis's book and the limits of its design, the game undercuts the theology embedded within Lewis's imagined world.

The diegetic world[5] constructed for the video game allows fans of Lewis to enter into Narnia and play as one or more of the four Pevensie siblings from the original novels. Players, however, are not free to explore Narnia at their leisure, but are pressured by respawning creatures and cold decrement to complete objectives and progress through the game. I will begin this chapter by providing a brief explication of the relevant parts of the theological framework from which Lewis writes. Like any writer, theorist, or philosopher, Lewis's beliefs about the world changed as he matured. Consequently, his writings on the problem of predestination and free will in particular are more easily expressed as a narrative than mere fact. Predestination, as well as the other concepts addressed in this chapter, plays a significant role in the structure of *The Lion, the Witch and the Wardrobe* and the Narnia series as a whole. To understand how this affects the novels, I will examine Lewis's approach to storytelling and conclude by applying these principles to *The Lion, the Witch and the Wardrobe* and the video game, elucidating what in fact happened to his theology as it was translated into the game.

Lewis's totalizing theology: sovereignty, determinism, and glory

Of all contemporary theology, Lewis's beliefs most closely mirror those of conservative Christians in the United States, so my research will focus primarily on them. As Polly Toynbee notes in her review of *The Lion, the Witch and the Wardrobe* Disney film in the *Guardian*, "This new Disney film is a remarkably faithful rendition of the book,"[6] referring both to the film's portrayal of the characters and to the embedded system of beliefs. Toybee concludes that "Most British children will be utterly clueless about any message beyond the age-old mythic battle between good and evil."[7] Consequently, readers may not be familiar with Lewis's theology, and I will use the next few paragraphs to elaborate on these beliefs.

For Lewis, Christianity is not simply a lens through which one can understand and interpret the world. In his 1943 book *The Abolition of Man*, Lewis spends a considerable amount of time distinguishing the concept of a totalizing philosophical system from the limited philosophical critiques of his contemporaries, stating, "What purport to be new systems or (as they now call them) 'ideologies', all consist of fragments from the *Tao* itself, arbitrarily wrenched from their context in the whole and then swollen to madness in their isolation."[8] While later in the essay Lewis claims he is not in fact arguing specifically for his Christian theism,[9] he is arguing for a form of objectivism that allows for and affirms his religious beliefs. What I find most interesting about Lewis's aim here is that he is (1) deliberately rejecting any kind of subjective or relativistic grounds for value, which for him is meaningful as morality; and (2), more importantly, asserting that a philosophical system must in fact take into account the whole of nature and everything in it to be valid. Several years later, in 1947, Lewis makes a similar point in a book called *Miracles*. In this text, Lewis sets up the Naturalist and Supernaturalist as polar opposites and argues that the Naturalist fails because s/he believes in a system that is unable to answer for all phenomena.[10]

In a similar way, Lewis uses the 1945 essay "The Laws of Nature," collected in *God in the Dock*, to deal with the problem of nature and to explore how his beliefs in Christianity inform his understanding of it.[11] He argues that it isn't the laws of nature that make things happen, but instead these laws are the rules by or boundaries within which God sets things into motion. Lewis articulates this by stating, "It is His act alone that gives the laws any events to apply to."[12] This will have implications later in the essay as I examine how Lewis portrays God's sovereignty or determination over the events of history. For now, however, it is necessary to keep in mind that Lewis perceives nature as an instrument by which God accomplishes his work. What is most important about the relationship between Lewis's reading of nature's laws and theology is the evidence Lewis finds for God within nature. In a letter to Arthur Greeves, Lewis explains that the theological concept of vicariousness or Christ's suffering for mankind can be found within nature. According to Lewis, man's necessary reliance on others is not only evidence for the existence of God, but also evidence for the presence of a greater spiritual law, which determines natural law.[13]

While vicariousness is one of the theological concepts present within *The Lion, the Witch and the Wardrobe*, it is not one that I intend to focus on in this essay. My only concern here is that Lewis believed with enough confidence to put the idea into writing that evidence not just for the existence of God, but also for a particular theology, was observed in the natural world. I am first interested in his understanding of God's sovereignty[14] because out of all of Lewis's beliefs, it has the most meaningful implications in the game. In his book *Mere Theology*, Will Vaus provides an insightful portrayal of Lewis's lifelong struggle, which begins with Arminianism and moves toward Calvinism in his later years.[15] In the chapter titled "God's Sovereignty and Human Responsibility," Vaus identifies a significant letter to Mary Van Deusen where Lewis expresses his frustration with the issue and makes the claim that "I suspect it is really a *meaningless* question."[16] While Lewis clearly isn't interested in staking out a position, I do find it revealing that he does in fact choose a side. Just a few sentences earlier he states, "Of course (say us) if a man repents God will accept him. Ah yes, (say they) but the fact of his repenting shows that God has already moved him to do so."[17] The "us" locates him as at the very least identifying himself with Van Deusen as Arminian, even if he does negate the significance of that distinction later in the letter.[18]

Lewis's distinction between the two grows even murkier in the letters that follow after the one to Van Deusen and signifies a shift toward Calvinist doctrine. When Emily McLay asks Lewis a similar question about God's sovereignty, Lewis writes in response, "I find the best plan is to take the Calvinist view of my own virtues and other people's vices: and the other view of my own vices and other people's virtues."[19] In essence, Lewis is arguing to attribute virtues to God, take responsibility for all faults, and do the exact opposite for others in order to always think the best of them. Here Lewis privileges neither view but instead finds it more valuable to emphasize humility when it comes to one's own faith. Lastly, in an interview titled "Cross-examination" that took place the same year as the letter to McLay, Sherwood Wirt of the Billy Graham Evangelistic Association asks Lewis about how he treats this issue in the autobiographical work *Surprised by Joy*. Wirt asks Lewis, "You suggest that you were compelled, as it were, to become a Christian. Do you feel that you made a decision at the time of your conversion?"[20] The operative move in Wirt's question is the shift from passive to active voice, concealing and unconcealing the person or being performing the action. Lewis responds, "I was the object rather than the subject of this affair. I was decided upon."[21] In this final example, Lewis appears to be leaning toward the Calvinist doctrine of predestination by indicating that God initiated the conversion.

Another theological concept that plays a significant role in *The Chronicles of Narnia* is that of determinism. While similar to God's sovereignty in the conversion of Christians, determinism differs in that it is a problem that needs be resolved, rather that one that needs to be decided upon. Outside the procedure of conversion, most Christians like Lewis believe and act as though they have agency. However, according to most Christians, God's omnipotence allows him to know all of a person's choices before these decisions are made. This raises the question that if God can foresee all events, how is it possible that humans have any free will, or simply not do what God has already foreseen? Lewis addresses this problem in *Mere Christianity* by theorizing that God is outside of time and experiences all moments as an infinite present. He writes, "In a sense, He does not know your action till you have done it: but then the moment at which you have done it is already "Now" for Him."[22] This notion of the infinite present eliminates foreknowledge altogether because, according to Lewis, God is not seeing anything before it happens; he is experiencing it all simultaneously.

What makes determinism even more complicated is the role of prayer. In an essay titled "Work and Prayer," Lewis contends that these two practices give a Christian authority over his own life and can consequently affect God's actions.[23] Lewis has to be careful with his explication of determinism because he does not want to negate the notion of a purposeful creation, so he cautions that there are limitations to the extent that Christians have over the will of God. He writes, "It is like a play in which the scene and the general outline of the story is fixed by the author, but certain minor details are left for the actors to improvise."[24] Like the previous point on God's sovereignty in conversion, Lewis makes room for both personal responsibility and action, and determinism.

Through the actions of work and prayer, Christians can achieve what Lewis defines as glory. He clarifies his own understanding of this concept in a sermon titled "The Weight of Glory." In this sermon, Lewis distinguishes true spiritual glory from his initial false notions of it, fame and luminosity.[25] Both of these notions are limited in the sense that these pertain only to the temporal or physical world, not the spiritual. Lewis concludes that despite its seeming childishness, "glory meant good report with God, acceptance by God, response, acknowledgment, and welcome into the heart of things."[26] In other words, according to Lewis, glory means recognition by God.

The final theological concept relevant to this analysis of *The Lion, the Witch and the Wardrobe* is moral objectivity. Under the rubric of moral objectivity, all human thought and action can be judged by God and determined to deserve glory or repulse it. While Lewis's rendering of it is nothing new, he does not limit objectivity simply to morality, but to all value. In the aforementioned work *The Abolition of Man*, Lewis states that objective value "is something we cannot neglect. It is ... the belief that certain attitudes are really true, and others really false, to the kind of thing the universe is and the kind of things we are."[27] Unlike the developmentalism of H. G. Wells, which Lewis is arguing against and which I read as a kind of structuralism, Lewis believes that a hierarchical philosophical system must be totalizing and encompass not only the physical world but also the spiritual, in a way that gives value to each moral and ethical decision made by individuals in the limited sense of autonomy permitted within a determined reality.

Storytelling as world-making

As I now turn to Lewis's approach to storytelling, I contend that the imagined worlds he created for readers reflect an embedded theology similar to that which Lewis identifies in his own perception of reality. And while I do not think it is possible to argue that the theology of Narnia is an exact representation of Lewis's beliefs, because Lewis claimed evidence of Christ's vicariousness within nature[28] and that any philosophical system must be totalizing like the *Tao*, we can approach the diegetic world of his imagination with that same critical eye and identify the theological structures embedded there. In this sense, it is even appropriate that Lewis repeatedly claims he did not at the start intend to promote Christian ideals through his fiction. One of the many letters he composed asserting his initially nondidactic aims for *The Lion, the Witch and the Wardrobe* reads:

> No, of course it was not unconscious. So far as I can remember it was not at first intentional either. That is, when I started *The Lion, Witch and Wardrobe* I don't think I foresaw what Aslan was going to do and suffer. I think He just insisted on behaving in His own way. This of course I did understand and the whole series became Christian. But it is not, as some people think, an *allegory*. That is, I don't say "Let us represent Christ as Aslan." I say, "Supposing there was a world like Narnia, and supposing, like ours, it needed redemption, let us imagine what sort of Incarnation and Passion and Resurrection Christ would have there." See?[29]

However, I would argue that in light of Lewis's Taoist claims, the act of storytelling will always be informed by his worldview, and the similarities between Lewis's own theology and that of the structure of Narnia is simply a consequence of this fact. This quotation also proves to be so interesting because of Lewis's use of the word "foresaw." It resonates with the previous discussion about God's sovereignty and locates Lewis in the role of God as creator of this Narnian universe. It also resonates with Lewis's claims about work and prayer, specifically the metaphor of the play where the actors have the ability to make minor changes while remaining within the framework designed and constructed by the creator. Consequently, the principal actors in *The Lion, the Witch and the Wardrobe* are endowed with agency and can make choices for themselves without changing the events of history. The difference here is that Aslan—who Lewis admits represents something like Christ the Son of God, as illustrated in the second half of the quotation above—does in fact do something quite significant that Lewis did not anticipate or plan out, whereas Lewis's view of God, who molded Christ's suffering into the laws of nature, would insist that God was well aware of what Christ would have to do. When it comes to determining whether or not the stories are allegories of the Christian faith, the quotation above demonstrates one of the several occasions where Lewis flatly denies it. While I agree with

Lewis that the *Chronicles* do not in fact read like allegory or tend toward the didacticism of his sermons, letters, and other nonfiction, the denials themselves are remarkably unconvincing. Even more striking is the fact that Lewis appears uncertain about whether the stories are allegorical. Like the quotation above, these denials are frequently concluded with rhetorical questions, concessions, and other statements that may simply be a vehicle for his frustration, but more likely signify equivocation or doubt about his claims.[30]

Whether the allegory is present or intentional, the fact remains that *The Chronicles of Narnia* are deeply indebted to the Christian faith and thematically organized by their correspondence to significant events and teachings of the Christian church. Lewis admits as much when he describes the thematic outline of the *Chronicles* in a letter to Anne Jenkins in 1961. While I won't quote the outline for the entire series here, I will list the first few points and draw attention to Lewis's arrangement of the outline in the chronological order of the events set in Narnia, not the order of writing or publication. Lewis writes: "*The Magician's Nephew* tells the creation and how evil entered Narnia. *The Lion etc* _____ the Crucifixion and Resurrection[,] *Prince Caspian* _____ restoration of the true religion after corruption [, and] *The Horse and his Boy* _____ the calling and conversion of a heathen."[31] Lewis may still be able to argue that storytelling remains at the forefront of these works; however, it is clear that the story Lewis finds most compelling is that of the faith in which he believes.

From the pen to the controller

Juxtaposing *The Lion, the Witch and the Wardrobe* novel and video game reveals some interesting connections and departures from Lewis's theology as articulated in the paragraphs above. Beginning with God's sovereignty, close analysis reveals that *The Lion, the Witch and the Wardrobe* aligns closer to Calvinist doctrine than Lewis does, predicting his move toward belief in predestination in the years that followed. In the aforementioned chapter on God's sovereignty, Vaus offers a compelling interpretation of Edmund's conversion in *The Lion, the Witch and the Wardrobe*. Vaus accurately recognizes that after Edmund allies himself with Jadis, the White Witch, he never chooses for himself to rejoin his siblings on the side of Aslan. There are several distinct moments of doubt, where Edmund consciously pushes down his feelings of guilt for his actions, but he never in fact chooses Aslan. It is only after Aslan sacrifices himself like Christ on the Stone Table that Aslan has a conversation with Edmund. This conversation is informed by Lewis's essay "On Forgiveness," written three years prior to the publication of *The Lion, the Witch and the Wardrobe* and collected in *The Weight of Glory*. In this essay, Lewis cautions the reader about the futility of making excuses to God because, according to Lewis, God would already know to overlook valid "extenuating circumstances."[32] To receive true forgiveness, one must submit the "inexcusable bit, the sin" to God.[33] Taking this into account, Edmund's conversation with Aslan most likely consisted of Aslan showing Edmund the "horror, dirt, meanness, and malice"[34] of his betrayal and forgiving it. Vaus also points out that the animals and other creatures Jadis turned into stone statues do not ask Aslan to be returned to their original form because they are unable to. In a sense, this signifies the concept of total depravity within Calvinist doctrine that asserts no one is able to come to Christ of their own accord because they are incapable of choosing God. This suggests that some of the theology of Narnia may in fact have been unconscious despite Lewis's claim and that his fiction articulated what he was not prepared to admit yet in reality, or it at least provided him the space to play out ideas that he wasn't yet fully convinced of, but still considering.

The video game designed for mass consumption by an American audience half a century later unsurprisingly relocates God's sovereignty to the background of gameplay.[35] However, there are some interesting problems that arise. In his book *Gaming: Essays on Algorithmic Culture*, Alexander Galloway spatializes gameplay on two axes of diegetic and nondiegetic action, and action controlled by the operator and action controlled by the machine. The result is what Galloway describes as four moments of gaming: diegetic machine acts, diegetic operator acts, nondiegetic machine acts, and nondiegetic operator acts.[36] While the lines between these categories are not as rigid as they first seem, the ability to at least theoretically distinguish between acts proves exceptionally useful, particularly when determining the limits of the game and the operator's ability to engage with or alter the environment of the game. Aslan's calling of Edmund, sacrifice, and hidden conversation all occur as diegetic machine acts and consequently have no impact on the gamer's experience. What is interesting, however, is that Jadis's statues do have a significant role in gameplay. Throughout every level preceding "The Great Battle" between the forces of good and evil, the player has the opportunity to locate and mark statues for Aslan, so that when he returns he will rescue them. During "The Great Battle," these statues come to aid the player in the form of reinforcements. The more statues a player marks for Aslan, the more assistance s/he has in the battle. If returning the statued creatures to their natural form is in fact a symbol of Christian conversion as Vaus suggests, then it is not Aslan or God who is calling these creatures, it is the player. By integrating statues in such a way into the gameplay, the game designers have imposed the Arminian doctrine of God's sovereignty, which emphasizes the value of Christians going out into the world and proselytizing so that more may come to know Christ of their own accord. The game therefore offers two methods of conversion, Edmund's and the statues', and foregrounds the Arminian method by reiterating it multiple times throughout almost every level of the game.[37] Because it is in fact still Aslan who completes the process of returning the creatures to their original form, the game more closely mirrors what Lewis *said* he believed at the time of writing *The Lion, the Witch and the Wardrobe*, than what he wrote in his composition of the novel.

Even though the principle of God's sovereignty in conversion is no different than his sovereignty at any other time, in an ironic twist, *The Lion, the Witch and the Wardrobe* novel matches Lewis's own beliefs where the game goes off in a completely different direction. As previously stated, Lewis explained the problem of determinism using the metaphor of a play. This aptly describes how the Pevensie children act within Lewis's novel. There are certain predetermined events that will take place, but the characters are free to make decisions and act as though they themselves determine history. Edmund's alliance with Jadis does not prevent her downfall or the return of Aslan. To illustrate that this was in fact the trajectory of Narnian history all along, Lewis uses Mr. Beaver to speak the old rhymes of prophecy. Beaver repeats them, saying, "Wrong will be right, when Aslan comes in sight."[38] Later on Beaver adds,

> When Adam's flesh and Adam's bone
> Sits at Cair Paravel in throne,
> The evil time will be over and done.[39]

These rhymes foretell the return of Aslan and the coming of the Sons of Adam and Daughters of Eve, demonstrating that at least the significant events of history have already been written.

The video game takes a much stricter approach to determinism, allowing the player little room to employ any kind of agency.[40] Because cut-scenes are literally taken from the film and used to tell the narrative of the adventure, the player is simply left with filling in the gaps. The film opens with a scene not in the original book where the Pevensie children must hide with their mother from a German bombing raid. The game expands this scene so that the first level encompasses running through the house, breaking down burning doors, discovering each member of the family, and escaping from the house. Similarly, each level of the game takes a moment from the film and stretches it into a 5–30-minute action sequence of smashing furniture, beating off waves of wolves and other respawning minions of Jadis, or enduring the harsh elements of Jadis's unnatural winter. Consequently, the player's goal is to struggle through the minor errata that don't even make it onto the page of the film script. On the rare occasions that the player's character has the opportunity to experience a moment from the film, the player's agency is severely constrained to a predetermined pattern for success. For example, to defeat Jadis—or rather to defeat her enough that the player reaches a cut-scene where Aslan comes to the rescue—the player only needs to hit her about a dozen times. However, this could easily take an hour of gameplay to complete because the player must hit Jadis by switching to the proper character, wielding the appropriate weapon from that character's inventory or surroundings, and striking all at the right moment. Otherwise the game resets to the previous checkpoint and the player must start over again. The player finds him/herself struggling to complete the game as it has been predetermined to happen by the game designers. While the option to relive a mistake has no implications in Lewis's theology, the lack of diegetic operator acts removes any possibility for players to influence God's will as Lewis purports through work or prayer.

The principle of glory functions in a similar way to determinism in the book and video game in the sense that the book underscores Lewis's beliefs, while the game embodies exactly what Lewis argues against. As illustrated above, Lewis understands glory as recognition by God, not society. In a double move, the Pevensie children receive glory in both of these senses, yet have the latter revoked at the same time. While in Narnia, the siblings enjoy Aslan's presence and are rewarded by his praise and admiration.[41] For his courage and insight in the battle against Jadis and her army, Edmund is knighted by Aslan on the battlefield.[42] Additionally, all the children are crowned Kings and Queens of Narnia—titles they will retain eternally, as the Professor points out a few pages later: "Once a King in Narnia, always a King in Narnia."[43] The crowning of the Pevensies not only confers recognition from Aslan, but also fame and luminosity. While this may appear to contradict Lewis's beliefs about glory, the fame and luminosity each child receives is stripped away as they leave Narnia and return to the Professor's home through the wardrobe. Any hope of rejoicing in their titles is denied them when the Professor cautions the children not to mention their adventures in Narnia to anyone who has not been there themselves. Consequently, all the children are left with is the recognition Aslan bestowed on them by offering them such rewards, but they are not able to retain the social recognition that must be left behind in Narnia. And while it is true that the children return to Narnia in the other novels, Lewis himself admits that he never planned on writing a sequel until after this first volume was completed. As a result, we can read this text as an isolated work, and this interpretation of glory in the novel is unaffected by circumstances in the other novels in the series.

The video game, on the other hand, offers the player no recognition from Aslan, and instead, his/her rewards come from the game itself and the bragging rights one earns from the completion percentage ratio. The more successful players are at the game, the more bonus levels and special features are unlocked. Success is dependent upon locating hidden shields throughout the game as well as completing levels to progress through the storyline. Even before the game is won, players begin to unlock the special features based on their completion percentage ratio. The special features resemble the behind-the-scenes addenda packaged with most film DVDs. Players are rewarded with video clips of the actors' recording voices for the characters, a brief documentary on how the game was developed, and, strangely enough, even an interview about the game with Douglas Gresham, a stepson of Lewis who was co-producer of the Disney film and had an advisory role in the creation of the game.[44] The bonus levels constitute part of the game as well, so the player finds herself slugging through these tedious onslaughts of Jadis's minions just to unlock more levels with stricter expectations. The coveted final special feature is a disappointing slideshow of unused models developed for the game. While the details of the bonus content itself are not necessarily significant, the fact that players are distinguished for their achievements with concrete rewards denotes a conception of glory that contradicts Lewis's.

The last theological concept that this essay will analyze in the book and the game is moral objectivity. In a comparison between the British and American editions of *The Lion, the Witch and the Wardrobe*, Walter Hooper writes that "We would probably be right in saying that the Deep Magic 'put into Narnia at the very beginning' is the moral order, the Moral or Natural Law of Narnia."[45] Hooper connects this to Lewis's explanation of the *Tao* in *The Abolition of Man*, which reinforces my previous argument about how Narnia is, in Lewis's mind, a world like ours that contains within it laws that speak to the existence and sovereignty of God. More importantly, this connection brings with it the objective value Lewis candidly spoke of in *The Abolition of Man* and insisted was a part of any comprehensive conception of the world. This emerges from *The Lion, the Witch and the Wardrobe* in two distinct forms. First, there is the clear-cut distinction between good and evil represented through the foils of Aslan and Jadis respectively. Moreover, with the exception of Edmund, any creature or person that allies him/herself with Jadis is irredeemably evil. Even after she has lost and is killed by Aslan, the Pevensies as kings and queens hunt down and exterminate the last vestiges of her army. There is no amnesty or forgiveness offered to those who collaborated with her, and I believe it can be easily argued that even Edmund is not a true exception to this because he never willfully served her. His acts were always influenced by the thrall of her magic, which consequently reduces his complicity. Second, Lewis offers characters distinct moral choices that are made transparent to the reader. Two instances of this are Mr. Tumnus's decision not to give Lucy over to Jadis[46]—which results in him turning into a statue[47]—and Edmund's decision to lie to Susan and Peter about entering Narnia with Lucy.[48] During each of these situations, Lewis makes the reader privy to these characters' thoughts as they weigh both options and make a decision, proving that once again the book synthesizes the physical and spiritual in a way that parallels Lewis's view of the world.

On this principle the game also echoes Lewis's theology, but not quite to the extent of the book. There is still the clear-cut distinction between good and evil via the forces that ally with Aslan and the forces that ally with Jadis. However, the moments of moral choice are omitted, as that would permit a course of action that could ultimately change the outcome of the narrative. To maintain synchronicity with the film, these moments are relegated to the cut-scenes. If the game designers had offered the player more autonomy, Aslan's suffering and the redemption of Edmund may not have been necessary.[49] Regardless of this fact, the gamer loses a substantial aspect of the Narnian experience that Lewis certainly would have regretted. Moreover, the game presents another irresolvable problem that puts at risk the moral objectivity of the diegetic game-world. There is no existential change within Edmund after Aslan's sacrifice. In the book, Susan and Lucy point out how much Edmund matured after his *conversion*, noting specifically his selfless techniques in combat with Jadis.[50] However, in gameplay, there is no distinguishable difference in Edmund pre-Aslan and Edmund post-Aslan. While there is evidence in Lewis's letters to substantiate a claim that the actions of a good person appear no different than the actions of an evil person,[51] the inclusion of the conversation between Lucy and Susan suggests that Lewis felt it necessary to provide concrete evidence for the change in Edmund's nature. The removal of moral choice and evidence of Edmund's redemption do not undermine the moral objectivity within the Narnian game-world, but it certainly reduces the effectiveness of Lewis's message and puts at risk the value of such a moral system because it was not significant enough to enter into gameplay.

The revival of Lewis's series in a changed cultural context provides those new to *The Chronicles of Narnia* and those familiar with it a different experience with Lewis's world. No one would have expected a video game released approximately 40 years after his death to align with his belief system, but neither should an audience pass up the opportunity of experiencing a text in an entirely different medium, particularly when that experience offers critical questions that may lead to a different understanding of Lewis's imagination. Because Lewis's Taoist conception of the world binds theology with Natural Law, readers and gamers may confidently search for and distinguish a particular theology within the novel and the game in comparison to Lewis's own beliefs. While the theology of the novel seems to be either a subconscious iteration of what Lewis would come to terms with over the next decade of his life[52] (or at least his rendering of one permutation of this thoughts on the subject), the theology of the game deviates significantly from that of the book and Lewis's beliefs—partially in its attempt to remain faithful to the story as opposed to its intent, and partially because of the limits imposed by the game designers.

Notes

1. One frequent question that Lewis received from readers was whether or not Aslan represented Christ. While Lewis's responses resisted a yes/no answer, he typically stated that Aslan was to Narnia what Christ was to our world. See Walter Hooper (ed.), *The Collected Letters of C. S. Lewis*, 3 vols. (San Francisco, CA: HarperSanFrancisco, 2004–7), vol. 3 (2007): at 230, 334–5, 602–3.

2. C. S. Lewis, *The Lion, the Witch and the Wardrobe* (New York: HarperCollins, 1994).

3. Buena Vista Games, *Disney's The Chronicles of Narnia: The Lion, the Witch, and the Wardrobe* (Disney, 2005).

4. *The Chronicles of Narnia: The Lion, the Witch and the Wardrobe*, directed by Andrew Adamson (Disney, 2005).

5. The term "diegetic world" is borrowed from Mark J. P. Wolf's use of the term in *The Medium of the Video Game*. He inherits the term *diegesis* from

film theory, a term that signifies an Aristotelian understanding of plot. This term has become extremely valuable to video game theory as most games developed in the past two decades depend heavily on constructing realistic universes within which the player or operator acts. These diegetic universes allow for multiple games, all with varying and distinct storylines and characters, to be created. Fully understanding the ideological structures informing the characters and story in a game necessarily involves understanding the environment where the game unfolds. Mark J. P. Wolf (ed.), *The Medium of the Video Game* (Austin: Texas University Press, 2001).

6. Polly Toynbee, "Narnia Represents Everything That Is Most Hateful about Religion," *Guardian*,December 4, 2005: www.guardian.co.uk/ books/2005/dec/05/cslewis.booksforchildrenandteenagers (accessed December 11, 2011).

7. *Ibid.*

8. C. S. Lewis, *The Abolition of Man*, in *The Complete C. S. Lewis Signature Classics* (San Francisco, CA: HarperSanFrancisco, 2002): 465–98, at 480.

9. Here Lewis clarifies the intent of the work: "In order to avoid misunderstanding, I may add that though I myself am a Theist, and indeed a Christian, I am not here attempting any indirect argument for Theism. I am simply arguing that if we are to have values at all we must accept the ultimate platitudes of Practical Reason as having absolute validity: that any attempt … to reintroduce value lower down on some supposedly more 'realistic' basis, is doomed. Whether this position implies a supernatural origin for the *Tao* is a question I am not here concerned with." *The Abolition of Man*: 481–2.

10. C. S. Lewis, "Miracles," in *The Complete C. S. Lewis Signature Classics* (San Francisco, CA: HarperSanFrancisco, 2002): 205–309, at 216.

11. "The Laws of Nature," in *God in the Dock: Essays on Theology and Ethics*, ed. Walter Hooper (Grand Rapids, MI: Eerdmans, 1970): 76–9.

12. *Ibid.*: 79.

13. Hooper, vol. 2: 953.

14. Within Christianity, there is still much debate about whether the choice to become a Christian begins with God or with the individual. Does one have to be chosen or called? Or does each person make that decision of his/her own free will? For the sake of clarity, I identify this issue at stake in personal conversion as God's sovereignty, and God's role in historical events as determinism, even though the terms overlap.

15. Will Vaus, *Mere Theology: A Guide to the Thought of C. S. Lewis* (Downers Grove, IL: InterVarsity Press, 2004).

16. Hooper, vol. 3: 237.

17. *Ibid.*

18. Strangely enough, this issue also arises in a letter to Van Deusen's daughter a year earlier in 1951, and in this letter to Genia Goelz, Lewis straddles the fence even more ambiguously than he does in the letter cited above from 1952. He writes in the postscript: "Of course God does

not consider you hopeless. If He did He would not be moving you to seek Him (and He obviously is). What is going on in you at present is simply the beginning of the *treatment*. Continue seeking with cheerful seriousness. Unless He wanted you, you would not be wanting Him." Hooper, vol. 3: 127.   What is remarkable about this letter is (1) Lewis is speaking to this issue without solicitation, and (2) if anything this letter emphasizes a move toward Calvinism, which he clearly does not identify with in the letter to Goelz's mother; even he underemphasizes the distinction.

19. Hooper, vol. 3: 355.
20. C. S. Lewis, "Cross-examination," in *God in the Dock: Essays on Theology and Ethics*, ed. Walter Hooper (Grand Rapids, MI: Eerdmans, 1970): 258–67, at 263.
21. *Ibid.*
22. C. S. Lewis, *Mere Christianity*, in *The Complete C. S. Lewis Signature Classics* (San Francisco, CA: HarperSanFrancisco, 2002): 1–118, at 93.
23. C. S. Lewis, "Work and Prayer," in *God in the Dock: Essays on Theology and Ethics*, ed. Walter Hooper (Grand Rapids, MI: Eerdmans, 1970):104–7.
24. *Ibid.*
25. C. S. Lewis, "The Weight of Glory," in *The Weight of Glory* (San Francisco, CA: HarperSanFrancisco, 1980): 25–46.
26. *Ibid.*: 7.
27. *The Abolition of Man*: 473.
28. Remember that Lewis himself stated that this was the most important spiritual law that governed natural law.
29. Hooper, vol. 3: 1113.
30. See Lewis's denials in the letters addressed to a fifth-grade class in Maryland: Cynthia Donnelly and Patricia Mackey cited in Hooper, vol. 2: 479–80, 502–3, 1157–9.
31. Hooper, vol. 3: 1245.
32. "On Forgiveness," in *The Weight of Glory* (San Francisco, CA: HarperSanFrancisco, 1980): 177–83, at 180.
33. *Ibid.*
34. *Ibid.*: 181.
35. Buena Vista Games.
36. Alexander Galloway, "Gamic Action, Four Moments," in *Gaming: Essays on Algorithmic Culture* (Minnesota University Press: Minneapolis, 2006): 1–38.
37. Edmund's conversion is also diminished by the lack of any existential change in the game version. The unconverted Edmund is just as effective (or ineffective) at fighting off Jadis's minions as the converted Edmund. Similarly, there are no other distinguishing changes in how a gamer can play Edmund or what a gamer can do with him. Consequently, Edmund's conversion has no value to the gamer, and only the statues' conversion represented according to Arminian doctrine has any tangible meaning within the game.

38. *The Lion, the Witch and the Wardrobe*: 79.

39. *Ibid.*: 81.

40. Buena Vista Games.

41. One such instance is the praise Aslan offers Peter for anticipating Jadis's treachery; *The Lion, the Witch and the Wardrobe*: 147.

42. *Ibid.*: 180.

43. *Ibid.*: 188.

44. I say "strangely enough" because I doubt the target audience for the game would think an interview with anyone would be an appropriate reward for the additional painstaking hours it takes of replaying the game to unlock these features.

45. Walter Hooper, *C. S. Lewis: A Companion and Guide* (San Francisco, CA: HarperSanFrancisco, 1996): 412.

46. *The Lion, the Witch and the Wardrobe*: 20–1.

47. *Ibid.*: 77–8.

48. *Ibid.*: 45.

49. The deliberate omission of Edmund's moral choice brings into question what would have happened had he not betrayed his siblings in a way that could not be realized if the video game did not exist. While this in itself may not negate the free will of Edmund in the book, it certainly puts it at risk. Aslan would not have fulfilled his role as a Christ-like figure, and the children might have led the Narnians to victory over Jadis.

50. *The Lion, the Witch and the Wardrobe*: 178–9.

51. In a letter to Dom Bede Lewis writes: "The bad (natural) tree cannot produce good fruit. But oddly, it can produce fruits that by all *external* tests are indistinguishable from the good ones: the act done from one's own separate and unredeemed, tho' 'moral' will, *looks* exactly like the act done by Christ in us." Hooper, vol. 3: 62.

52. I am speaking here specifically of his belief in God's sovereignty on the question of predestination.

Part IV
Conflicts and Controversy

8

Lewis and Anti-Lewis: On the Influence of *The Chronicles of Narnia* on *His Dark Materials* by Philip Pullman

Gili Bar-Hillel

Pullman vs. Lewis

In October of 1998, as Britain prepared to celebrate the centenary of C. S. Lewis's birth, author Philip Pullman published an editorial in the *Guardian* denouncing the "tweedy medievalist" and *The Chronicles of Narnia*. "So Narnia sells by the lorry-load," wrote Pullman, but he claimed to be puzzled by the popularity of the series, "because there is no doubt in my mind that it is one of the most ugly and poisonous things I've ever read." Pullman then went on to condemn the Narnia books for exhibiting misogyny, racism, a "sado-masochistic relish for violence," and "the colossal impertinence, to put it mildly, of hijacking the emotions that are evoked by the story of the Crucifixion and Resurrection in order to boost the reader's concern about Aslan."[1]

This editorial was but one stone thrown in a debate that is still ongoing, in which it would seem that Pullman has pitted himself against the late C. S. Lewis, while supporters of Lewis attempt to retaliate in Lewis's name. "This is the most dangerous author in Britain," announced conservative columnist Peter Hitchens in 2002, in response to the news that Pullman had won the prestigious Whitbread award for *The Amber Spyglass*, the concluding volume of the *His Dark Materials* trilogy. In a later column he wrote: "many who buy these books would be surprised, and even shocked, if they knew just how vehemently Pullman despises the Christian Church, and how much he loathes his dead rival, Lewis. He is, in fact, the Anti-Lewis."[2] Pullman has continued to voice his loathing for Narnia in numerous writings and interviews, while several writers have joined Peter Hitchens in condemning Pullman and his books.[3] The Internet is now full of articles, blogs, Facebook groups, and so on, supporting one camp or the other in the "war" between Pullman the atheist and Lewis the Christian.

And yet, for readers of children's books, both Lewis's *The Chronicles of Narnia* series and Pullman's *His Dark Materials* trilogy are held in very high esteem, cherished, and loved. When the BBC conducted "The Big Read" in 2003, a survey in which over three-quarters of a million votes were collected in the attempt to determine "Britain's best-loved book," Pullman's *His Dark Materials* clocked in at number 3 on a list of 200 beloved novels, and Lewis's *The Lion, the Witch and the Wardrobe* appeared at number 9 (this despite an apparent bias in favor of current bestsellers).[4] Both authors won the prestigious Carnegie medal for children's books (Pullman in 1995 for *Northern Lights* aka *The Golden Compass*; Lewis in 1956 for *The Last Battle*). Both authors regularly star on lists of recommendations for young readers and for readers of fantasy.

If Pullman and Lewis are truly in opposition to each other, how is it that their books attract the same kind of readership? One would think that readers drawn to Lewis's Christian symbolism would be repelled by Pullman's staunch atheism, and vice versa. As Lewis himself wrote, "different beliefs about the universe lead to different behaviour. ... Religion involves a series of statements about facts, which must be either true or false. If they are true, one set of conclusions will follow ...: if they are false, quite a different set."[5] If Lewis's books are based on the premise that our lives are guided by a benevolent deity, while Pullman's books are based on the premise that there is no true God, wouldn't one expect the books to be fundamentally different, and to appeal to fundamentally different audiences? And yet this does not seem to be the case.

Why readers love both authors

I can offer several possible explanations for how the same readers would be able to love both the Narnia books and *His Dark Materials*:

1. Pullman's writing, despite his proclamations, is much more similar to that of Lewis than Pullman would have us believe. Perhaps Lewis can even be viewed as a sort of literary father to Pullman, and Pullman's renouncing of Lewis a classic attempt at rebellion and patricide.

2. Pullman is opposed to Lewis on matters of theology, but readers are attracted to the books for their literary merits, and ignore theology. Readers, in particular young readers, are not always sensitive to the theological subtext of a book, let alone aware of public debates conducted mainly through newspapers. The readers, in effect, do not know that they are "not supposed to" enjoy both authors.

3. Both works are of such merit that sticking points can be ignored in favor of enjoying that which is worthy in each of them.

4. Pullman's arguments are in such perfect opposition to those of Lewis that they end up like the negative space around an object in a picture, delineating the same objects. Pullman may be yang to Lewis's yin, but from the readers' perspective, each of them creates the same yin/yang pattern. None of these explanations is mutually exclusive, and indeed, I believe they all come into play, as I shall demonstrate.

The very fact that Pullman returns time after time to the matter of his loathing for the Narnia books shows that Narnia is very much on his mind—and, moreover, Narnia was on his mind at a time when he had still not completed the writing of his famous trilogy (his 1998 denouncement of Narnia preceded by two years the publication of *The Amber Spyglass*). As several reviewers have pointed out, there are some striking similarities between the Narnia books and *His Dark Materials*: both involve British children traveling between parallel worlds and encountering witches, talking animals, and other mythological creatures; in both the children play a pivotal heroic role in world-consuming battles between good and evil forces—but these general similarities are common to many novels in the genre of children's fantasy. Other similarities are more specific: of Lyra's hiding in a wardrobe at the very opening of *The Golden Compass*, critic Michael Ward wrote, "the echo of Lewis' Lucy is so loud you would think it an act of literary homage."[6]

The most telling similarities, to my mind, are neither the most general nor the superficially specific mentioned above, but are rather the choices of both authors to struggle with the same moral and religious issues through revisiting the same mythological materials. A good example of this is Lewis and Pullman's treatment of the Judeo-Christian myth of Eve and the serpent. Neither author retells the myth per se, but both authors make numerous allusions to it and place characters in situations that mirror the temptation of Eve.[7]

Treatment of the Adam and Eve myth

In the Narnia books, humans are consistently referred to as "sons of Adam" or "daughters of Eve," to distinguish them from nonhumans. That this is significant becomes evident when Aslan tells Caspian: "'You come of the Lord Adam and the Lady Eve ... and that is both honour enough to erect the head of the poorest beggar, and shame enough to bow the shoulders of the greatest emperor on earth.'"[8] Adam and Eve are the progenitors of the human race but also the committers of the Original Sin, the reason for human suffering.

A variation on the Adam and Eve story is part of the plot of *The Magician's Nephew*. Having inadvertently brought the witch Jadis to the world of Narnia in the first moments of its creation, Digory is laid a charge by Aslan: he must pick an apple from a tree in a certain garden and bring it back to Aslan, who will plant it for the protection of Narnia; thus will Digory compensate for bringing evil to Narnia. When Digory arrives at the garden, he finds the following injunction posted on the golden gates:

> Come in by the gold gates or not at all,
> Take of my fruit for others or forbear.
> For those who steal or those who climb my wall
> Shall find their heart's desire and find despair.

But Jadis the witch has entered the garden before Digory and eaten of the apples despite the injunction, and now she tempts Digory, trying to persuade him to eat of the forbidden fruit: "'Do you know what that fruit is? I will tell you. It is the apple of youth, the apple of life. I know, for I have tasted it; and I feel already such changes in myself that I know I shall never grow old and die. Eat it, Boy, eat it; and you and I will both live forever and be king and queen of this whole world.'" Digory refuses, saying, "'I'd rather live an ordinary time and die and go to Heaven,'" but the witch persists, playing on his greatest weakness—Digory's beloved mother is mortally ill: "'Do you not see, Fool, that one bite of that apple would save her? ... What would your Mother think if she knew that you *could* have taken her pain away and given her back her life and saved your Father's heart from being broken, and that you *wouldn't*?'"[9] Thus the Witch plays the serpent in Eden. Centuries later in Narnia, her successor, the Lady in the Green Kirtle, has the ability to turn into a green serpent in *The Silver Chair*.

Though Digory's test is much harder than that of Eve, for his mother's life lies in the balance, Digory, unlike Eve, does not give into temptation. He refuses to eat or steal an apple, and brings the only apple he picked to Aslan as promised. Aslan rewards him with another apple with which to save his mother's life. By remaining true to his word and obeying the injunctions laid upon him, Digory avoids the fate of Eve and does not bring upon Narnia a fall from grace; thus Narnia retains some aspects of paradise. And yet, apple or no apple, Digory has already introduced evil into Narnia in the form of the witch Jadis who followed him there; therefore Narnia is doomed to be visited by future evils.

Like Lewis, Pullman ascribes great significance to the story of Adam and Eve. According to the witches' prophecy, Lyra's secret name, "the name of her destiny" is Eve: "'She will be the mother—she will be life—mother—she will disobey.'"[10] Knowledge of this prophecy prompts the Church to send out an assassin, Father Gomez, charged with finding and killing Lyra before she brings about the fall: "'How much better for us if there had been a Father Gomez in the garden of Eden! We would never have left paradise.'"[11] Thus Lyra, formerly considered mostly a nuisance, becomes the focus and most urgent target of the war between the Kingdom of Heaven and Lord Asriel's rebel forces.

There is also a serpent in Lyra's story: the nun-turned-physicist Mary Malone, from our own world. At Lyra's prompting, Mary adapts her Oxford laboratory computer—nicknamed "the Cave" after Plato's allegory—so as to allow communication with "Shadows," conscious subparticles of dark matter. Increasingly incredulous Mary is informed by the Shadows that they are "uncountable billions" of "angels," and when she asks them about their motives and the part they played in the Garden of Eden, the Shadows lay upon her to "'Find the girl and boy. Waste no more time. You must play the serpent.'"[12] Mary follows the Shadows' instructions and finds herself in a preindustrial world peopled by the Mulefa, odd sentient beings who "look like a cross between antelopes and motorcycles" with "trunks like small elephants."[13] The Mulefa tell Mary their own version of the story of Eve and the serpent, regarding the wheel-shaped fruit of the giant trees with which the Mulefa live in symbiosis.[14] This version of the tale varies significantly from the biblical origin in that the serpent here is benign, and the contact with the fruit of knowledge is of unqualified benefit to the Mulefa race. It is a foreshadowing of the positive role that Pullman intends for Lyra and Mary as Eve and the serpent, respectively, in his restaging of the temptation of Eve.

Lyra's temptation is perhaps not as transparent as Digory's, because Mary does not persuade Lyra to eat a particular fruit. What she does instead is tell her a rather long story about how falling in love brought her to stop believing in God. Her story contains multiple subtle images of gardens and of eating sweet things.[15] Mary's story arouses in Lyra exciting physical sensations she has never felt before, and not long after, Lyra acts upon the sensations and extends the temptation to Will.[16]

Pullman is not explicit about whether 12-year-old Lyra and Will have actual sexual intercourse at this point, but the moment is clearly erotic, and the suggestion is there. Mary the serpent has seduced Lyra, Eve; Lyra in turn has seduced Will, Adam. Where Pullman's story varies most significantly from the biblical origin is, once again, in that the entire seduction is framed as a positive occurrence, and leads to extremely positive results. Following their physical interaction, such as it was, Mary notices a cessation in the disastrous migration of Dust (aka Shadows), the loss of which had been slowly but surely killing the world of the Mulefa: "The Dust pouring down from the stars had found a living home again, and these children-no-longer-children, saturated with love, were the cause of it all."[17] Rather than precipitating the downfall of mankind, Lyra and Will's love, the "knowledge" they have gained from "tasting" the forbidden fruit, has brought about salvation.

This example of the use of the Eve and the serpent myth demonstrates both the similarities and the differences between the approaches of Lewis and Pullman. Both are inspired by the biblical tale and choose to explore their own variations upon it, but while Lewis remains true to the moral framework of the original story—the belief that disobeying God and eating of the forbidden fruit was a calamitous sin—Pullman inverts this, and creates a scenario in which eating the fruit of knowledge averts calamity.

Treatment of the heaven or afterlife myth

Another such example of an issue explored extensively, and in similar fashion, by both authors, is the question of what happens to us—or to our spirit, or ghost, or immortal soul, or whatever we might call it—after we die. Both authors (even Pullman, the alleged atheist) have characters in their books travel to the realms of death, and both describe quite extensively what they see and experience there. Of all the Narnia books, *The Last Battle* is the one that has drawn the most ire from Pullman:

> One of the most vile moments in the whole of children's literature, to my mind, occurs at the end of *The Last Battle*, when Aslan reveals to

the children that "The term is over: the holidays have begun" because "There was a real railway accident. Your father and mother and all of you are—as you used to call it in the Shadowlands—dead." To solve a narrative problem by killing one of your characters is something many authors have done at one time or another. To slaughter the lot of them, and then claim they're better off, is not honest storytelling: it's propaganda in the service of life-hating ideology.[18]

Pullman is not alone in disliking *The Last Battle*: "I never could get on with *The Last Battle*," wrote Diana Wynne Jones, a master storyteller in her own right who studied under Lewis at Oxford and whose work, too, shows his influence.

> Reading as an adult, I recognized the Antichrist and the Apocalypse and too readily knew everyone was dead. But this was my nephew's favorite of them all, because—as he told me at length—it is so exciting, and, when you think everyone is dead, they all come alive again. No, not in Heaven, he insisted. For real. Well, this is the magic of the Narnia books for you.[19]

Accepting the ending of this book as a happy ending is conditional upon the ability to believe in a truer life in Heaven, a belief of which atheist Pullman seems to be incapable. Regarding Lewis's world, Pullman is in a sense rather like the Dwarfs Lewis describes in *The Last Battle*, who enter the Stable and are unable to see that they are actually in Paradise. While King Tirian and the "friends of Narnia" see around them a grove of wonderful fruit trees and above them a blue sky, the Dwarfs see nothing but darkness, and are convinced they are enclosed by walls. Aslan lays before the Dwarfs a "glorious feast" of "pies and tongues and pigeons and trifles and ices," but "it was clear that they couldn't taste it properly. They thought they were eating and drinking only the sort of things you might find in a Stable." Despondent Lucy tries to convince the Dwarfs to see the light—literally—and is answered by an angry Dwarf:

> "Well, if that doesn't beat everything! ... How *can* you go on talking all that rot? Your wonderful Lion didn't come and help you, did he? Thought not. And now—even now—when you've been beaten and shoved into this black hole, just the same as the rest of us, you're still at your old game. Starting a new lie! Trying to make us believe we're none of us shut up, and it ain't dark, and heaven knows what."

Nothing sways the Dwarfs, and at last Aslan explains to the children: "'They will not let us help them. They have chosen cunning instead of belief. Their prison is only in their own minds, yet they are in that prison, and so afraid of being taken in that they cannot be taken out.'"[20]

Pullman's Land of the Dead is the diametric opposite of Lewis's Paradise-in-a-Stable. It is a barren, colorless "prison camp," "a terrible place," "hopeless," guarded by vengeful harpies who torment the dead with reminders of their failings and failures in life. Unlike the Stable, which is a paradise to believers but a stable to unbelievers, and in which the righteous are sent into the light whereas the sinners are sent to the dark, the land of the dead is the same to all dead: "'[It] isn't a place of reward or a place of punishment. It's a place of nothing. The good come here as well as the wicked, and all of us languish in this gloom for ever, with no hope of freedom, or joy, or sleep or rest or peace.'"[21]

But Lyra has thought of a solution: Will can use his knife to cut a way out from the Land of the Dead and into another world, upon which, according to the omniscient alethiometer, all the particles of which the ghosts are composed will scatter and disperse. As one of the ghosts imagines it, "'we'll be alive again in a thousand blades of grass, and a million leaves, we'll be falling in the raindrops and blowing in the fresh breeze, we'll be glittering in the dew under the stars and moon out there in the physical world which is our true home and always was.'"[22]

Most of the dead are only too glad of this solution, and willingly follow Lyra, but one among them speaks out:

> "The Almighty has granted us this blessed place for all eternity, this para-dise, which to the fallen soul seems bleak and barren, but which the eyes of faith see as it is, overflowing with milk and honey and resounding with the sweet hymns of the angels. *This* is heaven, truly! What this evil girl promises is nothing but lies. She wants to lead you to hell! Go with her at your peril. My companions and I of the true faith will remain here in our blessed paradise, and spend eternity singing the praises of the Almighty, who has given us the judgment to tell the false from the true."[23]

On the one hand this seems the precise opposite of the scene described by Lewis: in *The Last Battle*, those who saw a prison were deluded, while those who saw heaven were seeing truly; here in Pullman's writing, those who see heaven are deluded, while those who see a prison which must be escaped are seeing truly. The oppo-sition is so perfect that one cannot help but imagine that Pullman had Lewis specifically in mind when he wrote the scene. And yet, from the perspective of a "simple" reader following plot and character as opposed to the fine points of theology, these two scenes are *exactly the same*. In each, the innocent child—Lewis's Lucy, Pullman's Lyra—wishes to lead as many souls as she can to a happy end; in each, a stubborn unbeliever refuses to go along with the child, thus punishing himself through his own disbelief. Whether the happy end is everlasting life in heaven or rejoining the cosmos and "living again" hardly seems to matter: it's mere semantics, splitting hairs. For a reader who has no vested interest in defending or attacking the Church—say, a little Jewish girl reading the books in Israel—the emotional impact of these two scenes is all but identical.

Pullman's Land of the Dead is also reminiscent of the subterranean land described in Lewis's *The Silver Chair*.[24] Escaping both lands involves several stages, the first of which is overcoming the lethargy and forgetfulness brought on by the surroundings. In *The Silver Chair*, this lethargy is the result of spells set by the Lady of the Green Kirtle, but when she attempts to enchant the travelers, Puddleglum discovers that some of her enchantment can be warded off by telling stories of the world above: "'You may have blotted it out and turned it dark like this, for all I know. Nothing is more likely. But I know I was there once. I've seen the sky full of stars. I've seen the sun coming up out of the sea in the morning and sinking behind the mountains at night. And I've seen him up in the midday sky when I couldn't look at him for brightness.'"[25] Lyra, too, discovers the power of such stories in the Land of the Dead, after her friend Roger tells her: "'There's some kids been here thousands of years. They're no older than us, and they've forgotten a whole lot. Except the sunshine. No one forgets that. And the wind.'"[26] Lyra then sets about telling the ghosts stories of "the sun and the wind and the sky, and the things they'd forgotten, such as how to play," gradually discovering that these stories also have a pacifying effect on the vicious guardian harpies. Lyra's Gallivespian escorts, Lady Salmakia and the Chevalier Tialys, negotiate with the harpies and convince them to allow the dead to leave their land in exchange for true stories told of what they have seen in their lives.[27]

Just as Jill, Eustace, Puddleglum, and Prince Rilian must then make their way up to a place where they can dig through to the surface of the world, so do Lyra, Will, and their cohort of ghosts make their way up to a place where Will will be able to cut through to another world. In both cases the path is treacherous, and they must avoid sudden changes in the landscape so as not to fall into a yawning, bottomless abyss. Just as Lyra and Will are rescuing the ghosts from their prison of gloom, so Jill and Eustace are setting free the denizens of Underland and allowing them to return to their homeland from the gloomy prison they inhabited under the Lady with the Green Kirtle. Pullman may be at cross-purposes with Lewis regarding the message he wishes to convey with his story, but the means he uses are remarkably similar.

God and Christ as literary characters

So far I have contrasted and compared the ways in which C. S. Lewis and Philip Pullman each make use of parts of the religious narrative in their works: the story of Adam and Eve, the belief in heaven and an afterlife. The two authors have also, unusually for children's fantasy, cast the actual Christian deities in their works. The books are not mere parables on religion, not allegories, but new stories in which God and Christ themselves have roles to play.

C. S. Lewis gives his readers rather broad hints about the identity shared between Aslan and Christ. In *The Voyage of the Dawn Treader*, Aslan appears before the children in the guise of a lamb, then shifts into his Lion form and tells Lucy and Edmund they will never come back to Narnia, but that they will meet him in their own world: "'there I have another name. You must learn to know me by that name. This was the very reason why you were brought to Narnia, that by knowing me here for a little, you may know me better there.'"[28] In *The Last Battle*, Lucy herself explicates: "in our world too, a Stable once had something inside it that was bigger than our whole world."[29] In case the books themselves were not hint enough for some readers, Lewis gave even broader hints that he was writing about Christ in his letters to child readers, for example in this much-quoted letter to an 11-year-old fan:

> As to Aslan's other name, well, I want you to guess. Has there ever been anyone in *this* world who (1) Arrived at the same time as Father Christmas. (2) Said he was the Son of the Great Emperor. (3) Gave himself up for someone else's fault to be jeered at and killed by wicked people. (4) Came to life again. (5) Is sometimes spoken of as a lamb."[30]

Pullman has cast in his book not the Son but the Father Himself: God, here named "The Authority," has a very small role to play in the books. He was being carried by angels as a banner or mascot in their war against Lord Asriel shortly before Lyra and Will encounter him and release him from the confines of his crystal litter.[31] Surely there could be no more pathetic a depiction of God than Pullman's, who describes the Authority as an "indescribably aged" angel of "terrifying decreptitude," lacking free will or speech, moaning, picking at himself, responding to kindness with babyish innocence and relieved to be freed of his physical existence. On first glance this would appear, again, to be the diametric opposite to Lewis's God: the unseen Emperor-Beyond-the-Sea, father of the all-powerful, all-knowing, and glorious Aslan/Christ. But is the pathetic Authority in Pullman's trilogy truly God? Some of the characters deny this: "'It shocked some of us too to learn that the Authority is not the creator. There may have been a creator, or there may not: we don't know.'" If the so-called Authority is merely an angel who "set himself above the rest of the angels," what does this make Dust (aka Shadows), which is supposedly comprised of "countless billions" of angels?[32] Dust moves the hands of the alethiometer, which can tell truths past, present, and future. Dust is a part of everything, particularly anything to do with human or nonhuman consciousness: "Dust came into being when living things became conscious of themselves; but it needed some feedback system to reinforce it and make it safe. … Without something like that, it would all vanish. Thought, imagination, feeling, would all wither and blow away, leaving nothing but a brutish automatism." While observing Dust, Mary Malone realizes: "Matter *loved* Dust. It didn't want to see it go. … Had she thought there was no meaning in life, no purpose, when God had gone? Yes, she had thought that. 'Well, there is now,' she said aloud, and again, louder: 'There is now!'"[33] Omniscient, omnipresent, essential, benevolent—I would argue that in Pullman's multiverse, Dust *is* God.

If one accepts the premise that Dust is God, Pullman's story can no longer be interpreted as a tale of a rebellion against God, but rather as a rebellion against a particular religious establishment (the Authority and his followers) acting oppressively in the name of a false God, and a return to the true God (Dust). One reviewer noted this and was disappointed:

> I discovered that these are not antireligious novels. Certainly, there are some bad Christians, but there are also a god and tons of angels. Plus, all the universes are united via a spiritual substance called Dust, … a kind of psychic life-essence that fuels angels and souls. The Dust thing really bugged me. I expect magic in fantasy worlds, but Pullman turns astrophysics into spiritual goo. It was a rhetorical move right out of Jesusland.[34]

In the Narnia chronicles, we see a similar rejection of particular religious establishments acting oppressively in the name of a false God. In *The Last Battle*, Shift the ape dresses Puzzle the simple-minded donkey in a lion skin, and parades him as Aslan, ordering atrocities to be done in Aslan's name, such as the massacre of sentient trees and enslavement of sentient beasts. Shift does all this for his personal gain, while he sits around wearing a scarlet jacket, eating the fruit of forced labor and scratching himself. He explains to the other animals that they cannot speak to Aslan directly, only through him: "'I'm so wise that I'm the only one Aslan is ever going to speak to. He can't be bothered talking to a lot of stupid animals.'"[35] This description has led several critics to a similar conclusion: "I find it hard to see the ape Shift in *The Last Battle* as anything other than a satire of Roman Catholicism in general and the papacy in particular."[36] Lewis himself acknowledged the parallel between Shift's promotion of a false Aslan and the Antichrist's promotion of a false God.[37] Whether it is specifically the Catholic Church which Lewis is targeting with his portrayal of Shift, or some other church or interpretation of Christianity, he is clearly not attacking Aslan, Christ, or God themselves: "if any man do a cruelty in my name, then, though he says the name Aslan, it is Tash whom he serves and by Tash his deed is accepted"[38] (Tash being for all intents and purposes the Narnian equivalent of Satan).

Thus, though Pullman is more focused on tearing down the false Church than Lewis is, both writers are motivated by an essentially religious belief in a divinity above and beyond the Church, whether that divinity be a patriarchal entity such as Aslan (or his father), or an amorphous, plural, omniscient/omnipresent *something* such as the Dust. Lewis does not refrain from criticizing the Church in his books, nor are Pullman's books devoid of divine intervention. A conflict between Pullman and Lewis might be perceived if one were to take at face value that the character of the Authority in Pullman's books is meant to be God; but if one realizes that, rather, the feeble Authority is much more like the donkey Puzzle—an impostor God like the phony Aslan—then Pullman and Lewis's worldviews are much more in line with each other.

How prominent is Christian symbolism?

Returning to my original points about the similarities between *The Chronicles of Narnia* and *His Dark Materials*, I believe I have demonstrated amply that Pullman's writing is very much in the tradition of Lewis, as far as influences, imagery, and devices are concerned. On matters theological, Pullman and Lewis are like two fish arguing the nature of water: they may seem to be in conflict with each other, but to the eyes of a nonaquatic creature, they are actually quite similar. As Annalee Newitz put it, "Perhaps the West is so steeped in Christian mythology that we can't imagine an outside to Christianity."[39] People who don't care very much or are not knowledgeable about the fine points of Christian theology would need to have the differences between Pullman and Lewis explained to them, whereas the literary similarities of plot and style are much easier to appreciate.

In fact, it is quite possible to read the Narnia books without being at all aware of the Christian allusions within the text. This was demonstrated for me quite neatly in the discussions that developed on my blog when I wrote about a new translation of *The Lion, the Witch and the Wardrobe* into Hebrew. Roni, an educated, erudite novelist and a mother of several well-read children, wrote the following: "I read this book once when I was very young and again as a teenager, and when I discovered—I was quite grown up by then—that people claim this is a Christian book, I was stunned. Aslan as Jesus? Jesus!"[40] Tali, an educator and reviewer of children's books, responded: "Jewish children growing up in Israel can't decipher the proselytizing of the Christian symbolism in the book and so perhaps will be less disturbed by it." A few days later, Tali watched the film version of *The Lion, the Witch and the Wardrobe* in a cinema, and returned to the blog to add the following comment:

> After stating my educated opinion that the Christian clues in the books won't spoil the fun for Jewish children, because they'll be understood only by those in the know who are sensitive to hidden Christian symbolism, along come the great and mighty Disney studios and stick Santa Claus in Narnia! The actual Santa Claus! ... Spoon-feeding the message is one thing, did they have to chew it up for us first?

Tali had simply blocked out the presence of Father Christmas in the book. She had to go back and reread the chapter before she was convinced that Father Christmas was not a Disney addition, upon which she returned to the blog for a third time and wrote: "How embarrassing! I was convinced the gifts had been given to them by Aslan, and was quite annoyed to see Santa in the film ... *Mea culpa*, I take back what I wrote and am quite disappointed. To think I had claimed that the Christian messages remain on a complex symbolic level!"[41] I believe this example proves that even the most sophisticated reader, exposed to the Narnia books as a child, can enjoy them purely on the level of story, ignoring Christian symbolism to the point of *actively blocking out* memories of explicit Christian references.

Conclusion

The Narnia books are enjoyed by children of different religions from all over the world. In the film version of *The Golden Compass*, all references to the Church are replaced with references to the Authority, and yet the story works. It is on the level of *story* that these books—both the Narnia series and the *His Dark Materials* trilogy—work their magic most powerfully, especially when the readers are children. The talking animals, the witches, the travel between worlds (some young, some dying), the plucky children sticking up for their friends in the face of great powers, the adventure, the suspense, the heroism—these common elements by far outweigh whatever philosophical differences Pullman might think he has with Lewis. Anti-Lewis or not, Philip Pullman's *His Dark Materials* is successful primarily because of Pullman's skills as a storyteller, regardless of his religious beliefs. And it is as a storyteller than Pullman owes a certain debt to Lewis, like it or not.

Notes

1. Philip Pullman, "The Dark Side of Narnia," *Cumberland River Lamp Post*, September 2, 2001: www.crlamppost.org/darkside.htm (accessed May 15, 2011).
2. Peter Hitchens, "This is the Most Dangerous Author in Britain" *Mail on Sunday*, January 27, 2002: 63: http://home.wlv.ac.uk/~bu1895/hitchens.htm (accessed May 15, 2011); Hitchens, "A Labour of Loathing," *Spectator.co.uk*, January 18, 2003: www.spectator.co.uk/-spectator/thisweek/10760/part_3/a-labour-of-loathing.thtml (accessed 15 May 2011).
3. It can hardly be a coincidence that Hitchens' own 2009 book about what he sees as the decline of British society is called *The Broken Compass* and bears a striking visual resemblance to some editions of Pullman's *The Golden Compass*.
4. "The Big Read" 2003: www.bbc.co.uk/arts/bigread/top100.shtml (accessed May 15, 2011).
5. C. S. Lewis, *Mere Christianity*, in *The Complete C. S. Lewis Signature Classics* (San Francisco, CA: HarperSanFrancisco, 2002): 47.
6. Michael Ward, "C. S. Lewis and Philip Pullman," *Mars Hill Review* 21 (2003): www.planetnarnia.com (accessed May 15, 2011).
7. It is noteworthy that both authors in doing so allude also to Milton's *Paradise Lost*, about which Lewis wrote *A Preface to Paradise Lost* (1941) based on a series of lectures he gave on Milton's theology, and from which Pullman drew the name and motto for his trilogy: "Unless the almighty maker them ordain / His dark materials to create more worlds"

(*Paradise Lost*, Book II, qtd. in *The Golden Compass*). An examination of Lewis and Pullman's different approaches to Milton would no doubt yield fascinating results, but it is outside the scope of what I hope to achieve here.

8. C. S. Lewis, *Prince Caspian* (London: Penguin, 1965): 185.
9. C. S. Lewis, *The Magician's Nephew* (London: Penguin, 1965): 146, 150, 150–1.
10. Philip Pullman, *The Subtle Knife* (London: Scholastic UK, 2007): 313.
11. Philip Pullman, *The Amber Spyglass* (London: Scholastic UK, 2000): 75.
12. *The Subtle Knife*: 249.
13. *The Amber Spyglass*: 445–6.
14. *Ibid.*: 236–7.
15. *Ibid.*: 467–8.
16. *Ibid.*: 491–2.
17. *Ibid.*: 497.
18. Pullman: "The Dark Side of Narnia."
19. Diana Wynne Jones, "The Magic of Narnia," Amazon.com, 2000: www.amazon.com/exec/obidos/tg/feature/-/91955/103-7685759-6425428 (accessed May 15, 2011).
20. C. S. Lewis, *The Last Battle* (London: Penguin, 1965): 135, 133, 135.
21. *The Amber Spyglass*: 336.
22. *Ibid.*: 336.
23. *Ibid.*: 336–7.
24. Which, in turn, seems clearly inspired by George McDonald's underground kingdom in *The Princess and the Goblin*.
25. C. S. Lewis, *The Silver Chair* (London: Penguin, 1965): 152.
26. *The Amber Spyglass*: 328.
27. This is a scene modeled after Orestes' negotiation with the Furies in Aeschylus's classic play, *The Eumenides*.
28. C. S. Lewis, *The Voyage of the Dawn Treader* (London: Penguin, 1965): 209.
29. *The Last Battle*: 128.
30. C. S. Lewis, *Letters to Children* ed. Lyle W. Dorsett and Marjorie Lamp Mead (New York: Touchstone, 1995): 32.
31. *The Amber Spyglass*: 432.
32. *Ibid.*: 221, 222, 249.
33. *Ibid.*: 476.
34. Annalee Newitz, "The Anti-Christian Mythology of Philip Pullman," *AlterNet*, January 23, 2007: www.alternet.org/story/47131/ (accessed May 15, 2011).
35. *The Last Battle*: 32.
36. John J. Miller, "Back to Narnia, Harry Potter's Mother Country," *National Review*, July 8, 2005: www.freerepublic.com/focus/f-news/1440224/posts (accessed May 15, 2011).
37. *Letters to Children*: 93.

38. *The Last Battle*: 149.
39. Newitz.
40. Roni [Roni Gelbfish], "Re: *The Lion, the Witch and the Wardrobe*," December 19, 2005: http://gilibarhillel.wordpress.com עוד דף אחד ודי My translation (accessed May 15, 2011).
41. Tali [Tali Kochavi], "Re: The Lion, the Witch and the Wardrobe," December 19, 24, 27, 2005: http://gilibarhillel.wordpress.com עוד דף אחד ודי My translation (accessed May 15, 2011).

9

"Beautiful Barbarians": Anti-Racism in *The Horse and His Boy* and Other *Chronicles of Narnia*

Jennifer Taylor

In a chapter called "Garlic and Onions," Laura Miller observes that in Britain, garlic is often perceived as "the symbol of the dirty foreigner." She asserts, "Lewis expected his description of the Calormenes and their reek of onions and garlic to provoke an unthinking disgust in his readers."[1] Miller's remarks typify current discourse on *The Chronicles of Narnia*. Since at least the late 1990s, scholars, critics, and the general public have steadily discussed the apparent racism in the stories. Critics have focused largely on *The Horse and His Boy* and *The Last Battle* because these books carry detailed descriptions of the Calormenes, a desert-dwelling people who "are the archenemies of the free Narnians."[2]

For the most part, charges of racism fall under the broad umbrella of racial ethnocentrism, which is the "belief in the superiority of one's own ethnic group."[3] Critics alternate between denouncing the scientific theories driving this racism and censoring the social prejudices that result from them. For example, John Goldthwaite attacks the science-driven theory of Nordic Supremacy, commenting that the Narnia books are full of "the gospel of Northernness."[4] Gregg Easterbrook calls Lewis's imaginary world a place where "Brits must rule"[5] while David Holbrook writes that the *Chronicles* encourage "racism, antiSemitism [*sic*], legitimized war against 'gooks,' [where] the 'enemy' is hardly human."[6] Philip Pullman has stated that in Lewis, "light coloured people are better than dark coloured people," and Kyrie O'Connor writes, "Swarthy, freedom-hating Calormenes versus light-skinned, freedom-loving Narnians—which would you like better?"[7] Constance Classen sees the "stereotype of the fragrant foreigner" in *The Horse and His Boy*,[8] while Andrew Blake, Philip Hensher, and Tessa Laird, and Victor Watson find in it a "demonization of Islam."[9] Even some of Lewis's defenders, like Paul Ford, Kathryn Lindskoog, and David C. Downing,[10] apologize for what seems to be "cultural blindness."[11]

To assume Lewis had racist leanings is certainly logical. Lewis was born during the height of the British Empire's power. Racist stereotyping of Middle Eastern peoples would have been part of the culture, partly because of the traditional rivalry between Europe and the Ottoman Empire, and partly because this rivalry materialized into real war during this era. Further, Lewis wrote *The Chronicles of Narnia* at the start of the British Empire's decline when, piece by piece, various colonies began to win their independence, starting with India in 1947. Nostalgia could conceivably tempt anyone during these times to resent once-subjugated peoples and to view this attitude as patriotic. In any case, one underlying assumption commonly made is that "Lewis was a man of his time and socioeconomic class"[12] and could not help but soak in the racial-supremacist attitudes of his era.

However, not everyone agrees that the *Chronicles* support and promote racism. For example, Nelson and Downing effectively produce evidence to demonstrate that the Calormene religion does not resemble Islam, that "every objectionable trait associated with the Calormenes can easily be found in Lewis's source materials, which arose among Middle Easterners themselves,"[13] that some of the Calormenes are heroes in the stories, and that Lewis presents many "races" such as "fauns, naiads, centaurs, satyrs, … giants, … [and] dwarfs" that can "live together, work together, and, when necessary, fight side by side for the good."[14] Alan Jacobs and Elizabeth Baird Hardy believe that the Calormenes are not racial stereotypes at all, but instead represent traditional literary figures.[15] However, both sides have at times seemed less concerned about the fiction than about Lewis himself and whether he was racist or not. Neither side has examined racial elements for their thematic purpose in the books. Perhaps it is time to broaden the discussion to examine what purpose, other than racism, Lewis could have had when he included racial references in his children's fiction, and to do so within the framework of his other writings and the history of racist thought. Although racial references abound in the *Chronicles,* most notably in *The Last Battle* and *The Horse and His Boy*, overall these elements work together to expose and condemn offensive racial viewpoints.

White skin, black skin, and Platonic forms: does physical appearance reflect inner character?

Platonism undergirded the earliest seeds of scientific racism. Jonathan Marks explains that "early taxonomic practice relied on an intellectual framework that was largely intact since the time of the ancient Greeks. Real, existing creatures, human or otherwise, were considered to be deviants or degenerates from an ideal form, whose true nature was perfect, transcendent, and otherworldly."[16] For example, Linnaeus described Europeans as "white, hearty, muscular, [having] long blond hair [and] blue eyes." He did not base his description on observation. Rather, these details were meant to reflect the European's basic nature: "sensitive, very smart, creative [and] ruled by law." Other races were assigned negative traits: laziness, greed, indiscipline, slyness, and rule by caprice.[17] According to C. Loring Brace, a later scientist named Samuel George Morton arranged the races in a hierarchy of better to worse. His chart was meant to reflect "the differences in innate capabilities and 'worth' that characterized his various 'races.'"[18] Unfortunately, "because the attributes of [a people group] were Platonic essences taken to be inscribed in the very cores of the people in question ... it did not much matter what an individual representative looked like or acted like."[19] With the authority of science backing these ideas, it became common to uncritically assign character traits to people based upon their racial classification.[20] Because the Narnian heroes have white skin and their Calormene enemies have dark skin in the *Chronicles*, it is tempting to think that Lewis has created two races and that their physical appearances symbolize their moral character.

Clearly Lewis has set up a division between Narnia, which is inhabited by clean, white European humans, and Calormen, which is filled with swarthy, dirty, garlicky citizens. The Narnians are the heroes while the Calormenes are the liars, slave traders, and colonizers. However, Lewis demonstrates that he knows how black and white symbolism will come across and how to identify racist stereotyping. He writes, "Some readers, seeing (and disliking) [Tolkien's] rigid demarcation of black and white, imagine they have seen a rigid demarcation between black and white people. ... [But] motives, even on the right side, are mixed."[21] Furthermore, in a letter to Arthur Greeves, Lewis complains about bogey villains in literature. He abominates "put[ting] absolutely *all* the right, with no snags or reservations, on the side of the hero ... and all the wrong on the side of the villain." In the same letter, Lewis condemns a "fixed hatred" of opponents that causes a person to think of "the enemy" as "unredeemed black."[22] Given Lewis's awareness of

racial stereotyping and his opinions about how to present a moral
world in fiction, it is unlikely that light-skinned Narnians embody
unblemished righteousness or dark Calormenes pure evil.

Rather, in *The Horse and His Boy*, the light and dark skin types of
the characters reflect the racist manner in which both Narnians and
Calormenes view each other. Racial xenophobia exists on both sides.
Though some Calormenes find Narnians physically attractive, others
see whiteness as a deformity; either way, it always symbolizes evil.
The Tarkaan Anradin states that the Narnians are "cursed but beautiful barbarians who inhabit the remote north."[23] Lasaraleen quali-
fies his words, stating, "The Narnian *men* are lovely,"[24] but "Narnia
[is] a country of perpetual snow and ice inhabited by demons and
sorcerers."[25] She finds Narnians' maleness, not their color, attractive;
otherwise whiteness retains its associations with demonic evil. When
the Narnian royals arrive in Tashbaan, criers make way for them
through the streets crying, "Way! Way! Way! … for the White Barbarian
King, the guest of the Tisroc."[26] Instead of saying, "make way for King
Peter," the criers suppress his individual name and emphasize his skin
color and the traits of fierceness and brutality that whiteness symbolizes for them. Like Lasaraleen, Rabadash refers to whiteness as a curse
on Nature when he says, "the ice and snow have vanished, so that
Narnia is now wholesome [and ripe for our exploitation]."[27] But the
Tisroc argues that the curse goes deeper than whiteness. He believes
"the High King of Narnia is supported by a demon of hideous aspect
and irresistible maleficence [*sic*] who appears in the shape of a Lion."[28]
Overall, the Calormenes associate whiteness with evil enchantment
and believe the people who have white skin are barbaric.

Similarly, many citizens of Narnia see dark skin as the Calormenes'
chief trait. Narnian racism is most blatant against the Calormenes in
The Last Battle. Much of it is in the mouths of the evil characters such
as the treacherous group of dwarfs who refer to the Calormenes as
"Darkies"[29] and the ape Shift who refers to them as "our dark-faced
friends."[30] But even the heroes are guilty of it. King Tirian refers
to a Calormene messenger as "that dark Man with the beard,"[31]
and he murders two Calormenes rashly, in anger. When a group of
Calormene workmen bind him up for this violence, he sees them
as a pack of "dark men … smelling of garlic and onions, their white
eyes flashing dreadfully in their brown faces."[32] Similarly, during the
last great battle, Eustace sees the enemy not as soldiers but as a "line
of dark-faced bright-eyed men."[33] After the fighting, Jill and Eustace
patronizingly perceive Emeth, a noble Calormene soldier, as "rather
beautiful in the dark, haughty, Calormene way."[34] Even King Edmund

is guilty of racial rhetoric. In *The Horse and His Boy*, he refers to Prince Rabadash, with some irony, as "this dark-faced lover of yours."[35]

Throughout these stories, Lewis challenges his characters' views of the "white barbarians" and the "dark men." For example, Tirian, Eustace, and Jill learn from Emeth that Aslan has accepted him as an equal with them into the Real Narnia. Tirian's rash violence toward Calormenes permanently costs him a throne. In *The Horse and His Boy,* Aravis, a dark-skinned Calormene, and Shasta, a white-skinned slave, are forced to travel together and defend each other. Though their class differences make their friendship unlikely, during the journey each learns to see the other as an equally valuable fellow human being. In the same story, King Lune reproaches King Edmund when he fails to show Prince Rabadash, his mortal enemy, courtesy. And Prince Rabadash learns that his "white" enemies can be noble-hearted when the King of Archenland extends mercy to him instead of the execution he has merited. At first, the Tarkaan Anradin seems to betray the author's racialist assumption that darker-skinned people will find light-skinned ones attractive, yet not all Calormenes do so, and Shasta's marriage to Aravis demonstrates that the attraction can work both ways. Overall, most of the heroes are Narnian and "white," but some of the major villains, notably the White Witch, are white too. Good and evil are mixed within groups and even within single characters. Color imagery supports the idea that vice and virtue are not tied to race.

But, most importantly, Lewis overturns the Platonic basis for racial hierarchy through the character of Aslan. Like the nature of any Platonic Ideal, the nature of Aslan the Great Lion is "perfect, transcendent, and otherworldly."[36] The fact that he is a beast illustrates that the relationship between physical appearance and moral excellence is completely arbitrary. Not one of the other "good" *dramatis personae* resembles a lion at all. This ideal character also functions as the norm; his viewpoint and actions are the measuring stick against which every other character is judged. One scene in *The Last Battle* dramatically illustrates his role. When the residents of the Narnian world, including animals and mythic creatures, pass through the stable door to be judged by him alone, all must look him "straight in his face." Those who look at him in "fear and hatred" pass "into his huge black shadow", but those who look on him in love "[come] in at the Door … on Aslan's right."[37] Significantly, some Narnians end up in the shadow, proving that who you love and serve matters more than where you were born or even what color and shape you possess. Because Aslan is the final measure of all creatures, no other character can be regarded as a completely perfect example, and, as we have seen, Lewis does not shirk from representing racism in supposedly "good" people. As the norm, Aslan provides a model for how to treat people of different appearance and background. He extends an offer of pardon to both Edmund in *The Lion, the Witch and the Wardrobe* and to Rabadash in *The Horse and His Boy*. He welcomes both Narnians and Calormenes into the Real Narnia. He protects both white-skinned Shasta and dark-skinned Aravis as they journey toward a safe haven. Narnian or Calormene, light or dark makes no difference to him.

North and South: the spiritual sins that lead to physical slavery

However, critics of *The Chronicles of Narnia* have also noted the presence of a more recent development in scientific racism: Nordic Supremacy. The idea of a superior northern race took hold after Count Arthur de Gobineau published his revolutionary analysis of civilization, *Essay on the Inequality of the Human Race* (1854). In this work, Gobineau argues that "the white intellect is higher than the black or yellow, and … within the white race, the Aryans are the intellectually superior subrace."[38] Within 20 years, this theory of racial hierarchy had taken root and blossomed. Jacques Barzun describes the Nordic racialist mindset pervasive "from 1870 to 1914," as "the notion of a superior Anglo-Saxon race of which Britain England produced the fine flower. The decadence of France, Italy, and Spain [i.e. of southern nations] was contrasted with the political and economic success of the Teutonic sister-nations, England and Germany."[39] During the 1930s and 1940s, the Nazi regime adopted "the doctrines of human progress culminating in the Nordic race … that had been promoted for decades in the name of science"[40] and joined these to the popular theory of eugenics.[41] From their point of view, encouraging the reproduction of Aryans and exterminating the unfit was a duty toward humanity. Born in 1898, Lewis grew up in this milieu, and for some people it seems only natural that his fiction would reflect prejudices he learned in his formative years.

There can be no doubt that Lewis uses imagery that smacks of Nordic racialism. For one thing, the North acts as both a geographical and a political rallying point for Narnian characters. In *The Horse and His Boy*, Narnians constantly cry out, "Narnia and the North!" as their spur to heroic action. The horse, Bree, talks proudly about good blood and "true northern stock."[42] He says the Calormenes use "slaves' and fools' talk" and "southern jargon,"[43] and "an hour's life [in Narnia] is better than a thousand years in Calormen."[44] However, evidence in Lewis's other fiction contradicts the idea that any earthbound "race," especially the British, is intrinsically superior to any other. For example, the three "races" on Malacandra in *Out of the Silent Planet* do not rule one another. Ransom is continually surprised by this reality, thinking that surely the sorns must rule the hrossa and the pfifltriggi because they are "the intelligentsia." Later, he discovers that all three "races" obey one supernatural being named Oyarsa who has "no death and no young."[45] Outside of this creature, no group has any authority over the others, and there is no hierarchy within kinds; each group is highly intelligent yet uniquely so. In *That Hideous Strength*, Dimble explains what is wrong with viewing one's own nation as special in some way from all the others. He says, "There's no special privilege for England—no nonsense about a chosen nation. ... If one is thinking simply of goodness in the abstract, one soon reaches the fatal idea of something standardised—some common kind of life to which all nations ought to progress."[46] Moreover, the scientists who plan to exterminate the population of Malacandra to make living room for humans end up either thrown into hell or buried alive.[47] Incidentally, Bree in *The Horse and His Boy* learns not to be proud of his northern racial identity. He enters Narnia only after his pride in being Narnian has been rebuked. Shasta admits that the North is not quite the paradise he has been anticipating. In Calormen he thinks of the Narnians as paragons,[48] but later he says, "Most remarkable people, but I can't say I feel quite at home with them yet. I say, Aravis, there are going to be a lot of things to get used to in these Northern countries."[49]

Why then, does Lewis employ such distinctive North/South geographical imagery in the *Chronicles*? One explanation is that, in Lewis's fiction, North often represents the spiritual sins in human character, including pride. For example, Paul Ford explains that "the two railways [in *Pilgrim's Regress*], one from the north (the region of the mind) and one from the south (the region of the body), are the devil's routes into 'the country of Man's Soul.'"[50] Lewis gives greater detail in *Mere Christianity* when he writes, "There are two things inside me competing with the human self which I must try to become. ... They are the Animal self, and the Diabolical self." The Animal self includes the physical appetites, but the Diabolical self involves intellectual sins: "the pleasure of putting other people in the wrong, of bossing and patronising and spoiling sport, and back-biting, the pleasures of power, [and] of hatred".[51] In the *Chronicles*, the directions of "North" and "South" represent two types of tyranny.

Through the White Queen and the Tisroc, Lewis demonstrates that pride and greed both lead to slavery.

To begin with, the wicked rulers of Narnia and Calormen embody both types of vice. For example, the Tisroc, who rules the southern country of Calormen, in many ways represents an extreme of the visceral appetites. Aravis notices that "the least of the jewels with which he [is] covered [is] worth more than all the clothes and weapons of the Narnian lords put together," [and] "[his clothes seem] … a mass of frills and pleats and bobbles and buttons and tassels."[52] Later, he orders the third cook executed when he experiences indigestion, showing that he thinks of other people as tools to feed his physical comfort. Using him as their moral guide, his nobles echo his values by enslaving others to serve their every whim.[53] As Lasaraleen says, "'It must be right if *he's* going to do it!'"[54] By contrast, Narnia's recently deposed invader, the White Witch, represents the diabolical sins of the North, notably pride, hatred, and spoiling all growth and happiness.[55] Her removal from power is so recent that the Calormenes still think of Narnia as "a country of perpetual snow and ice."[56] During her repressive rule, "it is always winter … and never Christmas."[57] Her subjects, even the loyal ones, are her slaves. When her driver remarks that her sleigh can go no further, she shouts, "'Are you my councillor or my slave? … Do as you're told.'"[58] The only proper response to her demands is, "'I hear and obey, O Queen.'"[59] She calls the squirrels' Christmas feast "'gluttony … waste … [and] self indulgence.'"[60] She believes in her own supreme power, even over Aslan. When faced with his return she scoffs, "'There need be no flying. … Have I not still my wand? Will not their ranks turn into stone even as they come on?'"[61]

However, as in his use of white and dark imagery, Lewis does not engage in crass stereotyping with North and South. Though dominated by one vice or the other, both rulers are a mixture of intellectual and physical sins. As Lewis himself observed, "Opposite evils, far from balancing, aggravate each other" and are usually found together.[62] No simple glutton, the Tisroc also hungers for power. He states that all other loves are as hate compared to how he loves "the glory and strength of [his] throne"[63] and that he cannot rest at night because "Narnia is still free."[64] Lewis writes, "Power is what Pride really enjoys: there is nothing makes a man feel so superior to others as being able to move them about like toy soldiers."[65] Likewise, visceral appetites coexist with cerebral ones in frozen Narnia. The Witch knows that combined pride and greed can act as a powerful weapon. She tempts Edmund through his greed for Turkish Delight as well as through his selfish desire to rule over his siblings. After the thaw, other "animal" appetites become apparent in Narnia. For example, the woodland creatures, on hearing of Rabadash's invasion, almost cannot be bothered to sound an alarm because they have grown lazy. As the narrator relates, "In that golden age when the Witch and the Winter had gone ... the smaller woodland people of Narnia were so safe and happy that they were getting a little careless."[66] Ultimately, in *The Last Battle*, irresponsibility has spread to the Narnian throne so that the ape Shift easily usurps control of the country by producing a fake Aslan figure. The government is so lax that the citizens turn to the first person who shows organizational skills. But Shift only wants power and luxury. Narnians, once oppressed by pride under the White Witch, are now sold into slavery by a Narnian ruler consumed by his physical appetites and by commercial greed.[67] He, in turn, becomes dominated by Rishdah Tarkaan and Ginger, who seek supreme political and religious power. King Tirian and the small band still loyal to freedom and justice are routed and killed. When it is clear that Narnia has rejected justice in favor of greed and pride, Aslan rescues the few loyal to his ways and then covers war-torn Narnia with all-encompassing ice, physically symbolizing the spiritual death its citizens have chosen.[68]

Clearly, the North in *The Chronicles of Narnia* is no unblemished ideal. It does not signify either moral or physical superiority as it does in Nordic racialist thought. Further, the mingling of superior with inferior people has nothing to do with the destruction of civilization. Instead, the country falls to two reprehensible groups dominated by vice. The stories demonstrate that intellectual and physical vices can overrun any person or any group of people. Interestingly, Lewis does not associate spirituality with asceticism. Citizens of Narnia, during brief and fragile periods of allegiance to Aslan, enjoy the freedoms of feasting, growing, and learning in an environment of peace and justice. Lewis writes that "with both the 'North' and the 'South' a man has ... only one concern—to avoid them and hold the Main Road. ... We were made to be neither cerebral men nor visceral men, but Men. Not beasts nor angels but Men—things at once rational and animal."[69]

Colonialism and orientalism: some social critiques

From the imagery of black, white, North, and South, it seems clear that Lewis intentionally exploited common stereotypes in order to criticize the foundations upon which racism is built.[70] However, he does not stop with the foundations. Like other writers and thinkers of the colonizing and decolonizing eras, he critiques the cultural effects of racism and colonial ideology.[71]

One way Lewis questions racist colonial thinking is through role reversal. During the colonial era, the assumed childishness and help-lessness of so-called inferior races led to the idea of "the White Man's Burden," or the concept that it is the white man's moral duty to conquer and rule over those who, by virtue of their ordained inferior-ity, cannot peaceably rule themselves in a civilized manner. However, in *The Horse and His Boy*, Aravis and Shasta reverse typical race roles of colonial-era fiction. Dark-skinned Aravis is a smart, independent noblewoman. Shasta, the white boy, is the flunkey. Shasta eventually inherits the throne of Archenland, and as a prince his character is all the better for his having spent time as a slave. He says to Aravis, "I do hope you won't think I'm got up like this ... to try to impress you or make out that I'm different or any rot of that sort. Because I'd far rather have come in my old clothes, but they're burnt now."[72] Upon finding out he is heir to the throne, he says, "Oh dear ... I don't want to at all. And Corin—I am most dreadfully sorry. I never dreamed my turning up was going to chisel you out of your kingdom."[73] His background has left him with no sense of entitlement. Additionally, the story does not present the eventual "natural" subjugation of nonwhite races. Though Shasta eventually assumes his rightful place on the throne and Aravis eventually marries him, it is clear from the text that she is not subdued into a "proper place" for a dark-skinned person. She is never made a servant and even when married, there is no sense of her white-skinned husband ruling over her, of her being forced to marry, or of her being "tamed." Lewis writes, "Aravis also had many quarrels (and, I'm afraid even fights) with [Shasta], but they always made it up again: so that years later, when they were grown up they were so used to quarrelling and making it up again that they got married so as to go on doing it more conveniently. ... They made a good King and Queen of Archenland."[74]

Lewis also uses role reversal with countries to examine the cultural and economic problems caused by colonization. Throughout the novels, the country of Calormen appears as a powerful empire. For example, the men of the country are all-powerful, controlling the government, their slaves, and their women; in Calormen, Aravis has no choice about whom she will marry. The nation also has land armies that are "wonderfully trained"[75] and an emperor who schemes to increase his territory. To the Calormenes, Narnia is the "idle, disordered, and unprofitable" land that is "inhabited by demons." The little country needs a strong government to harness its "wholesome, fruitful, and delicious" resources.[76] Narnia offends the Calormenes because it is not under its control. Because Narnia is free, "it is an unseemly blot on the skirts of [their] empire."[77] Through Calormen's invasion plan, Lewis demonstrates that colonial ambitions foster treachery and unnecessary war. Rabadash proposes an attack on a mutual ally, Archenland, to draw the army away from Cair Paravel. He reasons, "'They are at peace with us and unprepared and I shall take Anvard before they have bestirred themselves.'"[78] This first time the Tisroc tries to annex Narnia, a runaway girl and an escaped slave defeat the military might of Calormen—a rather humiliating irony. But as the last days of Narnia reveal, commercial ambitions also lead to national problems. The second time the Calormenes invade, smaller and weaker Narnia invites them. Shift the ape makes a commercial expansion agreement with them that allows them to cut down the Narnian forests for logs.[79] Through his phony Aslan, he orders the holy trees cut down for logging, thus "murdering the dryads" who live in them and providing an excuse for the Calormenes to press the Talking Horses into slavery.[80] When Shift turns to drinking, the Calormene captain Rishdah takes over the government with Ginger the cat. These two villains suppress all freedom of speech and religion, executing anyone who dares to challenge their authority. Through role reversal, Lewis does not merely imply that rulers of any color, especially white ones, should develop a suitable degree of humility by imagining what it is like to be in the place of those they oppress. He also directly attacks the hypocrisy of foreign policies that produce slaves and grub for profit in the name of spreading civilization and order. By allowing commercial interests to be a direct cause of both Narnia and Calormen's destruction, he demonstrates that exploiting people and natural resources eventually brings about the downfall of nations.

But even though exploitation is condemned in *The Chronicles of Narnia*, the apparent stereotyping of the Middle East in the books jars strangely with the themes of anti-colonization, anti-imperialism, and anti-slavery. By endowing Calormen with an Arabian Nights flavor and by projecting the disagreeable colonial qualities of the West onto it, Lewis opens himself up to the charge of Orientalism. This by-product of racist colonial thinking views all the cultures of the Middle and Far East as "the Orient." Bari and Eaglestone explain that in the process of affirming itself the West romanticizes the East, exploits it as an "imaginative resource," and casts onto it "the rejected image of itself."[81] By employing Oriental stereotypes, Lewis seems to be guilty of undermining his own cultural critique.

However, a closer look at the world of the *Chronicles* reveals that Narnians and Calormenes are ethnically the same. Both groups are descendants of the same two people: King Frank and Queen Helen of Narnia. According to the "Outline of Narnian History So Far As It Is Known" drawn up for Walter Hooper, Calormen was established in the year 204 by "certain outlaws from Archenland" who escaped "across the Southern desert and set up the new kingdom of Calormen." All Archenlanders are descended from "Prince Col, younger son of K[ing] Frank V of Narnia" and his "followers" who travel "into Archenland (not then inhabited)" and establish that kingdom in the year 180.[82] Frank V is presumably a direct descendant of Frank I and Queen Helen, whom Aslan transported from England where they used to be a cockney cab driver and his wife. This family tree illustrates that both Narnians and Calormenes are ethnically English.[83] These facts would not be obvious to a casual reader of the *Chronicles*. However, they at least demonstrate that Lewis did not consciously project negative Western ideology onto an Eastern people and that he thought of Narnians and Calormenes as one "race."

Furthermore, he encourages his readers to accept foreigners as brothers. Several studies have pointed out that racism against Jews and other nonwhite peoples has persisted in Christian theology throughout the twentieth century.[84] In portraying an Arabian Nights type of kingdom along with negative cultural markers like garlic and onions, Lewis leads readers from the prejudices that they may bring with them to a place where they can acknowledge the equal worth of Westerners and non-Westerners. For example, in the final book in the series, garlic and onions are no longer a symbol of dirt and foreignness. When talking dogs detect Emeth beyond the stable door because of how he smells, they identify him as Calormene, but the smell is no longer repulsive and he is no longer an outsider. He is on the threshold of the Real Narnia and he belongs there along with all the things that distinguish him from Narnians. When the dogs tell King Peter about him, Peter says, "Whether he meets us in peace or war, he shall be welcome."[85] By the time Peter and his friends find Emeth, Aslan has already greeted him with the words, "Son, thou art welcome."[86] Through Emeth, Lewis suggests that members of nonwhite and non-European cultures will make it to heaven on equal footing and will have no need to be wiped clean or made more presentable.

However, there is no doubt that Lewis romanticizes the East and plunders it for "imaginative resources." Critics have noted how Lewis deliberately mythologizes the East through the Calormenes. Downing points out that Aslan's name and many details of Tashbaan come from Lane's *Arabian Nights*. He cites

> narrow, walled streets ... with wealthy nobles and their viziers carried on litters, forcing their way through the crowds. ... In several stories, slaves, or even wives, are whipped for real or imagined offenses. In one story a man is punished by being transformed into a donkey . ... [The] voluminous notes also describe the extensive burial grounds outside an Arabian city in terms similar to those Lewis uses to describe the tombs where Shasta spends the night. ... In many ways, the exotic scenes of Calormen re-present the *Arabian Nights*, transposed into the world of the chronicles.[87]

Alan Jacobs says "the Calormenes ... are but slightly disguised versions of the ravaging Turk who filled the nightmares of European children for more than half a millennium—but whose 'exotic' culture ... had also been an endless source of fascinated delight."[88] Elizabeth Baird Hardy agrees that "[The Calormenes] are traditional literary antagonists for Western knights,"[89] and Mervyn Nicholson writes that the Calormene religion has aspects of Babylonian lore in it. He compares Tash to the god Nisroch who also appears in an E. Nesbit story.[90] In *The Horse and His Boy*, Lewis heightens the exotic nature of Calormene culture when he describes the food and the architecture. Whereas in Narnia Shasta eats "bacon and eggs and mushrooms ... coffee ... hot milk ... toast ... [and] butter,"[91] in Tashbaan he samples "lobsters, and salad, and snipe stuffed with almonds and truffles ... and every kind of nice thing that can be made with ice."[92] As he and his companions enter Tashbaan, they see "balconies, deep archways, pillared colonnades, spires, battlements, minarets, [and] pinnacles." These are surrounded by gardens "smell[ing] of flowers and fruit."[93]

However, Lewis does not single out the East as exotic and mysterious. He also mines Western myths for fantastical details. Green and Hooper describe the land of Narnia as a mixture of "classical [myth] ... Arthurian myth and legend [and] the Bible."[94] Lindskoog finds a "mixed bag of sources: Homer, Plato, Virgil ... Beowulf, the Middle English romances of *Sir Orfeo*, *Sir* Gawain, and *Havelock*, Malory's *Morte d'Arthur*, at least three of Chaucer's poems, Dante, Shakespeare, Milton, Wagner" and others.[95] Instead of a cityscape, Narnia has the unspoiled sublime grandeur of "heathery mountains ... thymy downs, ... plashing glens ... mossy caverns and ... deep forests."[96]

Since Lewis mythologizes and romanticizes each nation liberally, it is clear that he does not privilege the West as a realm of reality while depicting the East as a realm of fantasy.[97] Additionally, Narnia never invades Calormen or attempts to colonize it, so the Eastern fantastic elements in the *Chronicles* cannot thematically "[facilitate] the justification of the [Western] colonial power to itself."[98] Therefore, the *Chronicles* do not meet the most important qualification for racist Orientalism as defined by Edward Said and others. In his essay *On Science Fiction*, Lewis explains his artistic reasons for using exotic elements. He writes that fantastic details infuse a story with "wonder, or beauty, or suggestiveness."[99] Due to "increasing geographical knowledge," the regular world provides fewer and fewer places that are unfamiliar enough to elicit this aesthetic response.[100] Tales full of marvels have value because they are not just "comments on life," but "are actual additions to life; they give, like certain rare dreams, sensations we never had before, and enlarge our conception of the range of possible experience."[101] The best of wonder tales provide "keen, lasting, and solemn pleasure. ... [It] does something to us at a deep level."[102]

Of course, part of the experience Lewis wanted readers to have is that of seeing the truths of Christianity without all of the "stained-glass and Sunday school associations" that inhibit understanding and feeling. He wondered if "by casting all these things into an imaginary world ... [he could] make them for the first time appear in their real potency."[103] Many people's conversions over many decades testify to the success of this goal. But the *Chronicles* accomplish something in addition. For example, the mythologies of both Narnia and Calormen illustrate the value of diverse literatures and cultures.

It is important to note that while to Lewis "atheist" and "theist" represented opposites, "pagan" and "Christian" had a close ideological relationship. Downing explains that "Lewis saw no such antithesis [between pagan and Christian]. ... He associated paganism with myth and romance, and Christianity with the reality that myth and romance point to."[104] In the *Chronicles*, the Eastern mythic figures in Calormen are equally as capable of pointing to Aslan as the Western Narnian gods. However, knowing either set of deities never takes the place of an actual relationship with the Great Lion.[105] The story of the noble Calormene Emeth illustrates this type of spiritual journey. The great myth of his people says that Tash is the Supreme God. Emeth follows Tash with true faith, but finds he has served an inferior god when he meets Aslan.[106] Aslan tells him, "Beloved ... unless thy desire had been for me thou wouldst not have sought so long and so truly. For all find what they truly seek."[107] Importantly, Emeth's story is not one of Western culture and religion conquering a non-Western man. Lewis concurred with Dom Bede Griffiths that "Christ has to become incarnate in the East, not as a Western teacher come to destroy what they have learned from tradition, but as He came to the Jews, as the fulfilment of all their hopes and desires,"[108] in other words, just as Aslan fulfilled all hopes and desires for Emeth.[109] By showing different mythologies and literatures to be equally capable of pointing to transcendent Truth, Lewis affirms the value of non-Western art.

Additionally, the value of cultural distinctions is upheld in other ways throughout the *Chronicles*. To have fellowship with Aslan is not to become uniformly Narnian. For example, in *The Horse and His Boy*, Archenland is at peace with Aslan, but has its own identity as suggested by the unique character of its land. Though Narnia is a wild romantic wilderness, Archenland is all "open park-like country."[110] Intriguingly, Tashbaan exists as a magnificent city in the Real Narnia, signaling "that there is something good in the Calormene culture (as symbolized by its chief city) that allows it to pass into eternity."[111] As Aslan would say, Tashbaan in the Real Narnia stands for the Real Calormen within Calormen, distinctly and gloriously recognizable, where "no good thing is destroyed."[112] Human freedom must be a part of this vision, for Lewis insists, "although I believe in an omnipotent God I do not consider that His omnipotence could in itself create the least obligation to obey Him."[113] By contrast, rebellion against Truth (represented by Aslan) results in the disappearance of cultural distinctions and individual liberties. When Shift, Ginger, and Rishdah Tarkaan deny the existence of Aslan, they end up creating laws that violate the truth, justice, and freedom that he stands for. At the end of the series, their political union has dissolved the national sovereignty of Narnia and has destroyed all freedom of speech and individuality. Even Calormenes are executed for disagreeing with the dictators. These examples suggest that Lewis believed in acknowledging and preserving the unique qualities and diversity of human cultures, but he also believed in a common humanity that could be freed from the burdens of selfish appetites, racial schisms, and spiritual ignorance through the power of Aslan/Christ.[114] Significantly, Aslan belongs to no country but his own, and it exists not in the North, South, or West, but in the East.

In conclusion, racial imagery in *The Chronicles of Narnia* highlights racism in Western culture and the roots of tyranny in the human heart. Lewis's own remarks reveal that he was on guard against the impulses associated with racial oppression. He writes, "I believe that no man or group of men is good enough to be trusted with uncontrolled power over others."[115] He warns against "the growing exaltation of the collective and the growing indifference to persons."[116]

And he cautions against political movements that are "trying to obey an impersonal force: that [believe] Nature, or Evolution, or the dialectic, or the Race, is carrying them on ... [and] that the forwarding of this process is the supreme duty."[117] In *The Abolition of Man* (1944), Lewis points out that though "a Jingoist, a Racialist, [or] an extreme nationalist" may argue "that the advancement of his own people is the object to which all else ought to yield," this idea of "duty to our own kin" must be restricted by "the inflexible demands of justice, and the rule that, in the long run, all men are our brothers"[118] In addition, Lewis's attitude toward children suggests his distaste for racist thinking. He writes, "Not long ago I saw in some periodical the statement that 'Children are a distinct race.'[119] ... [But] the right sort [of writers for children] work from the common, universally human, ground they share with the children."[120] An anti-racialist theme in Lewis's other fiction matches his prose statements. For example, Lewis sharply satirizes racialist and imperialist attitudes in his *Space* trilogy through the character of Weston, a scientist determined to make room for human expansion by conquering and annihilating intelligent life on other planets. Weston ends up in hell and the aliens survive. In fact, Martha Sammons points out that an important "difference [in Lewis] is that traditional writers of science fiction seem always to show aliens as monsters or ogres and terrestrial invaders as good and ever in the right. For Lewis, his trilogy began the trend of showing the opposite to be true."[121] Instead of mirroring onto foreigners the qualities Western culture or humanity at large wishes to reject, Lewis gives the various creature on Malacandra "a startling 'otherness' that turns out to be wise, innocent, brave, and good."[122] Given the evidence in his other writings, charges of racism against Lewis could be easily dismissed if the racial elements in the *Chronicles* were less striking.

However, the heated discussion of race surrounding Lewis's fantasy works for children raises concerns for contemporary fantasy writers. For example, considering the potential misunderstandings and the current political climate, is it appropriate for authors to manipulate offensive racial stereotypes or to employ conventions of Arabian/Asian fantasy in their work? Celestine Woo remarks that using conventions from Asian fantasy can help those "cut off or marginalized from their past or origins or homeland." She praises *The Horse and His Boy* because it "uses the mask of exotic foreignness to facilitate a moment of cultural critique."[123] Yet Lewis's bold attempt to blend cultural critique, racist imagery, and literary conventions from *The Arabian Nights* has led to great misunderstandings. In this regard, it is important to remember the context in which Lewis wrote *The Chronicles of Narnia*. Within the period of Lewis's lifetime, racist attitudes would have been widely accepted. It is feasible that Lewis's strategy to "steal past … watchful dragons" included setting up racial stereotypes and bringing his audience to reject them gradually through their experiencing of the stories.[124] The problem with reading the *Chronicles* in our times is that Lewis and others have succeeded too well in transforming public attitudes toward racism, and now the dragons on watch have changed. Gradually older works like *The Chronicles of Narnia* have become the victims of their authors' success. Yet in spite of the dissonance between our times and Lewis's, we should recognize the *Chronicles* for successfully showing how things were and for pointing to the way things should be. All these years later, the Narnia books still demonstrate that when it comes to discussing sensitive issues, "sometimes fairy stories may say best what's to be said."[125]

Notes

1. Laura Miller, *The Magician's Book: A Skeptic's Adventures in Narnia* (New York: Little, Brown and Company, 2008): 121.
2. Paul F. Ford, *Companion to Narnia* (San Francisco, CA: HarperSanFrancisco, 1994): 92.
3. "Ethnocentrism," *American Heritage College Dictionary*, 3rd ed. (Boston, MA: Houghton Mifflin, 1997): 471.
4. John Goldthwaite, *The Natural History of Make-Believe: A Guide to the Principal Works of Britain, Europe, and America* (New York: Oxford University Press, 1996): 238.
5. Gregg Easterbrook, "In Defense of Lewis," *Atlantic Monthly*, October 2001: 46–9: www.theatlantic.com/past/docs/issues/2001/10/easterbrook.htm (accessed January 3, 2010).
6. David Holbrook, "The Problem of C. S. Lewis," *Children's Literature in Education* (March 1973): 3–25, at 10.
7. Philip Pullman, "The Dark Side of Narnia," *Guardian*, October 1, 1998: www.crlamppost.org/darkside.htm (accessed May 17, 2012); Kyrie O'Connor, "Lewis' Prejudice Tarnishes Fifth Narnia Book," *Houston Chronicle*, December 2, 2005: www.seattlepi.com/ae/books/article/Lewis-prejudices-tarnish-fifth-Narnia-book-1188939.php (accessed January 3, 2010).
8. Constance Classen, "The Odor of the Other: Olfactory Symbolism and Cultural Categories," *Ethos* 20(2) (1992): 133–66, at 148. Classen writes that *The Horse and His Boy* is a good example of "the fragrant foreigner. … The repulsive aspect of the other is conveyed through the symbolism of corrupting stench, and the seductive aspect through the symbolism of corrupting fragrance."

9. Andrew Blake qtd. in David C. Downing, *Into the Wardrobe: C. S. Lewis and the Narnia Chronicles* (San Francisco, CA: Jossey-Bass, 2005): 159. Hensher writes, "The racism is extreme, even by the standards of the time (you would probably gather from *A Horse and His Boy* and *The Last Battle* that Islam was some kind of Satanic cult)." Philip Hensher, "Don't Let Your Children Go To Narnia," *Independent*, December 4, 1998: www.independent. co.uk/arts-entertainment/dont-let-your-children-go-to-narnia-1189015. html (accessed December 3, 2009). Laird and Rousseau write, "The 'bad' religion in the Narnia books really is (by virtue of being the invention of a Christian author) what Christianity … has always tried to make Islam be. … It is proved to be not really a separate religion, but the worship of the devil." Tessa Laird and Naomi Rousseau, "Killing an Arab," in *LOG Illustrated Archives* (1997) in *The Physics Room*: www.physicsroom.org. nz/log/archive/2/arab/ (accessed January 20, 2009). Watson writes, "There is race-fear, too, for the Calormenes—cruel dark-skinned worshippers of Tash—express Lewis's hatred of Islam." Victor Watson, "Blind Spot: Snobberies, Sneers and Narnia," *Books for Keeps*, n.d.: http://booksforkeeps.co.uk/issue/83/childrens-books/articles/blind-spot/blind-spot-snobberies-sneers-and-narnia%E2%80%A6 (accessed January 3, 2010).

10. Lindskoog writes, "Although the Calormenes are given some good qualities, they have unattractive traits based on the personal habits of less respectable Middle Easterners." Kathryn Lindskoog, *Journey Into Narnia* (Pasadena, CA: Hope, 1998): 209. Downing concurs, "It was probably unwise for Lewis to generalize about a whole people, even a fictional people." Downing: 159.

11. Ford: 95n.

12. Ford qtd. in Dr. Devin Brown, "Are the *Chronicles of Narnia* Sexist and Racist?*" Keynote Address at the 12th Annual Conference of the C. S. Lewis and Inklings Society, Calvin College, 2009: www.narniaweb.com/resources-links/are-the-chronicles-of-narnia-sexist-and-racist/ (accessed April 3, 2012).

13. Downing: 159.

14. Michael Nelson, "For the Love of Narnia," *The Chronicle of Higher Education: The Chronicle Review* 52(15) (2002): B15. Additionally, David C. Downing writes, "For some critics, the main problem with the chronicles is … racism. Andrew Blake, for example, objects to Lewis's Calormenes … concluding that the Narnia books contribute to the contemporary 'demonization of Islam.' On this last point, Blake is surely mistaken. Islam is strictly monotheistic, its foundational teaching that there is no god but God (Allah). The Calormenes, by contrast, speak of their 'gods,' including Tash, Azaroth, and Zardeenah. Also, in the Islamic tradition, Allah speaks through his prophets. He does not come to earth as Tash does." Downing: 160.

15. Alan Jacobs says "the Calormenes … are but slightly disguised versions of the ravaging Turk who filled the nightmares of European children

for more than half a millennium—but whose 'exotic' culture … had also been an endless source of fascinated delight." Alan Jacobs, *The Narnian: The Life and Imagination of C. S. Lewis* (San Francisco, CA: HarperSanFrancisco, 2005): 17. Elizabeth Baird Hardy agrees that "[The Calormenes] are traditional literary antagonists for Western knights." Elizabeth Baird Hardy, *Milton, Spenser and the Chronicles of Narnia* (Jefferson, NC: McFarland, 2007): 56. See also notes 88 and 89.

16. Jonathan Marks, "Scientific Racism, History of," in John Hartwell Moore (ed.), *Encyclopedia of Race and Racism*, 3 vols. (Detroit, MI: Thomson Gale, 2008), vol. 3: 1–16, at 2.

17. See note 14.

18. C. Loring Brace, "Racial Hierarchy: Races Ranked By Early Scientists," in John Hartwell Moore (ed.), *Encyclopedia of Race and Racism*, 3 vols. (Detroit, MI: Thomson Gale, 2008), vol. 2: 463–4, at 464.

19. See note 14.

20. Colin Kidd, *The Forging of Races: Race and Scripture in the Protestant Atlantic World, 1600–2000* (Cambridge: Cambridge University Press, 2006): 168–9. Kidd notes, "British Orientalist Archibald Sayce" wrote that "racial traits … 'include not only physical characteristics but mental and moral qualities as well.'"

21. C. S. Lewis, "The Dethronement of Power," in *Tolkien and the Critics: Essays on J. R. R. Tolkien's Lord of the Rings*, ed. Neil D. Issacs and Rose A. Zimbardo (Notre Dame, IN: Notre Dame University Press, 1968): 12–16, at 12.

22. Roger Lancelyn Green and Walter Hooper (eds.), *C. S. Lewis: A Biography*, rev. ed. (London: HarperCollins, 2002): 113.

23. C. S. Lewis, *The Horse and His Boy* (New York: Scholastic, 1988): 5.

24. *The Horse and His Boy*: 94.

25. *Ibid.*: 99.

26. *Ibid.*: 53–4.

27. *Ibid.*: 108.

28. *Ibid.*: 109. Personal insults are also freely bandied about by the Calormenes toward the Narnians. Rabadash describes Queen Susan as a "black-hearted daughter of a dog" (106). He places Narnia in the same low category as "an idle slave or … a worn out horse" fit only "to be made into dog's meat" (107–8). The Vizier scoffs that "the gods have withheld from the barbarians the light of discretion" (113). And the Tisroc curses Peter the High King, saying, "may the gods utterly reject [him]" (109).

29. C. S. Lewis, *The Last Battle* (New York: Scholastic, 1988): 119.

30. *The Last Battle*: 29.

31. *Ibid.*: 13.

32. *Ibid.*: 25.

33. *Ibid.*: 118.

34. *Ibid.*: 110.

35. *The Horse and His Boy*: 61.

36. Marks: 2. According to Martha Sammons, "Lewis emphasizes that like heaven, God has become 'unreal'—like a 'gas diffused in space,' 'vaporous, vague, indefinable, shadowy.' Although we associate spirit with ghosts and shadows, spirit should be presented as even '*heavier* than matter' because Reality finds its center in a concrete but non-material Almighty, who is concrete Fact. With Aslan, Lewis takes an abstract concept of an Ideal and makes it concrete and living." Martha C. Sammons, *"A Better Country": The Worlds of Religious Fantasy and Science Fiction* (New York: Greenwood, 1988): 26.

37. *The Last Battle*: 153–4.

38. Marks: 4.

39. Jacques Barzun, *Race: A Study in Superstition* (New York: Harper & Row, 1937, repr. 1965): 74.

40. Marks: 10.

41. Peter N. Peregrine, "Racial Hierarchy: Overview," in John Hartwell Moore (ed.), *Encyclopedia of Race and Racism*, 3 vols. (Detroit, MI: Thomson Gale, 2008), vol. 2: 461–2, at 462. Eugenics, "a social and political movement aimed at manipulating racial hierarchy by selectively breeding humans with desirable characteristics and preventing those with undesirable ones from having offspring"(462) was also a major factor in the Nazi vision.

42. *The Horse and His Boy*: 12.

43. *Ibid.*: 11.

44. *Ibid.*: 9. Additionally, Bree gives Shasta the idea that all Narnians are racists. When Shasta finally runs into the royal Narnian party, he assumes that these foreigners will "hate Aravis, because she [is] a Calormene, and either sell her for a slave or send her back to her father" (70).

45. C. S. Lewis, *Out of the Silent Planet* (New York: Macmillan, 1973): 69.

46. C. S. Lewis, *That Hideous Strength* (New York: Macmillan, 1946): 443–4.

47. C. S. Lewis, "A Reply to Professor Haldane," *On Stories and Other Essays on Literature*, ed. Walter Hooper (New York: Harcourt Brace Jovanovich, 1982): 74–85, at 77. Lewis explains that he is not anti-science. Rather, he condemns "the belief that the supreme moral end is the perpetuation of our own species, and that this is to be pursued even if, in the process of being fitted for survival, our species has to be stripped of all those things for which we value it—of pity, of happiness, and of freedom."

48. Shasta, the Narnian orphan who has grown up as a slave in Calormen, has a hero-worshipping and somewhat racist reaction when he sees other Narnian humans for the first time. He notices that "they were all as fair-skinned as himself, and most of them had fair hair. And they were not dressed like men of Calormen. Most of them had legs bare to the knee. Their tunics were of fine, bright, hardy colours—woodland green, or gay yellow, or fresh blue. Instead of turbans they wore steel or silver caps, some of them set with jewels, and one with little wings on each side of it. A few were bare-headed. The swords at their sides were long and straight, not curved like Calormene scimitars. And instead

of being grave and mysterious like most Calormenes, they walked with a swing and let their arms and shoulders go free, and chatted and laughed. One was whistling. You could see that they were ready to be friends with anyone who was friendly and didn't give a fig for anyone who wasn't. Shasta thought he had [never] seen anything so lovely in his life." Later he observes, "All of them, both men and women, had nicer faces and voices than most Calormenes." *The Horse and His Boy*: 54–5, 61.

49. *Ibid.*: 198.

50. Ford: 45n. Additionally, Chad Walsh observes that though "[*Pilgrim's Regress*] has never enjoyed the popularity of many of [Lewis's] later works … it was the source of the ideas in most of them" (qtd. in Lindskoog: 81).

51. C. S. Lewis, *Mere Christianity*, in *The Complete C. S. Lewis Signature Classics* (San Francisco, CA: HarperSanFrancisco, 2002): 1–177, at 89.

52. *The Horse and His Boy*: 104.

53. It is interesting that in Lewis's view, the sins of the South were more pardonable than those of the North. He writes, "The other, and less bad, vices come from the devil working on us through our animal nature." *Mere Christianity*: 105.

54. *The Horse and His Boy*: 120.

55. The White Queen is not a native Narnian who is being displaced. As revealed in *The Magician's Nephew*, she is Jadis, Queen of Charn. She is not human. She has destroyed her native world and has invaded Narnia, setting herself up as its ruler in place of Aslan. However, her character is relevant to discussions of racism and Lewis. She is from a race that is probably older than that descended from Adam and Eve. Her ancestry is monstrous: her mother is Lilith, a Jinn, and her father is a giant. Therefore, she is an important link to theories of race based on Pre-Adamism and theories of the monstrous. Unfortunately, this discussion could not be fitted into the length of this project.

56. *The Horse and His Boy*: 99.

57. C. S. Lewis, *The Lion, the Witch and the Wardrobe* (New York: Scholastic, 1987): 56.

58. *The Lion, the Witch and the Wardrobe*: 115.

59. *Ibid.*: 109.

60. *Ibid.*: 112.

61. *Ibid.*: 132.

62. C. S. Lewis, *The Pilgrim's Regress* [1933] (London: Geoffrey Bles, 1950): 12.

63. *The Horse and His Boy*: 116.

64. *Ibid.*: 110.

65. *Mere Christianity*: 104.

66. *The Horse and His Boy*: 164–5.

67. Shift is a ruler consumed by greed, as symbolized by his chronic alcohol abuse. His habit consumes him to the point that a Calormene captain

and a Narnian cat take over. They say, "'Do you, like me, grow a little weary of the Ape?' 'A stupid, greedy brute … but we must use him for the present.'" *The Last Battle*: 79. The carelessness, greed, and pride of both Narnians and Calormenes destroy the country.

68. These defenders include two Narnians, two British children, a Calormene, and even an ungrateful group of Dwarfs who refuse to appreciate their rescue or to acknowledge their rescuer.

69. *Pilgrim's Regress*: 13. Lewis does not differentiate human into male and female here, but sexism in Lewis's writings, while an important topic, is not within the scope of this paper's discussion.

70. Marks observes that "Scientific racism … is the result of a conjunction of two cultural values or ideologies: (1) that natural categories of the human species exist and are of different overall worth; and (2) that science provides a source of authoritative knowledge." Marks: 1. Lewis deals more directly with the second basis in his *Space Trilogy*. In *The Chronicles of Narnia* he focuses more on the first.

71. Marina Aguiar, Mrinalini Greedharry, and Khachig Tololyan, "Post-colonial Studies and Diaspora Studies," in Michael Ryan and Robert Eaglestone (eds.), *Encyclopedia of Literary and Cultural Theory*, 3 vols. (Malden, MA: Wiley-Blackwell, 2011), vol. 2: 765–80, at 766. Some of these writers include "J. A. Hobson, V. I. Lenin, … Jean-Paul Sartre … Frantz Fanon, Aime Cesaire, Mohandas Gandhi, Albert Memmi, and C. L. R. James."

72. *The Horse and His Boy*: 196.

73. *Ibid.*: 215.

74. *Ibid.*: 216.

75. *Ibid.*: 178.

76. *Ibid.*: 108.

77. See note 73.

78. *The Horse and His Boy*: 110.

79. From a certain point of view, Shift could seem like an unkind description of black people straight out of Linnaeus or Virey. A talking ape, he could be placed on an imaginary Chain of Being halfway between animal and human. He is black with kinky hair and he is sly. However, the Narnian world is monogenist; all people come from the same source, in this case, a pair of people. Shift does not represent a human being or even a missing link because Narnia is not an evolutionary universe. Aslan sings all beasts into existence in *The Magician's Nephew*, and he imports humans from elsewhere. Shift is a true beast just as Aslan is a true beast. Shift is not sluggish or lazy until he begins drinking, but rather has great administrative, organizational, and creative abilities. He steps in to govern when a government is needed in Narnia. Greed, pride, and overweening ambition are his downfall. Interestingly, monogenists have traditionally been associated with abolition on the grounds that all people are equally human.

80. *The Last Battle*: 20.

81. Shahidha Bari and Robert Eaglestone, "Orientalism," in Michael Ryan and Robert Eaglestone (eds.), *Encyclopedia of Literary and Cultural Theory*, 3 vols. (Malden, MA: Wiley-Blackwell, 2011), vol. 2: 756–7, at 756.

82. Walter Hooper, *Past Watchful Dragons: The Narnian Chronicles of C. S. Lewis* (New York: Collier Books, 1979): 41.

83. The race fear of extinction that can be read into *The Last Battle* (when Tirian and friends are overcome by the dark men with white eyes) would actually be a self-extinction. Their fight is against brothers, almost a civil war.

84. See especially David N. Livingstone, *Adam's Ancestors: Race, Religion, and the Politics of Human Origins* (Baltimore, MD: Johns Hopkins University Press, 2008); Kidd; Elazar Barkan, *The Retreat of Scientific Racism* (Cambridge: Cambridge University Press, 1996).

85. *The Last Battle*: 159.

86. *Ibid.*: 164.

87. Downing: 50–1.

88. Jacobs: 308.

89. Hardy: 56.

90. Mervyn Nicholson, "What C. S. Lewis Took From E. Nesbit," *Children's Literature Association Quarterly* 16(1) (1991): 16–22, in *Project Muse*: http://0-muse.jhu.edu.fintel.roanoke.edu/journals/childrens_ literature_association_quarterly/v016/16.1.nicholson.html (accessed January 3, 2010).

91. *The Horse and His Boy*: 167.

92. *Ibid.*: 71.

93. *Ibid.*: 49.

94. Green and Hooper: 325.

95. Lindskoog: 213.

96. *The Horse and His Boy*: 9.

97. In *The Horse and His Boy* Lewis probes the assumption that the East is feminine, weak, cowardly, and driven by emotion. For example, he shows a Calormene woman to be courageous and intrepid. Aravis appropriates her brother's armor, creates a false trail, and runs away to Narnia with no one but her horse. She also shows a great deal of courage and intelligence in escaping the palace of the Tisroc. Additionally, Lewis challenges the idea that the East should be "feminized." He gives the East a masculine representative in the noble Calormene soldier Emeth. This man does not grow into nobility and turn Narnian. He never actually defects from his country. Instead, he insists on entering the stable to see Tash because he has longed for truth all his life. He is determined to see Tash or to prove his leaders have lied. He stands up to his commander on principle and insists that he be admitted into the stable even though threatened with death. These characters also show that courage, intelligence, and a love for truth are not limited by gender.

98. Bari and Eaglestone: 757.

99. C. S. Lewis, "On Science Fiction," in *On Stories and Other Essays on Literature*, ed. Walter Hooper (New York: Harcourt Brace Jovanovich, 1982): 59–73, at 69.

100. *Ibid.*: 68.

101. *Ibid.*: 70.

102. *Ibid.*: 71–2.

103. C. S. Lewis, "Sometimes Fairy Stories May Say Best What's To Be Said," *On Stories and Other Essays on Literature*, ed. Walter Hooper (New York: Harcourt Brace Jovanovich, 1982): 45–8, at 37.

104. Downing: 109. Nelson adds, "Lewis became persuaded that the many … ancient myths in which a god dies and is reborn to save his people had 'really happened' when Jesus was crucified and resurrected, placing Christianity squarely at the intersection of myth and history. Lewis had an enormous regard for pagan myths, both for their marvellous stories and for the truths about origins, aspirations, and purpose he found embedded in them." Nelson: B14.

105. This is just one way that Lewis illustrates the value of diverse literatures. Lewis's *The Horse and His Boy* is a positive example for Celestine Woo because "Aravis, the Calormene ('Arab') girl, displays her finely honed storytelling skills. Lewis observes drolly, 'In Calormen story-telling … is a thing you're taught just as English boys and girls are taught essay-writing. The difference is that people want to hear the stories, whereas I never heard of anyone who wanted to read the essays.'" Celestine Woo, "Toward a Poetics of Asian American Fantasy: Laurence Yep's Construction of a Bicultural Mythology," *The Lion and the Unicorn* 30 (2006): 250–64, at 251. At the end of *The Horse and His Boy*, Lewis gives Narnia the credit for more beautiful poetry.

106. When asked "what pagan gods and goddesses are doing in a Christian universe … Lewis [replied] that it is only in God's name that the spirits of nature can rule their domains with 'beauty and security.' Without God, they would disappear or 'become demons.'" Ford: 204. Tash is a picture of this process, for, though ultimately subordinate to Aslan in *The Last Battle*, previously he has been set up as an independent god in Tashbaan, and when he does appear, he is in a demonic form: "A terrible figure … [with] a vulture's head and four arms. Its beak was open and its eyes blazed. A croaking voice came from its beak" (132). However, though the Calormenes incorrectly worship a group of subordinate beings, Lewis does not condemn them for believing in the existence of these gods. For example, in *The Last Battle*, Lewis vindicates the Calormenes' faith when Tash materializes as an existing supernatural being. Actually, one of the praiseworthy traits of the religion is its sincere belief in the concrete reality of the supernatural. Lewis shows the Calormenes to be superior to Narnians like Bree, who think of deity as an abstract, nonsubstantial reality.

107. *The Last Battle*: 165.

108. Griffiths qtd. in Walter Hooper (ed.), *The Collected Letters of C. S. Lewis: Narnia, Cambridge, and Joy 1950–1963*, 3 vols. (San Francisco, CA: HarperCollins, 2007), vol. 3: 408n. Lewis agreed, adding the cautionary remark to Griffiths, "We must beware of thinking of 'the East' as if it were homogenous" (408).

109. C. S. Lewis, *Till We Have Faces: A Myth Retold* (New York: Harcourt, Brace & Co., 1956). Another illustration of this idea occurs in Lewis's *Till We Have Faces*. Queen Orual, ruler of a kingdom on the outskirts of pre-Christian Greek culture, encounters Christ but through a manifestation of one she identifies as Ungit's (Aphrodite's) son, the God of Love.

110. *The Horse and His Boy*: 134.

111. Ford: 408.

112. *Last Battle*: 181.

113. "A Reply to Professor Haldane": 74–85, at 74.

114. Edward Said's *Beginnings* argues that "narratives of a singular human history" bolster oppressive authoritarian systems of thought. Shahidha Bari, "Said, Edward," in Michael Ryan and Robert Eaglestone (eds.), *Encyclopedia of Literary and Cultural Theory*, 3 vols (Malden, MA: Wiley-Blackwell, 2011), vol. 2: 822–7, at 822–3. Though Lewis affirmed a single origin for the people of Narnia that is ordained by a Christian deity figure, he clearly did not believe in obliterating human freedom of choice. In "A Reply to Professor Haldane," he denounces Theocracy as "the worst of all governments" (81).

115. "A Reply to Professor Haldane": 81.

116. *Ibid.*: 83.

117. *Ibid.*: 83–4.

118. C. S. Lewis, *The Abolition of Man*, in *The Complete C. S. Lewis Signature Classics* (San Francisco, CA: HarperSanFrancisco, 2002): 689–730, at 713.

119. C. S. Lewis, "On Juvenile Tastes," *On Stories and Other Essays on Literature*, ed. Walter Hooper (New York: Harcourt Brace Jovanovich, 1982): 49–51, at 49.

120. *Ibid.*: 51.

121. Martha Sammons, *War of the Fantasy Worlds: C. S. Lewis and J. R. R. Tolkien on Art and Imagination* (Santa Barbara, CA: Praeger, 2010): 33.

122. Thomas Howard, "Out of the Silent Planet," in Jeffrey D. Schultz and John G. West Jr. (eds.), *C. S. Lewis Reader's Encyclopedia* (Grand Rapids, MI: Zondervan, 1998): 308–9, at 309.

123. Woo: 251.

124. "Sometimes Fairy Stories": 37.

125. *Ibid.*: 45.

10

Boy-Girls and Girl-Beasts: The Gender Paradox in C. S. Lewis's *The Chronicles of Narnia*

Susana Rodriguez

I first came to the world of Narnia well past my childhood, as an early 20-something poking about stacks at a book fair. I saw the cover of the edition I call my own now, a lion's head burning out of a dark background, and remember thinking, "It's about time." I had grown up with the Children's Television Workshop cartoon adaptation of *The Lion, the Witch and the Wardrobe*, never wanting a copy of the book until about seventh grade. That year, I was one of very few of my friends who didn't get a chance to read about the Pevensies in school for class. Girls and boys talked at lunch about what Turkish Delight must taste like and how they wanted to be their favorite Pevensie, while I slogged through a book about a 13-year-old girl who kept making up excuses about how she lost her gym clothes because she was uncomfortable in her body. I didn't want to read about my life—I wanted to escape it. Ten years after middle school, I found myself stretched out on my couch devouring the Narnia stories and not at all understanding why they felt so wonderful but so odd at the same time: why were there just as many girls as boys and yet the boys had all the fun, fighting battles and leading revolutions?

C. S. Lewis's *The Chronicles of Narnia* appear to present adventure stories led by girls and boys who hold individually enough power and knowledge to confront Narnia's troubles without falling into traditional, oppressive female and male gender role stereotypes—at least on the surface. Each story in the series pairs an equal number of boys and girls to adventure in Narnia. We are introduced to the first set of pairings, the four Pevensie siblings, in *The Lion, the Witch and the Wardrobe*, who are shaved down to two and eventually replaced by their cousin Eustace Stubbs and his school friend Jill Pole. They too are also switched for Digory and Polly in *The Magician's Nephew* flashback, but all (except for Susan) return to close out the series in *The Last Battle*.

In having an equal number of girls and boys leading the *Chronicles'* stories, Lewis masks the reinforced female and subverted male gender role stereotypes that the narratives promote. By examining three of the main female and male protagonist pairings in the series—Lucy and Edmund; Polly and Digory; and Jill and Eustace—I intend to show the Narnia stories' gender paradox: worlds where boys are empowered by performing female roles and girls are disserviced through stereotyping, relegated to perform as *deus ex machina*s. A close look at the series' male and female gender models—Aslan and Jadis, the White Witch—will help show how these patterns form and shape other characters' performances.

Lucy's adventure becomes Edmund's salvation

In *The Lion, the Witch and the Wardrobe*, the journey to Narnia begins with Lucy's wanting to try the wardrobe door during the rainy afternoon she and her siblings spend indoors exploring the Professor's home. When she ventures in and out of Narnia this first time, her siblings refuse to believe her because only a moment has passed in their world since Lucy had stepped into the wardrobe. All three siblings deny her story, but, interestingly, Peter and Susan attempt to find rational explanations for the report, while Edmund flatly calls Lucy "batty." Even when Edmund follows Lucy into Narnia and sees for himself that the country does exist, he still denies the venture to his siblings: he lies and says they have been pretending for fun.[1] This rug pulling from under Lucy's feet transforms the potential girl adventure into a boy's one, with Edmund stepping in to helm the ship as villain cum tragic repentive hero. His change from being the spiteful sibling begins the moment he and Lucy return from their journey into Narnia, feeling the mistake he's made in meeting the White Witch as Lucy recounts all she's learned from Mr. Tumnus. This uncomfortableness is physically apparent to Lucy, who comments on Edmund's not looking well. From here on, Edmund's redemption story separates from Peter, Susan, and Lucy's journey to save Narnia, both narrative threads paralleling each other in being freedom quests to liberate bodies that have been corrupted by the White Witch: a boy and a country's soul.

And yet, *none* of this would have happened had Lucy not discovered the land beyond the back of the wardrobe. Worse still, the fact that Lucy's greatest denier, Edmund, takes center stage is offensive when considering that the story began with the siblings' adventures and then focused in on Lucy as the character the reader would follow. By calling her "batty" and denying her story, as well as never directly apologizing when Lucy's proven right,[2] Edmund is saying in effect that she can't have adventures. The shift to Edmund as a focalizer, replacing Lucy, then reinforces this idea and expands it through the implication made by the switch in the focalized character's gender: silly girls, adventures are for boys.

Polly's adventure becomes Digory's salvation, too

This pattern—a potential girl's adventure transformed into a boy's story—will repeat in the series again as Polly's attic explorations turn into Digory's Narnian quest in *The Magician's Nephew*. Polly has discovered the crawl space long before Digory moves to London, filling it with found objects like packing cases, a cash box with treasure, food, and drink to make it a smuggler's cave.[3] While Digory does long to explore, it is Polly's idea to try to get into the empty house beyond Digory's by walking along the attic rafters. Where he hesitates at venturing, she responds that she's game each time. Her curiosity to push forth is what allows Uncle Andrew to trick her into becoming his guinea pig, flattering her into trying on one of the yellow rings of transportation.

Rather than following Polly into the wood between worlds, the narrative stays with Digory in Uncle Andrew's study. This switch in focalization is abrupt and out of sync with the text's opening chapter where Polly was introduced, seemingly as the heroine of the story who happens to befriend her new neighbor, Digory, while out in the garden one day.[4] Now, Polly needs saving because she has become "a lady in distress," and Digory, as a boy, should do so out of "honor and chivalry" and because it's the "decent" thing to do.[5] Like Edmund, Digory is tempted, falls, and begins a redemptive quest to atone for his sin in ringing the bell at Charn and bringing evil into the infant Narnia that he watches Aslan sing into existence. Just as in *The Lion, the Witch and the Wardrobe*, *The Magician's Nephew* falsely leads readers into the story through a female protagonist that is soon replaced by a male one embarking on a redemptive journey, when Aslan charges Digory with the blame for bringing Jadis into Narnia.[6] This further entrenches the story's focus on Digory rather than Polly as he journeys to find the seed for a tree that will protect Narnia from Jadis's evil for years before the events in *The Lion, the Witch and the*

Wardrobe unfold. The book's title does suggest that the focus would be on Digory as the protagonist, since he *is* the titular referent, yet the narrative's introduction of Polly and beginning the story from her point of view easily lends itself to the idea that this is a story about the magician's nephew as experienced by the girl next door.[7]

But what happens to Lucy and Polly, the two girls that led us into the adventures to begin with? Lucy, along with her sister Susan, witnesses events around her rather than performing as an active agent in their unfolding. These roles are hinted at in the gifts that Father Christmas gives the sisters: a cordial for Lucy and a horn for Susan.[8] Lucy's cordial is meant to heal hurt friends, while Susan's horn can call for help wherever she finds herself. Both girls are also given weapons—Lucy a small dagger and Susan a bow and arrows—but are told by Father Christmas to only use them "in great need" as neither "are meant to be in battle" because battles "are ugly when women fight."[9] The presents they are encouraged to use then demand that Lucy perform as a nurse ministering to others' wounds, and Susan as a damsel in distress calling for a rescuer.

Meanwhile, Polly floats between being Digory's conscience or foil. She is sensible enough to see that ringing the bell at Charn is not a good idea, and, when Digory doesn't listen, brave enough to use Jadis's words against her to escape back to London.[10] Yet, before this, she is characterized as easily distracted by Uncle Andrew's flattery and the allure of his rings, transforming into a damsel in distress for Digory to save.[11] All three girls also perform as witnesses to major events in their stories. Lucy and Susan watch silently as Jadis kills Aslan at the Stone Table,[12] while Polly watches as Digory rings the bell,[13] as Aslan sings Narnia into life,[14] and as Jadis attempts to tempt Digory a second time in the garden.[15] They now function as secondary, supporting characters rather than as the equal pairings their introductions suggested.

Jill and Eustace on (somewhat) equal footing

Of the major girl–boy protagonist pairs, it is Jill and Eustace in *The Silver Chair* that present the most believable façade of equality in the series. Like *The Lion, the Witch and the Wardrobe* and *The Magician's Nephew*, this story too begins by focusing on its female protagonist, Jill Pole. The narrative thread follows Jill even when Eustace comes into the story, staying with her as they travel from their alternative school, Experiment House, to Narnia through a door in the schoolyard's stone wall.[16] When she meets Aslan for the first time, he sets her the task of finding Prince Caspian's lost son, Rilian.

The set of instructions that Aslan gives her is most interesting as they reveal who is really supposed to complete the quest: Eustace. The first command Aslan gives Jill is to ensure Eustace greets an old friend he'll see the moment he arrives in Narnia.[17] Eustace himself asserts that he is meant to complete the quest when called to conference with Glimfeather and the other owls, saying that Caspian would have sent him to search for the prince had he known Eustace was back in Narnia.[18] Jill reminds Eustace that she too would have been sent after Rilian, albeit parenthetically in a statement that is not acknowledged by Eustace or Glimfeather as they continue their conversation.[19] Eustace even speaks to Glimfeather about Jill in the third person despite her standing with them during this meeting.[20] When they find Prince Rilian in Underland, Jill has no part in helping to free the prince from the silver chair: it is Eustace and Puddleglum, the Marsh-wiggle, who use their swords to cut Rilian's bonds.[21] Even in the battle against the Lady of the Green Kirtle, Jill's agency is snatched from her by the transformed witch who coils her serpent's tail around young Jill, leaving the girl constrained while Prince Rilian, Eustace, and Puddleglum fell the witch with their swords.[22]

Like Lucy and Polly, Jill only serves to lead the reader into the story despite having been presented as a main protagonist. Although much of *The Silver Chair* focalizes more on Jill than it does on Eustace, she is merely a witness to events in which Eustace effects change. The instance she can claim some action in is in discovering the recipe for Man Pie in the cookbook at Harfang, the house of giants they overnight at near the end of their journey.[23] While this discovery prompts their escape from the house, it is as preventative and passive in function as Lucy's cordial and Susan's horn are in the battles against the White Witch: not a strike against would-be attackers, but aid in a time of need. This further reinforces the idea of girls in the series being secondary to the boys, supporting their male counterparts by coming to their aid when needed, but never standing alongside them when action is called for.

Susan grows up and is cast out of Narnia

According to these three texts, Narnia is a boy's world. Even the prophetic rhyme Mr. Beaver shares with the children gives preference to boys over girls: "When Adam's flesh and Adam's bone / Sits at Cair Paravel in throne / The evil time will be over and done."[24] While this is a reference to the series' Christian roots, with Eve having been crafted from Adam's rib,[25] the feminine half of the binary is regardless still linguistically coded as a masculine possession. Perhaps the most disheartening, even grossest, blow against girls in the series is Susan's fate at the end of *The Last Battle*. Peter explains her absence in the gathering beyond the stable door, saying she "is no longer a friend of Narnia."[26] Eustace offers that Susan sees Narnia as a "funny game" they all played when they were children, a place that doesn't exist outside of the mind. Jill adds that her only interests are "nylons and lipstick and invitations" and "being grown-up," while Polly contends that Susan isn't maturing but rather "[racing] on to the silliest time in one's life." This exchange shows that Susan's place amongst the elect is nullified because of her desire to appear and perform more like an adult, or at least what she *thinks* an adult is. It is also apparent that Susan freely chooses to distance herself from Narnia by relegating it to a childhood memory, yet here she is shunned by her family and friends, her own elected absence silencing her and denying her an opportunity to speak for herself while those closest to her disassociate themselves from her physically and spiritually. Susan is effectively punished by proxy, disowned by her brothers and sister for choosing to have a differing idea of Narnia than their own.

The punishing of Susan's actions without allowing for her redemption is absurd when compared to Edmund's transgression in *The Lion, the Witch and the Wardrobe*: he exchanged his brother and sisters to the White Witch for Turkish Delight, much like Judas Iscariot exchanging Jesus Christ to the priests for thirty pieces of silver.[27] According to Mark 3:28–9, "whoever blasphemes against the Holy Spirit never has forgiveness, but is guilty of an eternal sin." Susan would fall into this category *if* she had denied Aslan, which she doesn't: she denies Narnia.[28] If she had denied him, she would also be denying Aslan's Breath, which Paul Ford argues represents the Holy Spirit when considering the texts as a Christian allegory,[29] and would damn herself for doing so. In allowing Edmund salvation despite the gravity of his crime but depriving Susan for a lesser fault, the texts underscore their bias in the male protagonists' favor while disempowering and damning the females for performing conventionally feminine roles[30] that they were groomed for from the beginning with being given defensive rather than offensive weapons.

On the other hand, Sally Adair Rigsbee notes in her cross-examination of *The Lion, the Witch and the Wardrobe* and George MacDonald's *The Princess and The Goblin* that female protagonists like Lucy Pevensie are empowered because of their suspension of disbelief: "Both authors create heroines who are gifted in imagination and, therefore, readily accept a fantasy realm as a valid reality.

The heroines proceed without hesitation to explore the strange new worlds they encounter, and then teach their secret knowledge to their less enlightened companions."[31] These ideas suggest that the girl protagonists innately breach fantastic spaces, readily accepting what others around them may reject upon a first encounter. Applying this to the Narnia texts, then, the girl protagonists function as gateways for the boy protagonists, opening up the fantasy realm for the others to step through. What is most interesting about this repeating imbalanced dynamic is its dependence on this symbiotic relationship to push the stories forward. Without Lucy discovering the wardrobe, Edmund wouldn't follow to be tempted by Turkish Delight, thereby never catalyzing the Narnian revolt against the White Witch. If Polly had not discovered the attic crawl space, Digory would never find himself in Uncle Andrew's study on that fateful rainy afternoon to begin a rescue mission that brings evil into the nascent Narnia. Jill's wanting to escape being bullied at Experiment House prompts Eustace to share his stories of Narnia and to find a way for them both to get there. This would therefore suggest that the girls act as generative forces, creating the conditions for the story to play out.

Yet deeper reading of the series nullifies this idea when examining the male and female gender models, Aslan and Jadis. Aslan and Jadis construct gender types and expectations for the series, the authority of their performance enhanced by their positions as adult characters and representatives of the poles of good and evil. The masculine Aslan is good and the feminine Jadis is evil. What helps define good and evil is their ability to create or destroy, Aslan a creative, generative force in birthing Narnia contrasting with Jadis's destructive and corruptive nature. His singing the Narnian animals into being resembles pregnancy:

> Can you imagine a stretch of grassy land bubbling like water in a pot? For that is really what was happening. In all directions it was swelling into humps. ... And the humps moved and swelled till they burst, and the crumbled earth poured out of them, and from each hump there came out an animal. The moles came out just as you might see a mole come out in England. The dogs came out, barking the moment their heads were free, and struggling as you've seen them do when they are getting through a narrow hole in the hedge.[32]

Creation as, biologically, a female ability characterizes Aslan's maleness with an inherent femaleness. While this is expected of his performance as the God figure within the context of the *Chronicles* as a Christian allegory, it is unexpected if read by an audience unfamiliar with the source text who may not recognize the parallels and allu-sions. The descriptions of the ground swelling into humps resemble an accelerated pregnancy, the gestation period contracted into the seconds it takes water to pop and bubble up again in a boil. Like water breaking, the bursting humps pour out placental earth before nascent animals—heads first like infants—cry out life. Narnia born is the product of Aslan's dual male and female sex, being both seen as physically masculine in appearance and performing feminine embodi-ment in carrying out pregnancy and birth through song.

In contrast, Jadis only appears and performs as feminine but does not embody the biological capabilities. She is introduced in her native Charn. The world has long died out, Jadis having spoken the decimat-ing Deplorable Word because her sister wouldn't let her be queen. Jadis is pure artifice, as her description reveals:

> The last figure of all was the most interesting—a woman even more richly dressed than the others, very tall ...with a look of fierceness and pride that it took your breath away. Yet she was beautiful too. Years after-wards when he was an old man, Digory said he had never in all his life known a woman so beautiful. It is only fair to add that Polly always said she couldn't see anything specially beautiful about her.[33]

Unlike Aslan, Jadis's strength lies in her ability not to create, but to destroy, her incredible beauty facilitating destruction by enchanting others—usually males—to obey her. Like the serpent in the Garden of Eden,[34] Jadis too tempts those around her through language. She commands Polly and Digory to obey her, changes her demeanor and tone of voice to bait Edmund, and spreads these abilities to her meta-phorical descendent,[35] the Lady of the Green Kirtle, who will use them to ensnare Jill, Eustace, and Prince Rilian. This sharp contrast between Aslan and Jadis provides a foundation within Narnia's chro-nology for preference to masculine forces over feminine ones, further underscoring the divide between the child protagonists and their agency, or lack of, in the series.

As male and female gender role models, Aslan and Jadis's perfor-mances attribute expectations of the female protagonists to the males: like Aslan, boys in the series are generative, restorative forces while also performing traditionally masculine roles. Edmund gives Peter's army the upper hand by destroying the White Witch's wand,[36] Digory retrieves and plants the silver apple in Narnia to guard against Jadis,[37] and Eustace helps Puddleglum and Prince Rilian destroy the Lady of the Green Kirtle.[38] By contrast, the girls are agentially neutered, accompanying the boys on their ventures but relegated to standing on the sidelines once the switch in either focalization (as happens to Lucy and Polly) or role (like Jill) is made.

A corrupted fantasy: imagining limited possibilities

These patterns bring the series into dangerous and disempowering ideological territory. Girls are allowed to discover new spaces, but they cannot lead its exploration. Girls can stand by and bear witness to events, coming in after the fact to tidy loose ends, but they cannot perform in an active role to enact real change. Girls are second to boys. This is especially troubling when considering David Gooderham's posing of fantasy as a metaphor:

> [Fantasy] works by substitution of the purely imaginary for realistic description, in the sense not that common human experiences, feeling, and ideas are removed from the text, but that metaphorical images become the vehicle by which these are rendered. ... The conceptualization of *fantasy* is thus seen not so much a collection of marvels which divert readers from ordinary human concerns, but a distinctive and fruitful way of speaking about just these concerns.[39]

The Chronicles of Narnia, then, as metaphors for common human experience, espouse that adventures are for boys only; girls just tag along for the ride. Yet this too furthers an ideology of disempowerment: do boys always have to lead the venture? Do they always have to be in the thick of a battle? What if they would prefer to switch roles? Where is choice in the matter for either sex in texts that by nature—as fantastic adventure stories—should brim with possibility?

If fantasy functions as "a distinctive and fruitful way of speaking" about human conditions, the *Chronicles* reflect and reinforce traditional gender role stereotypes through the agency given to the male protagonists that is denied to the females. This idea is supported by Anna E. Altmann's understanding of the hero's journey and its function: "symbolic or actual, [it] is a leaving behind of the structures and roles of the social order and a move into a liminal space where the self may be developed."[40] While Jean E. Graham argues that "puberty ends the freedom of girls to assume nontraditional roles" in the series,[41] what is happening in the Narnia texts is that the children are leaving their real worlds—spaces that we are only briefly introduced to—to venture to a fantastic space that inculcates them with traditional feminine and subverted masculine roles. This ties back to Altmann's assertion that "the quest of the hero, however, is for *self*-recognition, and her reintegration into society is for society's benefit rather than her own,"[42] making the submersion into traditional gender roles for Lucy, Polly, and Jill that much more sinister because of the fantasy space's ability to allow for difference and possibility for something other than and even subversive to cultural expectations. Yet boys are allowed to subvert masculine expectations, bringing both destruction and redemption to Narnia, the fantastic space allowing them a fluidity denied to the girls.

What is for society's benefit rather than the girls' own, to borrow Altmann's phrasing, is a desexualized little girl rather than a sexualized woman. This is clear when looking again at Susan through Jadis/the White Witch and the Lady of the Green Kirtle. The list that Jill draws up for King Tirian to explain Susan's absence on the other side of the stable door in *The Last Battle* includes "nylons, lipstick, and invitations," a list that Polly chides for representing "a silly time in one's life" that Susan wants to rush to and "stop there as long as she can."[43] Paul Ford notes in *Companion to Narnia* that Susan wants "to be thought mature and attractive"[44]; Jill's list then illustrates that Susan defines these two ideals through superficial adornments like clothes and makeup as well as social status and popularity in being sought after to go out, more than likely by members of the opposite sex. I want to place special emphasis on Ford's note: Susan's wanting "*to be thought* mature and attractive" draws attention to a third party inclusion—it doesn't mean she wants to think of herself as these things but wants to have others perceive her as such, further underscoring the sexuality implicit in the definition she constructs for these goals in dressing up, painting her face, and dating. A sexualized girl, which Susan is running the risk of becoming quite willingly and quickly, cannot exist in Narnia for fear they grow into women like the antagonistic witches.

According to Jean E. Graham, it is expressed female sexuality that makes Jadis/the White Witch and the Lady of the Green Kirtle so dangerous and wicked in the *Chronicles*. Graham likens the two antagonists to Circe and Lilith, two classic femme fatale characters known for using their sexuality to gain power over men.[45] One of the greater fears attached specifically to Lilith is her desire to seduce men in order to "take control and dominate the world."[46] Superficial features tied to her sexuality are also a main focus, including her representation in a painting by Dante Gabriel Rossetti as a "beautiful but cold and self-absorbed woman" as well as allusions referring back to her in literature like Sin in John Milton's *Paradise Lost*, Satan's daughter and lover known as the "Snakie Sorceress" because of her scaly body and snake-like arms.[47] This equation between sex and serpents ties back to the Garden of Eden, connecting both female antagonists in the *Chronicles* to Satan tempting the innocent, which, in the series' context, translates into the male protagonists who are lured by both witches.[48]

The reason for Susan's exclusion at the series' end now becomes clear when we understand that her wanting to be mature and grown up includes and desires sexual maturity as part of her pull away from childhood. If Susan were to get what she wants, she would run the risk of becoming more like Jadis/the White Witch and the Lady of the Green Kirtle in being able to wield power over men through her sexuality. This agential, sexualized gender role does not fit with the accepted ones found at the other side of the stable door, seen in Lucy, Polly, and Jill. It is not that "puberty ends the freedom of girls to assume nontraditional roles"[49]; it is that puberty begins sexual awakening which ends the possibility that girls would remain powerless forever. Graham argues that the *Chronicles* damn female sexuality as the witches and Susan express it, but reward its suppression in a tomboy girl who "gives up [their] dreams and [has] children instead."[50]

But what I see the series actually damning is choice on the girls' parts to enact gender roles as they wish; they are restricted to perform as watchful companions to boys and to stand by, ready to help only if absolutely necessary. This is frightening territory indeed in a fantastic world where imagination and possibility should be the only limitations.

Notes

1. C. S. Lewis, *The Lion, the Witch and the Wardrobe. The Chronicles of Narnia* (New York: HarperCollins, 2001): 107–97, at 129.
2. *The Lion, the Witch and the Wardrobe*: 174.
3. C. S. Lewis, *The Magician's Nephew. The Chronicles of Narnia* (New York: HarperCollins, 2001): 7–106, at 13.
4. *The Magician's Nephew*: 11.
5. *Ibid.*: 22, 23, 24.
6. *Ibid.*: 79–80.
7. Many thanks are due to Lance E. Weldy for his pointing out that indeed the book's title lends itself too neatly to the idea that Digory is the intended star of the show despite its opening focalization on Polly.
8. *The Lion, the Witch and the Wardrobe*: 159–60.
9. *Ibid.*: 160.
10. *The Magician's Nephew*: 35, 45.
11. *Ibid.*: 17, 22.
12. Lewis, *The Lion, the Witch and the Wardrobe*: 181.

13. *The Magician's Nephew*: 36.
14. *Ibid.*: 64.
15. *Ibid.*: 93–5.
16. C. S. Lewis, *The Silver Chair. The Chronicles of Narnia* (New York: HarperCollins, 2001): 543–663, at 553–4.
17. *The Silver Chair*: 559.
18. *Ibid.*: 574.
19. *Ibid.*: 574.
20. *Ibid.*: 577.
21. *Ibid.*: 626.
22. *Ibid.*: 634.
23. *Ibid.*: 609–10.
24. *The Lion, the Witch and the Wardrobe*: 147.
25. Genesis 3:21–5.
26. C. S. Lewis, *The Last Battle. The Chronicles of Narnia* (New York: HarperCollins, 2001): 665–767, at 741.
27. Matthew 26:14–50.
28. *The Last Battle*: 741.
29. Paul F. Ford, *Companion to Narnia: A Complete Guide to the Enchanting World of C. S. Lewis's The Chronicles of Narnia* (New York: HarperCollins, 1994): 230–3.
30. I am indebted to Amy Hicks for her incisive observation that Susan is, in fact, performing a conventional feminine role in the ways that her siblings see her playing at maturity.
31. Sally Adair Rigsbee, "Fantasy Places and Imaginative Belief: *The Lion, the Witch and the Wardrobe* and *The Princess and The Goblin*," *Children's Literature Quarterly* 8(1) (1983): 10–11, at 10.
32. *The Magician's Nephew*: 68–9.
33. *Ibid.*: 34.
34. Genesis 3:1–7.
35. Here I mean to propose a metaphorical descendency between the two witches when considering the pattern of balance between sexes and power repeated throughout the series: for every boy found in the series there is a girl; for every representative power for good there is one for evil—a veritable Noah's Ark of Harmonic Antinomies. The villainous White Witch's defeat early in the series demands a new counterbalance to Aslan and the Narnian's goodness, appropriately restored by the Lady of the Green Kirtle in *The Silver Chair*.
36. *The Lion, the Witch and the Wardrobe*: 192.
37. *The Magician's Nephew*: 90–6.
38. *The Silver Chair*: 634.
39. David Gooderham, "Children's Fantasy Literature: Toward an Anatomy," *Children's Literature in Education* 26(3) (1995): 171–83, at 173.
40. Anna E. Altmann, "Welding Brass Tits on the Armor: An Examination of the Quest Metaphor in Robin McKinley's *The Hero and The Crown*," *Children's Literature in Education* 23(3) (1992): 143–56, at 147.

41. Jean E. Graham, "Women, Sex, and Power: Circe and Lilith in Narnia," *Children's Literature Association Quarterly* 29(1–2) (2004): 32–44, at 32.
42. Altmann: 149.
43. *The Last Battle*: 741.
44. Ford: 398.
45. Graham: 32.
46. *Ibid.*: 35.
47. *Ibid.*: 35–6.
48. *Ibid.*: 38.
49. *Ibid.*: 32.
50. *Ibid.*: 42.

Further Reading

Obviously, this is not an exhaustive list of the large body of existing critical commentary on Lewis and his Narnia series. It is not even an exhaustive summary list. In compiling this overview, I cannot underscore enough the sheer magnitude of scholarship available on Lewis and what a daunting challenge it has been to give a representative sampling of the kinds of extant critical commentary. As evidence of this, let me note that a simple MLA Bibliography search using the term "Lewis, C. S." revealed a staggering 1,500 entries, and this does not necessarily include book-length studies. I have tried to organize the criticism somewhat chronologically while simultaneously highlighting significant thematic emphases from the sources.

Walter Hooper's 1974 article, "Narnia: The Author, the Critics, and the Tale," which I referenced in the Introduction, explains that Lewis's stories are popular because fairy tales have become popular again.[1] However, he mentions that at the time of this article, people objected to the Narnia series because it was either too frightening or too Freudian. For the source of the latter reason, he refers to **David Holbrook's article, "The Problem of C. S. Lewis."**[2] As of 1982, James Como says that books published in the past few years about Lewis have been poorly done and admits he has little patience for Christian scholarship, saying that Lewis's "Christian substance [has been] ridden nearly unto death." However, Como lists quite a few books from the 1950s, 1960s, and 1970s about Lewis that he finds meritorious. One book that Como thinks highly of is **Walter Hooper's *Past Watchful Dragons*.** According to Como, it sets out to "establish a record of composition, to describe the milieu, especially Lewis' own life, interests, and temperament, out of which the Narnian world emerged, to suggest the appropriate *topoi* of criticism, and to locate Narnia in the larger world of Lewisian discourse."[3]

Sally Adair Rigsbee's 1983 article, "Fantasy Places and Imaginative Belief: *The Lion, the Witch and the Wardrobe* and *The Princess and the Goblin*," takes a comparative close reading of the two titular texts and applies a Jungian approach. Basically, she argues that "Lucy and Irene are the gifted visionaries, but the foibles of their close companions make them seem more human." She spends quite a bit of time discussing the psyche and the separation motifs, and believes the "plots of both novels focus on the struggle between good and evil. The destructive archetypes of the unconscious, the white witch and the goblins, must be overpowered by the heroines with the assistance of archetypal figures who embody virtue and wholeness." Near the end of her essay, she says that "Narnia is not simply an unreal fantasy land created to entertain children; it is a meaningful visualization of the inner landscape of the psyche where the internal conflicts that lead to personality growth are acted out." In other words, Rigsbee believes in traversing beyond the constraints of the narrative, suggesting that while Aslan created Narnia,

199

Lucy created Aslan through her creative imagination and unconscious. Such a stance would certainly diverge from the typical Christian-heaven interpretation.[4]

Dennis B. Quinn's 1984 article in *Children's Literature* scrutinizes the genre of fantasy and ultimately suggests that the genre is dangerous: "I would like to offer a few cautionary words about the genre itself and about one of its most popular practitioners, C.S. Lewis." He provides a distinction between the Platonic and Aristotelian philosophy of Art and Nature to establish the difference between the fantastic ("unreal") and the wonderful ("real but strange, mysterious, unexplained"). He does provide a "literary context in which Lewis wrote," referring to it as "the neoplatonic tradition in order to distinguish Plato himself from his later interpreters"; and goes on to say that the Aristotelian approach to literature is a "direct imitation of nature," while "the neoplatonic ideal demanded an imitation of an image in the artist's mind." Furthermore, Quinn provides Lewis's love of Spenser as one of the means by which he inscribes his Neoplatonic ideology, specifically with Lewis's attachment to *The Faerie Queene*. Quinn argues that Lewis rejected how scholars were interpreting Spenser's work, thereby promulgating an affinity toward fantasy rather than realism. He, of course, like many others, uses *The Last Battle* stable scene to support his assertions. Interestingly, he argues that Lewis's use of fantasy is quite detrimental to theology because "What is Platonic is the denial of the reality of this world, God's created universe."[5] Essentially, he makes an interesting question: If God created the world and called it "good," how can it not be real? While his position is quite thought provoking, I might humbly assert that "not real" does not necessarily mean "fake" or "artificial," but rather could mean "containing the essence in part but not the whole."

It would appear that Quinn believes that Lewis, to some degree, employs allegory in his Narnian writings, arguing that "allegory introduced a third world, the 'other world' of pure 'fancy.' It is clear that for Lewis and his school the actual world and the supernatural world are not enough. Mere reality—mere heaven and earth—is not enough. So be it. But there are consequences. Narnia is a *utopos*, a no place, a shadow-land, and as such, it is unlikely to endure." What Quinn says is true, in part, because Narnia, the initially created Narnia, truly does not endure. It is what Lewis provides in the last chapter of *The Last Battle* that we are told endures forever, as the "true" image of Narnia has been revealed to the readers. I wonder, almost 30 years later, just how seriously contemporary readers will take Quinn's overall argument concerning the fears of the fantasy genre, especially when they come across the statement on his last page: "Fantasy is harmful to the imagination, and especially to the youthful imagination, because it encourages the reader to turn inward and to distrust if not despise reality."[6]

A common approach I have noticed in surveying scholarship on Lewis is making a case for the resources that either influenced Lewis or that he incorporated into Narnia. In his **1986 article, "Platonic Shadows in C. S. Lewis's Narnia** *Chronicles***," William Johnson** claims that while Lewis does rely on Plato for his *Chronicles*, he does not rely solely on Plato, making it difficult to pinpoint where exactly and how much of Plato he used, especially because he incorporated so many others: "it is impossible to ascertain how much else Lewis takes directly from Plato, how much is 'second hand' through the Church Fathers, Neo-Platonists, and Renaisssance Christian Humanists, and how much is merely an amalgam developed by Lewis as part of his own creative processes."[7] Johnson is clear in pointing out that Lewis did not incorporate the Platonic idea of preexisting souls. However, as many other scholars have indicated, Johnson discusses the allegory of the cave and how some characters choose to stay in darkness, like the dwarves in *The Last Battle*.

In 1989, Frank P. Riga edited a special issue of the *Children's Literature Association Quarterly*, focusing on the topic of religion. His introduction to the special issue applies literary criticism to texts which contain varying degrees of religious emphasis, and it is significant that Riga expresses the importance of scrutinizing religious materials: "As the following papers demonstrate, the subject of religion in children's books involves us, not only in specific questions and themes, but in the social and critical perspectives of which children's books are a part." This is important to note in this special issue, especially when analyzing one of the general ways in which literary scholars latch onto the Narnia series, through religion or spirituality. In his overview of the special issue, Riga mentions his own article and argues that "Lewis uses fairy tale to show the real and consubstantial relationship of the terrestrial and spiritual realms. Our response to the Chronicles, then, cannot accord with one of the common views of Lewis's art: i.e., as a blatant Christian apologist, his work is both allegorically simple and overtly didactic."[8]

Moreover, in **Riga's own essay in the issue, "Mortals Call Their History Fable: Narnia and the Use of Fairy Tale,"** he discusses how the juxtaposition between Narnia and our primary world helps us to see different perspectives when we look at our world by "inverting the reality of the commonplace." He asserts that one of the primary functions of Lewis's fairy tale is to add a richness to our ordinary world. Also, Riga discusses one of the main critiques of Lewis, that "the Chronicles promulgate certain moral and ethical duties." Riga admits this is true, but that if we take the Narnia series as part of the fairy-tale genre, "it would be puzzling if the didactic impulse were missing." Interestingly enough, Riga argues that the link between our world and Narnia is not allegorical, but rather "consubstantial": "Should the mode of participation be allegorical or symbolic, then our participation is merely fictional: it may have truth in it, but in the final analysis, the mode is only make-believe. If, however, the mode of participation is with things that are real in both worlds, the participation is real."[9]

Another article that investigates the sources and writers that inspired Lewis is **"What C. S. Lewis Took from E. Nesbit" by Mervyn Nicholson in 1991**. Nicholson's convincing essay reveals how Lewis took a great deal of inspiration from his literary ancestors: Milton, Spenser, and Nesbit. Nicholson makes an interesting point that while many people look at Lewis's "place in the tradition of Christian romance and apologetic and of his links to Christian writers like MacDonald and Williams," not many talk about how he was inspired by non-Christian writers, like E. Nesbit. He provides quite a few examples of how Lewis draws on Nesbit's writings, arguing that *The Magician's Nephew* is "perhaps closest to Nesbit," even going so far as mentioning her at the beginning of the story.[10]

Hugh Crago has written one of the few articles I have seen that directly addresses the BBC TV adaptations from the late 1980s in his **1994 essay, "Such Was Charn, That Great City."** For the most part, Crago seems to ruminate anecdotally about the connections between *The Magician's Nephew* and C. S. Lewis's personal life. He poignantly notes, "There are fantasies better written and more consistently imagined than Narnia, but most of them have fallen into oblivion, whereas Lewis's world will endure because it has tapped something that unites people across times, places, and individual backgrounds. Not all people, of course, but surprisingly many."[11] He finishes his essay noting the popularity of the BBC Narnia video productions.

John Morgenstern's 2000 article, "Children and Other Talking Animals," aims to establish a theoretical framework whereby we may distinguish the difference between children's and adult literature because, as he claims, children's literature "tastes different than adult literature." To do so, Morgenstern uses Lewis's children's and adult literature as examples. I appreciate how he mentions early in his essay the issue of children's sexualities: "Presumably, for some reason, we wish to be able to think that children have no language although it may seem that what we wish to believe is that they have no bodies/sexuality. It would hardly be a very interesting, or very accurate, observation to suggest that the 'supposition' about children that constructs their literature is that children do not have bodies/sexuality."[12] This comment about the sexuality of the child reminds us of the complicated image of the faun that I mentioned at the beginning of my Introduction, but it also becomes a point of discussion in this New Casebook, specifically in Susana Rodriguez's chapter.

Writings about Lewis and Narnia have not slowed down in the twenty-first century, not even indirectly. As mentioned previously, Lewis and Tolkien are often grouped together in discussions of post-World War II fantasy, especially because of their friendship and their huge influence on the genre. **T. A. Shippey**, one of the leading Tolkien scholars, mentions Lewis quite a bit in his **2002 paperback, *J. R. R. Tolkien: Author of the Century***. For example, we learn that Tolkien received a professorship at Oxford and that "C.S. Lewis, despite the distinction of his scholarship, was one of the thirty or forty who never got one at Oxford, moving to Cambridge to take one up in 1954 when he was fifty-five." In terms of the historical context of the early twentieth century, Shippey notes that "The life experiences of many men and women in the twentieth century have left them with an unshakable conviction of something wrong, something irreducibly evil in the nature of humanity, but without any very satisfactory explanation for it. ... Twentieth-century fantasy can be seen as above all a response to this gap, this inadequacy."[13] Shippey maintains that for Lewis and Tolkien, both veterans of World War I, horrific life experiences turned their minds toward finding a way to cope with a shattered worldview, and the fantasy genre helped them do that.

As is suggested by the title of her **2004 article, "Women, Sex, and Power: Circe and Lilith in Narnia," Jean E. Graham** spends the majority of her essay making connections between Jadis (the White Witch) and Circe and Lilith as sources that Lewis drew from in creating the villainess in Narnia. She echoes Susana Rodriguez's chapter in this book when talking about how Jadis and the Emerald Witch "possess dangerous qualities—the qualities of female sexuality and power." This reinforces Susana Rodriguez's assertion about gender and sex, especially when Graham notes "that puberty ends the freedom of girls to assume nontraditional roles." More significantly, in light of my discussion in the Introduction about "The Problem of Susan," Graham spends some time making the connection between Circe and Susan, noting that "Susan is apparently prevented from entering heaven ... because on entering adolescence she has allowed stereotypically feminine interests to displace her spiritual life." But Graham does defend Lewis against sexism by saying that it "is an obvious temptation when examining his use of the Circe and Lilith myths, with which he inherited centuries of stereotypes that feminists have begun to undo ... only well after Lewis' 1963 death. To do so would be an oversimplification, since he also portrayed women positively, including the girls in the Narnia stories." However, she does provide a caveat to this defense by noting that the gender stereotype becomes enforced for the adult domesticated women, as evidenced by Queen Helen in *The Magician's Nephew.*[14]

What is unique about **Amanda Rogers Jones's article from 2004, "The Narnian Schism: Reading the Christian Subtext as Other in the Children's Stories of C. S. Lewis,"** is that she calls for an academic investigation of religious (specifically Christian) texts. According to Jones, we in academia tend to look at texts from a secular approach, and Narnia contains a Christian subtext that needs to be scrutinized, not ignored: "avoiding Lewis' Christian belief is an intellectual misstep because it is reasonable to regard Christianity as a belief system the secular academy excludes." Furthermore, she says, "Lewis' moral element constitutes a specific kind of bias, but critical responsibility can open a kind of 'Aslan's country' beyond the bias, by showing where secular and Christian meanings overlap and augment one another, as well as where they conflict."[15] Connected to Jones's focus on the secular criticism of religious texts is **Elissa McCormack's 2008 article, "Inclusivism of C. S. Lewis: The Case of Emeth,"** which essentially argues that the character of Emeth from *The Last Battle* supports Lewis's controversial theology that one can receive salvation outside of Christianity. Additionally, she claims, "it is possible, according to Lewis, to be saved from within a non-Christian religion as long as one does have this true longing for Truth." McCormack follows this reasoning and also addresses the "Problem of Susan": if one can be saved by searching for the truth, though misguided, could one also be saved while being backslidden within the "true" religion? As far as I am aware, she is one of the few who argues that Susan's behavior throughout the series demonstrates a track record of her being less sincere about Narnia than the rest. McCormack says that "her new attitude was not something that she only decided once she left Narnia," and she rests primarily on Susan's doubtful behavior in *Prince Caspian* as evidence of this. McCormack also addressed her belief about the fate of Susan: "we can still hope that she has a chance for salvation and she will find her way back to Narnia. She still has a chance to rekindle her desire for Truth."[16]

Though the points that **Alan Jacobs** brings up in his monograph are too numerous to discuss here, I would call attention to several parts where he refers to issues of racism and sexism. In *The Narnian: The Life and Imagination of C. S. Lewis* (2005), Jacobs argues that the Narnia stories have affected the fantasy genre, even into the twenty-first century. He discusses Philip Pullman's extreme hatred of the Narnia series, including the alleged racist and sexist elements in it. However, Jacobs argues that what really disturbs Pullman is "Lewis's whole vision of human life and its possibilities." Essentially, "Of all the Christian beliefs with which atheists disagree, the only one that seems to generate real and deep rage is the belief in eternal life ... and the corollary belief that the eternal life that some people choose is a miserable one." Jacobs also acknowledges and identifies problematic representations of race in his Afterword, chalking up Lewis and Tolkien's alleged racism to

> an Old Western Culture to which the chief threat, for hundreds of years, had been the Ottoman Empire. ... In short, Lewis and Tolkien had a ready-made source of "Oriental" imagery on which to draw to enrich their fictional worlds, and in a time less sensitive to cultural difference than our own, they saw no reason not to draw upon it. Perhaps this should count against them, but it rarely does. I think that is because readers ... can tell the difference between, on the one hand, an intentionally hostile depiction of some alien culture and, on the other, the use of cultural difference as a mere plot device.[17]

Jacobs also addresses the sexism allegations. He argues that the Narnia series shows gender equality because "there is a strong tendency toward pairing characters, a boy and a girl, of roughly equal narrative interest and with a general moral equality as well ... None of these characters is perfect: all are flawed, but flawed in very familiar ways, and all are capable of virtue when the going gets tough." Jacobs even goes so far as to say that the boys are "a little worse" than the girls, citing Edmund and Eustace as characters who needed desperate personality transformations, and also notes that Lucy has an extra special spiritual blessing over all the rest.[18]

As far as book-length studies of Lewis or Narnia go, it would be difficult to discuss or list them all, but, from the past half-decade, several are worth mentioning, especially to distinguish themselves from this current New Casebook. **David Colbert's** *The Magical Worlds of Narnia: A Treasury of Myths, Legends, and Fascinating Facts* **was published in 2005**; as is evident from the title, this book is concerned with giving facts and is written in a more popular style. **David C. Downing's *Into the Wardrobe: C. S. Lewis and the Narnia Chronicles*, also from 2005**, is still popular in style, but, as Andrew White notes, "Downing, like Colbert, includes a discussion of the apparently racist and chauvinist elements of the Chronicles, but he comes down on the opposite end of the spectrum. He successfully posits counterexamples to most of the more common issues raised by Colbert."[19] **Shanna Caughey has edited a collection called *Revisiting Narnia: Fantasy, Myth and Religion in C. S. Lewis' Chronicles* that was published in 2005**. Even though its tone is more academic than the previous two books mentioned and it contains an astounding 25 contributors, not all of the contributions are equally scholarly, such as the chapter written by the cofounder of PETA (People for the Ethical Treatment of Animals).[20] **Elizabeth Baird Hardy's book, *Milton, Spenser and The Chronicles of Narnia: Literary Sources for the C. S. Lewis Novels***, positions the Narnia stories in the context of both Milton and Spenser. For all of the positive elements of the book, Rebecca Davies says that Hardy is not convincing about defending the allegations of racism based on the "justification of courtly tradition." She argues that "her vindication of Lewis on this point is not a completely persuasive exoneration of him from accusations of racism."[21]

As proof that reader and scholarly interest about Lewis and Tolkien continues into the twenty-first century, **Diana Pavlac Glyer published in 2007 *The Company They Keep: C. S. Lewis and J. R. R. Tolkien as Writers in Community***, and her discussion essentially focuses on the type of influence the two writers had on each other.[22] **Michael Ward** has written what has been called a fascinating, albeit farfetched, book called ***Planet Narnia: The Seven Heavens in the Imagination of C. S. Lewis* (2008)**. As Judy Rosenbaum notes, Ward argues that "Lewis imposed an additional structure on his Narnia books, one based on the Medieval (Ptolomaic) view of the cosmos, with Earth at the center and seven heavenly bodies orbiting it."[23] Of course, as many scholars have noted, this theory goes against the commonly held view that Lewis did not initially plan on writing seven books at the onset of his composing Narnia. Finally, **Steven R. Loomis and Jacob P. Rodriguez coauthored a book called *C. S. Lewis: A Philosophy of Education*, in 2009**, which has a pedagogical perspective, and **Robert MacSwain and Michael Ward edited the *Cambridge Companion to C. S. Lewis* in 2010**, which is more of a literary biography.[24]

Notes

1. Walter Hooper, "Narnia: The Author, the Critics, and the Tale," *Children's Literature* 3 (1974): 12–22.

2. David Holbrook, "The Problem of C. S. Lewis," *Children's Literature in Education* 10 (1973): 3–25.

3. James Como, "Mediating Illusions: Three Studies of Narnia," *Children's Literature* 10 (1982): 163–8, at 163, 167; Walter Hooper, *Past Watchful Dragons* (New York: Macmillan, 1979).

4. Sally Adair Rigsbee, "Fantasy Places and Imaginative Belief: *The Lion, the Witch and the Wardrobe* and *The Princess and the Goblin,*" *Children's Literature Association Quarterly* 8(1) (1983): 10–11, at 10, 11.

5. Dennis B. Quinn, "The Narnia Books of C. S. Lewis: Fantastic or Wonderful?" *Children's Literature* 12 (1984): 105–21, at 105, 108, 112.

6. *Ibid.*: 118, 119.

7. William Johnson, "Platonic Shadows in C. S. Lewis' Narnia Chronicles," *Modern Fiction Studies* 32(1) (1986): 75–87, at 86.

8. Frank Riga, "Religion in Children's Literature: Introduction," *Children's Literature Association Quarterly* 14(1) (1989): 4–5, at 4, 5. Incidentally, more than 20 years later, the *Quarterly* published the most recent special issue on religion, edited by Jennifer M. Miskec.

9. Frank Riga, "Mortals Call Their History Fable: Narnia and the Use of Fairy Tale," *Children's Literature Association Quarterly* 14(1) (1989): 26–30, at 26, 27, 28.

10. Mervyn Nicholson, "What C. S. Lewis Took from E. Nesbit," *Children's Literature Association Quarterly* 16(1) (1991): 16–22, at 16, 19.

11. Hugh Crago, "Such Was Charn, That Great City," *Children's Literature Association Quarterly* 19(1) (1994): 41–5, at 44.

12. John Morgenstern, "Children and Other Talking Animals," *The Lion and the Unicorn* 24(1) (2000): 110–27, at 117, 114.

13. T. A. Shippey, *J. R. R. Tolkien: Author of the Century* (New York: Houghton Mifflin, 2002): 270, 120–1.

14. Jean E. Graham, "Women, Sex, and Power: Circe and Lilith in Narnia," *Children's Literature Association Quarterly* 29(1–2) (2004): 32–44, at 32, 41.

15. Amanda Rogers Jones, "The Narnian Schism: Reading the Christian Subtext as Other in the Children's Stories of C. S. Lewis," *Children's Literature Association Quarterly* 29(1–2) (2004): 45–61, at 54, 58.

16. Elissa McCormack, "Inclusivism of C. S. Lewis: The Case of Emeth," *Logos: A Journal of Catholic Thought and Culture* 11(4) (2008): 57–73, at 58, 64.

17. Alan Jacobs, *The Narnian: The Life and Imagination of C. S. Lewis* (San Francisco, CA: HarperSanFrancisco, 2005): 307, 308.

18. *Ibid.*: 259.

19. Andrew White, "Rev. of *The Magical Worlds of Narnia: A Treasury of Myths, Legends, and Fascinating Facts*, by David Colbert, and *Into the Wardrobe: C. S. Lewis and the Narnia Chronicles*, by David C. Downing," *The Lion and the Unicorn* 30(3) (2006): 427–30, at 429.

20. Shanna Caughey (ed.), *Revisiting Narnia: Fantasy, Myth and Religion in C. S. Lewis' Chronicles* (Dallas, TX: BenBella Books, 2005).

21. Rebecca Davies, "Rev. of *Milton, Spenser and The Chronicles of Narnia: Literary Sources for the C. S. Lewis Novels*, by Elizabeth Baird Hardy," *Children's Literature Association Quarterly* 32(4) (2007): 400–2, at 401.

22. Diana Pavlac Glyer, *The Company They Keep: C. S. Lewis and J. R. R. Tolkien as Writers in Community* (Kent, OH: Kent State University Press, 2007).

23. Judy Rosenbaum, "Rev. of *Planet Narnia: The Seven Heavens in the Imagination of C. S. Lewis*, by Michael Ward," *Children's Literature Association Quarterly* 33(4) (2008): 451–4, at 453.

24. Steven R. Loomis and Jacob P. Rodriguez, *C. S. Lewis: A Philosophy of Education* (New York: Palgrave Macmillan, 2009); Robert MacSawin and Michael Ward (eds.), *The Cambridge Companion to C. S. Lewis* (Cambridge: Cambridge University Press, 2010).

Index

adaptations, 6, 8, 9, 38, 46, 47, 113,
    115, 117, 118, 119, 120, 122,
    186, 202
allegory, 6, 7, 91, 92, 93, 94, 97, 99,
    117, 118, 121, 126, 131, 132,
    149, 191, 192, 200, 201
Aravis, 62, 63, 65, 165, 166, 167,
    168, 170
Aslan, 2, 4, 5, 6, 21, 22, 25, 28, 29,
    30, 31, 32, 39, 40, 41, 42, 43,
    44, 45, 46, 47, 48, 49, 53, 59,
    60–7, 81, 83, 84, 92, 93, 98,
    101, 102, 103, 105, 106, 115,
    116, 117, 118, 122, 131-7, 145,
    148, 149, 150, 151, 154, 155,
    156, 157, 165, 166, 168, 169,
    171, 172, 173, 174, 175,
    187-93, 199, 200, 203

Bahktin, M. M., 9
Beaver, Mr. and Mrs., 16, 17, 21,
    22, 23, 24, 26, 39, 40, 41, 44,
    45, 47, 65, 82, 83, 97, 115, 116,
    134, 190
Bettelheim, Bruno, 72, 73, 75,
Bosmajian, Hamida, 73, 79, 81
Brandt, Deborah, viii

Carnegie Medal, 4, 146
The Chronicles of Narnia, 2, 3, 5, 6,
    7, 53, 71, 73, 75, 82, 84, 91, 93,
    97, 132, 162
chronotope, 9, 90, 91, 98
colonialism, 169

"The Dark Side of Narnia," 4
determinism, 126, 129, 130, 134,
    135
Disney, 38, 47, 113, 120, 121,
    122, 123, 126, 127, 136,
    157

education, 9, 53, 57, 58, 59, 60, 61,
    64, 65, 96, 122, 123
Egoff, Sheila, 76
Experiment House, 60, 61, 62, 189,
    192

faun, 1, 2, 10, 17, 18, 56, 57, 91, 102,
    116, 162, 202
Freud, Sigmund, 73, 82, 83, 199

Gaiman, Neil, 4, 5, 58, 59
gender, 8, 9, 10, 15, 19, 22, 23, 24,
    25, 26, 33, 98, 116, 117, 186,
    187, 188, 192, 193, 194, 195,
    196, 203, 204
Girard, René, 38, 39, 40, 41, 42, 44,
    45, 46
Green, Roger Lancelyn, 1, 54, 91,
    173
Greeves, Arthur, 92, 94, 95, 96, 128,
    163

Hooper, Walter, 6, 54, 92, 136, 172,
    173, 199
The Horse and His Boy, 2, 3, 6, 9, 62,
    132, 161, 162, 164, 165, 166,
    167, 170, 173, 175, 176
Hunt, Peter, 2, 8
Hutcheon, Linda, 113, 118, 119,
    122, 123

Jadis, 93, 94, 102, 103, 132, 133,
    134, 135, 136, 137, 148, 149,
    187, 188, 189, 192, 193, 195,
    196, 203
Jones, Diana Wynne, 151

Kidd, Kenneth, 72, 73, 74
Kilmer, Martin, 5
King Tirian, 151, 164, 165, 169,
    195

Kirke, Digory, 6, 54, 58, 59, 76, 98, 105, 148, 149, 187, 188, 189, 192, 193
Krieg, Laurence, 3

Lacan, Jacques, 80
The Lady of the Green Kirtle, 148, 153, 190, 193, 195, 196
The Last Battle, 2, 3, 4, 6, 9, 100, 146, 150, 151, 152, 154, 155, 156, 161, 162, 164, 165, 169, 187, 191, 195, 200, 201, 203
Lewis, C. S., 48, 53, 75, 77, 90, 92, 94, 100, 126, 130, 154, 162, 174
    The Abolition of Man, 54, 55, 127, 130, 136, 137, 176
    That Hideous Strength, 167
    "The Laws of Nature," 128
    Mere Christianity, 55, 63, 66, 129, 167
    "On Forgiveness," 133
    On Science Fiction, 174
    "On Stories," 121
    "On Three Ways of Writing for Children," 90, 115
    Out of the Silent Planet, 167
    "The Weight of Glory," 130, 133
    "Work and Prayer," 129
Lilith, 7, 94, 102, 195, 203
liminal space, 71, 72, 74, 76, 86, 194
The Lion, the Witch and the Wardrobe, 1, 2, 3, 6, 7, 15, 19, 22, 28, 38, 39, 42, 45, 47, 48, 56, 65, 71, 72, 76, 79, 86, 100, 106, 113, 120, 126, 128, 132, 146, 157, 166, 186, 188, 191

The Magician's Nephew, 2, 3, 6, 39, 54, 58, 132, 148, 187, 188, 189, 202, 203
McGillis, Roderick, viii

Narnia themes, 6, 30, 171
Nikolajeva, Maria, 97, 101, 106
Nodelman, Perry, 75

orientalism, 171, 174

Pevensie, Edmund, 2, 6, 16, 17, 18, 19, 20, 21, 22, 23, 24, 25, 26, 27, 28, 29, 30, 32, 39, 42, 44-9, 59, 60, 63, 64, 76, 77, 79, 80-5, 97, 105, 114, 115, 117, 132, 133, 134, 135, 137, 138, 154, 164, 165, 166, 168, 187, 188, 191, 192, 193, 204
Pevensie, Lucy, 1, 2, 10, 16, 17, 18, 20, 23, 24, 26, 39, 40, 41, 44, 46, 56, 57, 59, 65, 66, 76, 77, 79, 80, 84, 98, 105, 106, 114, 116, 117, 118, 137, 138, 147, 151, 153, 154, 187, 188, 189, 191, 192, 194, 195, 196, 199, 200, 204
Pevensie, Peter, 16, 23, 24, 47, 59, 76, 77, 79, 80, 83, 84, 85, 103, 105, 114-17, 137, 164, 172, 187, 191, 193
Pevensie, Susan, 4, 16, 24, 25, 26, 43, 46, 47, 58, 76, 77, 79, 80, 81, 84, 98, 101, 106, 114, 116, 117, 118, 137, 138, 187, 189, 191, 195, 196
    "The Problem of Susan," 4, 5, 203
Plummer, Polly, 54, 57, 58, 59, 98, 187, 188, 189, 190, 191, 192, 193, 194, 195, 196
Pole, Jill, 6, 45, 54, 58, 62, 64, 153, 164, 165, 186, 187, 189, 190, 191, 192, 193, 194, 195, 196
predestination, 127, 129, 132
Prince Caspian, 3, 6, 7, 59, 98, 105, 132, 204
Prince Rilian, 6, 64, 153, 189, 190, 193
Puddleglum, 64, 153, 190, 193
Pullman, Philip, 4, 5, 9, 58, 92, 116, 145, 146, 147, 149, 150, 204

racism, 5, 10, 21, 145, 161, 162, 163, 164, 166, 169, 170, 172, 175, 176, 177
Rose, Jacqueline, 75
Rowling, J. K., 4, 5

Said, Edward, 174
scapegoat, 9, 38, 39, 40
Scrub, Eustace Clarence, 6, 58, 60-3, 64, 97, 153, 164, 165, 186, 187, 189, 190, 191, 193
sexism, 5, 203, 204
Shasta, 6, 62, 63, 165, 166, 167, 170, 173
The Silver Chair, 3, 6, 45, 61, 64, 148, 153, 189, 190
Stone Table, 6, 30, 31, 39, 40, 41, 42, 46, 84, 94, 132, 189

Tolkien, J. R. R., 1, 2, 5, 6, 7, 91, 92, 95, 116, 163, 202, 204, 205
Tom Brown's Schooldays, 61

trauma, 71, 72, 73, 74, 79, 81, 83
Tumnus, Mr., 1, 2, 10, 17, 18, 19, 23, 29, 39, 40, 41, 56, 57, 80, 82, 102, 116, 117, 137, 187
Turkish Delight, 18, 19, 20, 21, 24, 27, 28, 29, 80, 81, 115, 168, 186, 191, 192

violence, 8, 9, 38, 39, 41, 42, 72, 75, 118, 145, 164, 165
The Voyage of the Dawn Treader, 3, 6, 58, 60, 65, 154

Walden Media, 6, 9, 113, 115, 120, 121, 122, 123
war, 3, 18, 19, 21, 71, 72, 78, 97, 100, 102, 104, 114, 154, 162
The White Witch, 7, 17, 19, 20, 21, 22, 29, 39, 42, 44, 46, 57, 83, 115, 116, 117, 132, 165, 168, 169, 187, 190-3, 195, 203